The N
Employment
Contract

The New Employment Contract

Using employment contracts effectively

Patricia Leighton & Aidan ODonnell

NICHOLAS BREALEY
PUBLISHING

LONDON

This edition first published in Great Britain by
Nicholas Brealey Publishing Limited in 1995
21 Bloomsbury Way
London WC1A 2TH

ISBN 1-85788-021-8

British Library Cataloguing in Publication Data
A catalogue record for this book is available from the British Library.

Printed in Finland by Werner Söderström Oy

LAW AT WORK

Other Books in the Series

A GUIDE TO THE EMPLOYMENT ACTS
Joan Henderson

HANDLING REDUNDANCY
Sue Morris

INDUSTRIAL TRIBUNALS
Philip Parry

MANAGING THE PENSIONS REVOLUTION
Sue Ward

UNFAIR DISMISSAL
Richard Painter

THE WORK ENVIRONMENT
Patricia Leighton

Contents

Preface and Acknowledgements   viii

PART I   THE MANAGEMENT AND LEGAL FRAMEWORK
             OF CONTRACTS

Chapter 1   Introducing the Issues   **3**
What does an employment contract look like?   4
What about self-employment?   7
Why are employment contracts important?   8
Why is it important to get contracts right?   10
What are employment contracts for?   12

Chapter 2   The Role of Law in Employment Contracts   **14**
Employment law and 'atypical' workers   15
European employment law   15
Comparing regulation of contracts in the UK and other European states   17
Dealing with employment contract disputes   18
Can industrial tribunals deal with breaches of contract?   20
Organisational objectives and legal restraints: an illustration   21
Anti-discrimination legislation   22
Health and safety law   23

Chapter 3   Basic Legal Rules When Making Employment Contracts   **26**
The process of forming employment contracts   28
Offers of work   28
     Uncertainties about offers?   30
     Guidelines on offers   31
Acceptance of offers   33
     Time of acceptance   33
     Accepting offers but failing to turn up?   34
Creating a 'legally binding relationship'   34
     The law   35
     What if a contract is for an illegal purpose?   38
     The content of employment contracts   42
Contract types or contract terms?   44
Express terms: the sources   45
     Collective agreements as sources of contract terms   48
     Other sources of contract terms   52
     Policy development: suggested guidelines   53
Implied contract terms   56
     The new implied terms   58
     Pension schemes and good faith   59
     Implied terms: some detail   60

The relevant legal rules 61
Duties on the employee 62
The duty to obey lawful orders 62
Duty to work competently 64
Duty to act in faithful and honest service 64
The employer's obligations 65
To provide a safe and healthy workplace 65
To pay the agreed wage and protect from loss 67

PART II   EFFECTIVE CONTRACT MANAGEMENT

Chapter 4   Defining Employment Relationships 73
Changing role of the employee 74
The employee/self-employed divide 76
How important is the 'divide'? 78
Categorising working patterns: the leading cases 80
The 'business test' 81
Applying the legal tests 83
Implications for managers 84
Suggested guidelines 84

Chapter 5   Documenting Employment Contracts 87
The documents for employees 88
An approach to the task 88
Legal rules on documentation 91
Statement or contract? 92
What is a written contract? 93
Legal requirements on contract documentation 95
Practical points to note 98
Conclusion 98
Documents for self-employed staff 102

Chapter 6   Special Types of Employment Contracts 105
Types of contract 107
Identifying the appropriate contract type 107
Level and nature of demand 108
Labour costs 108
Production or service capacity 108
Centrality of function 108
Labour market factors 109
HRM factors 109
Industrial relations constraints 110
External policy constraints 110
Contracts charcterised by time 110
Part-time work 111
Job-sharing contracts 115
Annual hours contracts 121
Negotiated core and variable hours contracts 124
Contracts characterised by length 124
Fixed term contracts 128
Nil/zero hours contracts 131
Task contracts 134
Contracts characterised by location 134

The employment of homeworkers 135
Employment relationships based on status 143
    Contracts of self-employment and consultancy 143
    Public sector employment: the background 145
    Workers with tenure 147
    Training contracts 148

Chapter 7   Contract Terms **150**
Signposting the issues 150
Adopting a strategic approach 151
    Technical issues 151
    Management issues 152
    Presentational issues 153
Terms relating to remuneration 155
    What of smaller firms? 156
    Legal issues for terms relating to pay 156
Key legislative requirements 157
    Equal Pay Act 1970 157
    Defences to an equal pay claim 160
    The Wages Act 1986 161
    The itemised pay statement 163
Contractual problem areas: expectations of pay rises/bonuses etc 163
    How are uncertainties resolved? 163
    Performance related pay 164
    Payment through illness or injury 166
    The health and safety agenda 169
    Maternity and pay 169
    Deferred pay: occupational pensions 170
    Payment during periods when work is unavailable 170
    Statutory guaranteed pay 172
Terms relating to working time 172
    What is 'working time'? 174
    Basic working hours 175
    Overtime 175
    Shift working 176
    Night work 177
    'Unsocial' hours 178
    Sunday working 179
    Holidays 180
    Flexi hours 182
    Time off for specific duties or activities 182
Terms relating to job location 183
    Job location 183
    Split sites 184
    Travel and short visits 185
Occupational benefits 185
    Travel and subsistence expenses 188
    Cars and other vehicles 188
    Provision of accommodation 189
    Claw back clauses 190
Employee performance 190
    Legal issues 192
    The need for disciplinary procedures 194
    The advantages of fair and effective procedures 195

Drafting disciplinary rules and procedures 196
Some typical performance issues: applying the rules 197
Loyalty and commitment 198
Exclusivity and conflicts of interest 200
Whistle blowers! 201
Restraint of trade 201
'Garden leave' clauses 203

Chapter 8 Changing and Managing Contracts Effectively 205
Dealing with change 206
Major reasons for change 207
Changes to location, working hours, job content 207
Changes to the employing organisation 208
The basic legal rules of contract change 209
Where the contract authorises change 209
Where the change is not authorised by contract 211
Imposing new contracts? 213
Implications of unlawful 'change' 214
Changes to the employing organisation 215
Detailed issues 216

Chapter 9 Ending It All 220
The costs of legal action 220
The mechanics of termination 222
Notice 222
'Garden leave' 223
What is 'dismissal'? 224
Termination by the employer 224
Non renewal of fixed term contracts 225
Constructive dismissal 225
Summary dismissal 226
Justifying dismissal 227
The concept of unfair dismissal 228
Where do we find the law? 228
Who does the legislation apply to? 228
Two years continuous service 229
What is an associated employer? 230
'Temporary cessations' of work 230
Defending claims 230
Potentially fair reasons for dismissal 231
Behaviour driven and just cause dismissal 231
Capability or qualifications 232
Guidelines for 'capability' dismissals 232
Guidelines for 'qualification' dismissals 233
Ill health 233
Breach of statutory duty 237
Other substantial reasons for dismissal 237
Economically driven termination 237
Who the Act covers 238
The legal definition of redundancy 239
'Bumping' 240
Handling redundancy 240
Offers of alternative employment 240

The trial period   241
Consultation   243
Other issues surrounding the ending of employment contracts   244
Guidelines for lawful termination of contracts of self-employment   245

Endpiece   **246**
What does the future hold for employment contracts?   246

Index   247

Preface and Acknowledgements

Employment contracts underpin most organisational policies and practices concerned with people management. In recent years those policies have been much changed, especially through a growing emphasis on flexibility, diversity and adaptability. Employment contracts have altered correspondingly, both in their form (more part-time, fixed term and homebased contracts, for example) and in their detail.

Employment contracts are legal relationships and must operate within a legal framework. This framework has also undergone major change, not least from European law. New approaches and new priorities have emerged and challenged traditional UK employment practices. The law now looks for stable workforces, equality of opportunity, and protection for disadvantaged or 'atypical' employment groups. All this has direct significance for the development and management of contracts.

This book explains the legal framework, and also shows how employment contracts can reflect an organisation's people management agenda. It aims to help readers avoid legal and other problems caused by poorly-defined, documented and managed contracts. With employment relationships becoming increasingly diverse and the law gaining in complexity, it is vital for all those concerned with employment contracts to get everything right.

The book deals with the key elements of effective employment contracts - their formation, content, change and termination. It makes considerable use of examples and case studies from organisations that have devoted considerable energy and effort to developing particular contract types, documents or even useful clauses.

We are grateful to many individuals and organisations for the information and support they have given to this book. In particular, we would like to thank Crossaig Ltd, the Nationwide Building Society, United Biscuits plc, Forte Crest Hotels, Elaine Adkins, Jackie Bryden, Eileen Everitt, Jeanette Lysagh, Nicola Whatley and Pip Evans.

Patricia Leighton & Aidan ODonnell

Part I
The Management and
Legal Framework
of Contracts

1
Introducing the Issues

'Unit's manager refuses new contract'

'Doctor dismissed for divulging "scandal" at hospital'

'Hairdresser to the stars banned from competing with old boss'

'Inland Revenue prosecute over security company's "phoney" casual contracts

'Annual hours contracts are all the rage'

'Newspaper staff strike over imposed "personal" contracts'

'Football managers to job share'

When employment contracts hit the headlines like this it is often because the contract involves a celebrity, media personality, a group of workers with industrial clout or an allegation of criminal or scandalous behaviour. These headlines serve to illustrate the wide range of important issues which can surface over employment contracts.

At any given moment, approximately 20 million workers in the UK will have contracts of employment, with at least 3.5 million having contracts of self-employment of some sort. Each year millions of new contracts are entered into, and several million ended voluntarily or otherwise. It is impossible to estimate the overall number and scale of individual changes made to employment contract terms relating to pay, hours of work and job content.

An employment contract establishes a legally-regulated relationship whereby the parties to it, along with law itself, define rights and duties. Employment contracts underpin virtually all aspects of work relationships, defining what work has to be done, for what pay and other benefits or entitlements. Some lawyers simply define contracts as the 'wage - work' bargain, but all see employment contracts as the 'cornerstone' of employment law. Statutory protections, such as maternity rights, job security rights and an entitlement to equal pay for men and women, take as their base the contract of employment and build on it. Essentially, contract law establishes the framework for the relationship and other areas of law elaborate on it. For example, a contract may establish a weekly wage for a woman of £185.00 per week. If she then discovers that a comparable male colleague earns £215 per week, in principle she can rely on equal pay legislation to seek a pay rise to his level.

WHAT DOES AN EMPLOYMENT CONTRACT LOOK LIKE?

The simple answer is that it need not look like anything at all because an oral agreement can constitute a legally binding contract. An advert in a local shop window for bar staff in a wine bar might read:

'Wanted immediately. Experienced bar staff. Contact "The Happy Grape", High Street. Tel....'

If Mary visited the wine bar and spoke to the manager an employment contract would be made if the conversation went as follows:
Mary
'I want to apply for the bar job; I've worked for three years at "Winos" in Portvillle but I want to work closer to home.'
Manager
'The rate's £4.00 an hour, Monday to Friday 12-11pm. Start next Monday?'
Mary
'Yes, fine'.
This simple conversation would be adequate to create a contract of employment. It conforms to the basic elements of a binding contract. These are:

• an offer of work by the employer to work in the bar.

• acceptance of that offer by Mary.

• an agreement which is reasonably certain - i.e. can be defined with regard to the statements of the parties and the understood features of the occupation.

- an agreement which is not illegal, e.g not set up to defraud or mislead the Inland Revenue, or breach immigration controls.

In addition, in England and Wales (though not in Scotland) contracts must be supported by 'consideration', (pay) to be legally binding.

As Mary has experience in bar work and will know how the occupation works she can reasonably be expected to understand the demands and nature of the work. It is implicit that if she fails to turn up by 12 noon the following Monday, or is paid only £3.50 an hour, the contract has been broken and the victim can sue for breach of contract.

However, relatively few contracts are created as simply as this. Most contracts are entered into after interview, careful consideration and confirmation in writing of the main terms.

For example, Michael Thomas applied for a temporary post with the Great Northern University. He has been interviewed and has been provided with written information about the work and workplace. He is successful in his application and is written to as follows:

Mr M Thomas
Croft Cottage
Springtown
W Lenoxshire, Scotland

Dear Mr Thomas,

I have pleasure in offering you a Temporary Post at The Great Northern University with effect from 2nd March 199....

Your salary will be payable in arrears, by credit transfer on the 28th day of the month if it falls on a banking day; if it does not the payment date will be the first banking day immediately prior to the 28th day of the month. Your salary details are as follows:

Grade: Marketing Administrator (Temporary)
Salary: £15,750 p.a.

This appointment will terminate on 21st March 199... unless termi nated earlier by either party giving one week's notice, in writing.

A copy of your main terms and conditions of service is attached.

I also enclose Acceptance, Bank Details and Medical forms which should be completed and returned to indicate your acceptance of the post no later than return date of February 22nd 199...

Yours sincerely

Mrs Janette Porrage
Head of Personnel

Mr Thomas replies as follows:

Mrs Janette Porrage
Head of Personnel
Great Northern University
Sporran Drive
McTavish
Scotland

Dear Mrs Porrage,

Re: Marketing Administrator (Temporary)

I accept the offer of appointment for the above post together
with the Terms and Conditions set out in the attached document.

.........................Signature

...........................Date

Many contracts are even more detailed. They aim to fully express the expectations of the parties and to ensure that not only are documents unambiguous but are appropriate for both the type of work involved and the nature and culture of the employing organisation.

For example, in the banking and finance sector matters of personal appearance, honesty and commitment to the culture of the financial services industry will be seen as important. Contract terms will often spell out such matters in considerable detail and lead to complex, and lengthy contracts.

Beyond questions of pay, post, working hours, occupational benefits, notice periods etc some of the key terms might be as follows:

Clause 21
'The Bank attaches considerable importance to complete honesty by employees not only regarding their employment with the bank but also in their private life. Any failures to attain the highest standards will be considered a disciplinary matter and may lead to summary dismissal.'

In some occupations, engaging in outside activities which might rival the employer or be inappropriate are expressly dealt with. A typical clause might then read:

'You are required to devote your full time, attention and abilities to your duties during your working hours and act in the best interests of the company at all times. Accordingly, you must not, without the company's written consent undertake any employment   or engagement which might interfere with the performance of your duties or conflict with the company's interests'.

WHAT ABOUT SELF-EMPLOYMENT?

A growing number of workers in the UK are becoming self-employed. They may be establishing small businesses in the retail or service sectors, or perhaps be professionals working in partnerships. However, they may also be 'freelance' designers, hairdressers, writers, trainers or consultants, or construction workers - essentially 'one person businesses' hiring out their skills to a range of clients. The skill or service to be provided will be the essence of the contract, often for a one-off payment. Just as some refer to the contract of employment as the 'wage-work bargain', so the self-employed contract might be called the 'skill-fee' contract. However the parties will nonetheless want to establish 'ground rules' for their working relationship.

The basic legal rules are the same (offer, acceptance etc) but it will be implicit in the relationship that the worker has a high level of autonomy and will not wish to be integrated or even associated with the client organisation's policies, structures and culture. The self-employed worker wants an 'arms length' contract which clearly expresses the objectives of the contract (to develop a video, write advertising copy, advise on financial structures, review information technology at the company, provide a fleet of hire cars, clean the windows, develop an in-house training programme etc.) and determine other basics such as fee level, timing and access to or use of equipment.

Although the task to be performed or skill/service to be provided will be at the heart of the contract it is inevitable that other matters are often addressed. Clients may worry that a consultant will 'poach' contacts, make use of business intelligence gained while working with them, damage equipment or send a substitute worker/associate if business pressure becomes too great.

Freelance staff may worry about the contract being cancelled, varied or delayed. They may be anxious to have access to necessary organisational information and support while working for a client. They fear that without it the consequences may be a poor standard of work and a damaged reputation.

Self-employment contracts are finely balanced; they can generate many misunderstandings and disputes if they are not handled professionally and carefully. Typical terms of the contract of a management consultant to a large public sector employer are shown below:

An Agreement

Clause 1
The parties to this agreement are West Artery Health Authority (The Authority) and Roland Peters Associates (the Associates).........
Clause 2
The Associates are contracted to provide training courses, as and when required.........
Clause 6
We give no undertaking as to provision of work. When you are contracted for a specific training course we reserve the right to cancel the course up to two weeks before its scheduled date. Should we cancel within two weeks we

undertake to pay 50% of the agreed fee in addition to any necessary expenses associated with the particular course.

Clause 7

'The Associates should never use the training courses as an opportunity to promote their own business. Delegates lists for courses remain the property of the Authority. In no circumstances should they be reproduced, distributed or otherwise relied on other than with the express written consent of the Authority. Breach of this clause entitles the Authority to immediately terminate this Agreement'.

WHY ARE EMPLOYMENT CONTRACTS IMPORTANT?

Some reasons have already been touched on. Contracts are the basis of both employee relations and relations with self-employed persons and the primary vehicle in the UK for establishing legal rights and obligations. They also give out important signals to people inside as well as outside the organisation, such as job applicants and clients. Both the style and content of contract documentation are indicators of how much the organisation values its staff and how they are treated, and whether a professional approach to employment contracts exists.

However, employment contracts today have also to be set in and respond to their context if they are to be realistic and workable. In other words, those with responsibility for devising and managing employment contracts in an office, factory, restaurant, haulage company or hospital need to reflect carefully on the changing climate affecting contracts generally, and their own workplace in particular. It will be an unusual workplace indeed which has not been subject to change. There may have been changes to the role and status of trade unions and to collective agreements which have traditionally established the key terms of work for well over 50% of employees. Unions may have been de-recognised and 'personal contracts' introduced. Pay systems may have changed, or the workforce itself through increased numbers of part-timers etc. Perhaps there has been a tightening up of disciplinary rules to improve organisational efficiency, or promote excellence. An emphasis may have been placed on flexibility, multi-skilling or entrepreneurism.

Similarly, a new management style may have been introduced. There might now be emphasis on 'customer care', employee involvement or on eliminating waste. Some employees may have moved to an entirely different type of employment contract. Employment contracts may now offer less job security, reward performance more directly or expect staff to be more adaptable.

Typical among organisational developments are:

• The widespread use of performance related pay (PRP) or merit pay which links employee performance with pay levels.

• The extension of formal appraisal procedures into virtually all sectors of employment, whether or not linked to pay policies, whether or not linked to disciplinary procedures.

- A growing emphasis on organisational performance and improvement through adoption of total quality or, say, business process re-engineering continuous improvement.

- An emphasis in many organisation on employee participation in organi sations through team briefings, suggestion schemes, works/departmental committees and the like.

- Measures to provide flexibility in skills deployment through multi-skilling or the use of changing job structures, which have often challenged both the use of traditional skills and professional/craft demar cations.

Other policies have been explicitly or implicitly encouraged by government policy and the absence of a highly regulated labour market. The public sector has been particularly affected by policies such as the abandonment of national or sector-wide collective bargaining and contracting out of services, especially in areas such as cleaning, catering, security and maintenance. The message has been that jobs for life are a thing of the past, so that temporary and fixed term contracts have become widespread.

Overall, organisational objectives and policies have changed and the call is for flexibility, diversity and competitiveness. The expectations of employees have necessarily changed in accordance with these developments. Clearly, the concept of the simple 'wage-work bargain' is inadequate to discharge these complex yet focused new organisational goals. For example, contracts requiring employee flexibility will need to express flexibility in contract terms relating to job content, working hours, training and re-deployment. Organisations committed to quality need to emphasise their performance management/disciplinary contract provisions, perhaps even re-emphasising matters such as dress code, customer relations and the like.

Some management changes may require the whole basis of employment contracts to be reviewed. Examples include a policy that employees are replaced by consultants/freelance staff, or that numbers of full-timers be reduced and part-timers increased. The need to reduce operational overheads may lead to distance/home working, a need to reduce the overtime bill may lead to the introduction of annualised hours.

The options available are numerous. All require well-developed and well-executed employment contracts, or there will be a mismatch between organisational policy and reality for individual workers and their managers.

It is also important to reflect on how employing organisations themselves have recently changed. Many have become 'flatter' and have devolved responsibility for personnel matters to departmental managers, including recruiting and managing staff. This means contracts of employment as well as contracts for freelance, consultants and other self-employed staff are being increasingly handled by managers.

The last decade has also seen personnel management sometimes renamed human resources management, though many still prefer the original title. The change has signified a shift away from purely operational matters (pay, pensions and employment contract documentation itself) to a more central and strategic role for people management within organisations. This has moved the spotlight to the developmental aspects of individual employees and the workforce more generally - training, career management etc. It has also led to a more analytical view of skill needs, skill deployment and to linking employee performance to organisational performance, and vice-versa etc. Contracts need also to translate these goals into reality.

WHY IS IT IMPORTANT TO GET CONTRACTS RIGHT?

In this context 'contracts' includes not only their formation and day-to-day management but also the process of changing their terms.

A compelling reason today for getting contracts right is the growing awareness that poorly-drafted and managed employment contracts can be a cause of stress and related problems. Much of the literature on stress focuses on physical problems such as noise, overcrowding, or violence. It is now clear that the way employment contracts are operated in many organisations can also cause stress. Performance related pay, appraisal, secrecy clauses, clauses leading to a sense of precariousness, and excessively rigorous disciplinary codes can all add to the problem.

The causes of stress are well understood. Employment contracts, if oppressive and badly managed can have major impact. Managers must be aware of this and see that contracts have balance, clarity and are fairly managed to minimise the risks of harm.

A second, and vital, reason to get contracts right is that they define the parameters of the relationship and the nature and scope of authorisation to perform tasks and take decisions. When a employee uses a company van for private purposes or authorises expenses or payments the law asks whether such acts were 'within the scope of employment'. This question is especially relevant when an employee has injured or caused loss to a third party. The employer will be vicariously liable for the acts or decisions if it was within the scope of employment. Contracts need to be carefully considered and drafted to avoid uncertainties; employees need to know clearly through the contract just what they are empowered to do .

Thirdly, failure to express the original terms clearly and in accordance with what the parties thought they had agreed on can lead to disputes, employee de-motivation and perhaps legal action. An employee who thought they would obtain a bonus at Christmas, gain access to an occupational benefit scheme or have the opportunity to travel abroad on the basis of what was discussed at interview may react badly when nothing is forthcoming. Similarly, an employee disciplined for 'inappropriate dress and attitude' will feel aggrieved and may challenge the decision if the disciplinary code merely refers to 'misconduct' in a very generalised way and contains no provisions relating to dress.

An aggrieved employee may also complain to their union, seek meetings with managers, organise support at their department/unit/workplace or invoke the grievance procedure. This will be time consuming for managers and staff and possibly stressful. Indeed, some of the most recent and notorious industrial disputes have involved employee contracts and attempts by employers to change the basis of them, (withdrawing from collective agreements, de-recognising trade unions, imposing new terms, sacking staff and offering new contracts with very different terns etc.).

Included here is the famous 1993 TIMEX dispute in Dundee, widespread disputes involving teachers in further education colleges from 1993-5, and many disputes in the printing, transport, and television and related industries.

A dispute over a contract may reach the point where an employee or group of employees commences legal action, leading to:

• a claim for breach of contract in the County/Sheriff Court;

• a claim under the Wages Act 1986;

• a claim for unfair dismissal, based on a breach of contract providing evidence of constructive dismissal. This might also be accompanied by a breach of contract claim in the industrial tribunal.

These are by no means the only possible legal outcomes, but all have major cost implications. Legal advice is rarely cheap, and legal representation in courts and tribunals may work out at £1,000 a day or more (for further information see Chapter 9). Cases can also go on appeal at even higher cost. Trade unions and other organisations supporting employees and claimants are becoming increasingly active as well as innovative regarding the type of claims they will pursue.

While many employers have insurance protection against employment law claims with companies which offer legal advice as part of their cover arrangement, legal fees are probably not the major cost of disputes. The real costs will probably include the following:

• *Compensation*, whether determined by or out of court. Awards are getting higher with the 'normal' ceiling of around £12,000 removed for many types of tribunal claims.

- *Management and other employee time*, along with the stress and strain of disputes themselves. Litigation is almost inevitably divisive and usually creates a tense working environment.

- Unwelcome publicity, especially if the case has salacious facts, or involves dishonesty, or concerns a well known person.

- Damage to business reputation, especially today with more and more attention being paid to employment contracts and practices which some commentators and journalists consider unfair, oppressive or otherwise as evidence of bad practice.

The true costs of an employment contract (including one of self-employment) going 'wrong' are impossible to assess accurately; their reality can never be ignored.

Turning now to the effective development of employment contracts, it is important to address a vital preliminary question.

WHAT ARE EMPLOYMENT CONTRACTS FOR?

On the surface this is a simple question. Employment contracts regulate the working relationship and establish the key obligations of each side. Some of these obligations will be agreed and set down, some will be implied by law itself to make the contract workable (see Chapter 3).

Contracts can also perform different roles. For some, the contract is agreed and documented for the purpose of complying with legal rules, especially rules relating to its structure and content. It is a basic legal device which needs to be created and written down, but little more.

For others, the contract is about regulating the performance of the employee, employer and perhaps also the self-employed. In these circumstances, disciplinary/performance rules, appraisal, and all the clauses which deal with hours of work, productivity etc. will dominate.

Others will take this position further. The contract, they argue, is essentially there to protect the legitimate business interests of the employer. Such contracts will emphasise trade secrets, confidentiality, competition and perhaps put emphasis on clauses which highlight the dress and conduct of employees or even self-employed/freelance workers.

However, there is a fourth and increasingly popular perception of what contracts are about. This is where contracts are explicitly devised to reflect and implement organisational and HRM policies. Here, clauses emphasising involvement, team work or empowerment will be much in prominence, while others will incorporate policies on areas such as smoking, equal opportunities, well-being, dignity and effective home-work links.

Many managers see contracts performing all the above functions and possibly more, but will give different weights to the various roles. Contracts need to reflect these goals but they must nonetheless be underpinned by a clear understanding of legal rules and the way in which courts and tribunals interpret and apply them.

It is also important to remember that contracts are part of an organisation's communication system, not just with employees and the self-employed but to outsiders such as job applicants, work experience trainees, consultants, inspectors and visitors. They will pick up 'vibes' about the organisation's priorities and values from contract documents. Language and style are of crucial importance. Whether an employer adopts a relatively straightforward approach to the content and documentation of contracts or goes for glossy or computerised documentation the basic message is the same. Contracts must be clear, accurate, reflect both the expectations of the parties as well as the organisation itself, be consistent with other organisational policies and, just as with all other organisational communications, give out the right message.

This book explains these key legal and practical issues in the following order:

1   How the legal framework operates; employment law, the law relating to contracts (Chapters 2 & 3).

2   How to identify and articulate organisational needs through the choice, and the form of the employment relationship (Chapters 4 & 5).

3   How to reflect in the contract itself the key features of that employment relationship and to adopt a strategic approach to the process (Chapter 6).

4   How to deal with specific workplace issues, e.g. relating to pay, discipline and restraint of trade etc. (Chapter 7).

5   How to respond to change and adapt the terms of contract lawfully (Chapter 8).

6   How to deal with disputes arising and/or end the contract lawfully (Chapter 9).

7   Looking to the future for employment contracts (Endpiece).

2
The Role of Law in Employment Contracts

Anyone developing and managing employment contracts needs to understand and appreciate the nature and role of the law which regulates them.

Employment contracts must be set in the context of current UK employment law, which combines statute law with the common law rules applying to contracts. Traditionally, employment law, whether devised by judges or through legislation, has emphasised the need to operate contracts correctly and to follow agreed procedures or policies rigorously.

Many employment contracts are moulded by collective agreements drawn up by trade union(s) and employer(s). Typically, they deal with pay, hours of work, and occupational benefits, and are more prevalent in the public sector and in large organisations. In recent years the number of collective agreements has declined leading to fewer employment contracts being affected. Employers now have increased scope to determine contracts terms.

Although UK law has left wide discretions regarding contracts to employers, there are some statutory interventions which affect the contract. The major ones concern:

- recruitment and career management procedures, insofar as it is unlawful to discriminate on sexual or racial grounds.

- specified employee rights, e.g. regarding maternity, written particulars of employment, written information about contracts, pay, time off for trade union and public duties and guaranteed payments during lay-offs.

- job security, e.g. regarding unfair dismissal provisions, compensation for redundancy and protections for employees when organisations are taken over or merged.

- health, safety and welfare.

Beyond this there is relatively little statutory regulation of employment contracts. Anti-discrimination legislation and health and safety provisions have had particular impact. Their application to contracts will be considered at relevant points in this book.

EMPLOYMENT LAW AND 'ATYPICAL' WORKERS

Employment organisations in the UK make extensive use of 'atypical' staff - part-timers, casual, fixed term and similar work patterns. An attraction to some has been the traditional emphasis of employment rights on so-called 'core' workers and the corresponding difficulty of atypical staff in claiming statutory protections such as for unfair dismissal and redundancy. The '16 hour rule' has been a notable barrier to claims in the past. Much has changed, and part-timers are now covered by virtually all statutory protections. Short-term/temporary staff may also soon be included.

These legal changes have major implications for both labour use strategies and the nature, content and management of the contracts.

EUROPEAN EMPLOYMENT LAW

If UK statute law has been of limited effect, European (EU) law is having greater impact on both the law affecting contracts and the nature of employment law itself. In the early 1980s a significant European agenda emerged. At the heart of this agenda was recognition that economic progress has to be accompanied by a so-called 'social dimension' to employment practices. This implies that there should be minimum employment protections for all workers across Europe. It furthers two other vital European objectives.

The first is that common basic employment standards enable workers to move more easily between member states. The second is to avoid 'social dumping'. This is a situation whereby low wage and legally unprotected workforces can 'undercut' employees in parts of the Union where employees *are* provided with legal protections - hence the requirement by 1997 for Europe-wide regulation of working time and the intention to set a Europe-wide statutory minimum hourly wage.

The EU agenda has considerable practical impact. The 1993 Trade Union Reform and Employment Rights Act (TURERA) introduced no less than five substantial measures specifically required by European law. These included the maternity provisions to implement the 1992 Maternity Directive[1] and the consultation provisions to implement the 1992 Collective Redundancies Directive[2]. Most importantly TURER also implemented the Contract Documentation Directive 1991[3] (see Chapter 5). European law is thus creating a new and enlarged statutory framework for employment contracts.

The emphasis of law on the 'social dimension', involves setting employment relationships in their broader context of social protections, training and, perhaps family life. This implies that the employment contract is not simply a legal transaction but carries with it notions of trust, support and responsibility. However, of real practical importance is the fact that law derived from Europe is qualitatively different from traditional UK employment law. European law has explicit policy objectives, for example to protect health, avoid disadvantage for groups of workers, and to ensure employee involvement in decision-making. When UK legislation derived from European law is tested in UK courts it *must* be applied to a given factual situation in order to implement those explicit policy objectives.

Put simply, the benefit of any doubt must be given to those whom the law decided should receive protection. Hence, the Transfer of Undertakings (Protection of Employment) Regulations 1981 (TUPE) which implemented the Acquired Rights Directive 1977[4] should always be applied so as to protect workers affected by business transfers. It is the spirit of the law as much as the letter which must be taken note of.

There are a number of other ways in which European law differs from traditional UK employment law, all of which have considerable relevance for employment contracts.

- Law develops through the creation of *rights* for workers rather than *duties* on employers.

- Law increasingly questions *why* decisions are made (e.g. to declare redundancies, not appoint an applicant for a job or to give a fixed term rather than indefinite contract) as much as *how* decisions are made (e.g. by following contractual disciplinary procedures etc).

- Law aims to improve the position of the *'disadvantaged'* in the labour market by,for example, providing pro-rata benefits for part-timers in comparison with full-timers. Part-timers in the UK are now entitled to virtually all the same legal protections as full-timers. [5]

- Law aims to establish *generic* and broadly based *protections*, for example, to ensure 'dignity' at work for all staff regardless of sex, race, age, sexual orientation or disability. This is in contrast to the traditional approach of UK law under anti-discrimination legislation which is to create discrete and distinctive legal rules for individual situations.

- Law requires 'transparency' in policies and practices at the workplace.

This means that decision-making must be fair, open and well documented, with clear implications for employment contracts.

These differences are neither academic nor cosmetic. They have major and growing practical implications for those managing employment contracts. Specific examples of where European employment law has brought about important changes of details or emphasis will be considered at appropriate points in this book.

COMPARING REGULATION OF CONTRACTS IN THE UK AND OTHER EUROPEAN STATES

With the growing influence of European employment law, the increased movement of workers between states and the important role of multi-national organisations it is important to set employment contracts in an international, especially European, context.

Although there are many similarities between the UK and Eire, there are some major differences in law affecting contracts in the UK and other European states. They include the following:

- In many states basic legal rules affecting employment contracts are set down in a specific Labour Code. Examples are Germany, Italy, France, Spain, the Netherlands and Greece. This leaves less to individual negotiation.

- Large scale collective agreements are important or dominant in determining working conditions in many states. This is especially so in Denmark and Belgium.

- Laws for formalising employment contracts themselves are generally less stringent outside the UK. Exceptions are usually for atypical contracts, especially for temporary work where contracts have often to be in writing. Many managers stress the 'psychological' or trust basis of the relationship and reject over-formalisation.

- In some member states different rules apply depending on worker category, e.g. executives, manual, domestic staff or white collar. Denmark and Germany are examples of this, though in other states such demarcations are not such a feature.

Although some distinctions emerge it is important to note that many aspects of employment contracts are treated in a broadly similar way. This is true of the basic legal obligations on employers, such as provision of agreed pay and benefits, and a safe working environment. Fidelity, support and competence are expected from employees. Treatment of disciplinary matters, redundancy and other aspects of job termination have a similar common core, not least because this is an area where European employment law has had some impact.

In summary, UK managers have been responsible for negotiating a far wider range of topics than their European counterparts and doing so often within a different type of legal structure. This explains the 'battle' over much European Union legislation. However, the reality is that European ideas and standards are rapidly and significantly affecting the way in which contracts are devised and managed in the UK.

DEALING WITH EMPLOYMENT CONTRACT DISPUTES

The legal mechanisms which deal with disputes are many and varied. They are set out at Figure 2.1. 'Simple' claims for a breach of employment contract or one of self-employment, especially issues such as restraint of trade, confidentiality and fidelity are dealt with by the ordinary law courts. In the UK, lower courts hear claims where the compensation requested is less than £15,000; if higher, cases go the High Court or equivalents. These courts also have the power to award injunctions, ie a legal device to prevent a proposed action taking place, for example, termination of the contract. Cases are heard by ordinary judges sitting alone and appeals are taken to the Court of Appeal / Court of Session in Scotland, then to the House of Lords which is the final appeal court for the UK.

Since 1963 disputes over statutory employment protections, such as for unfair dismissal or sex discrimination, have been decided by industrial tribunals. Tribunals, unlike 'ordinary' law courts have lay members as well as a legally qualified chairperson. In effect, the tribunal acts as both judge and jury by combining law with the practical experience of lay members. Its decisions on matters of fact are final - for example, that a particular employee was regularly late for work or that a manager was rude to customers or inappropriately dressed for work. This means their factual decisions cannot be overturned by a higher court or tribunal on appeal unless an interpretation of law which conditioned their approach to the facts was faulty.

Procedures in tribunals are relatively speedy and informal but parties to actions are not eligible for Legal Aid. Another distinctive feature is that there is a statutory role for the Advisory, Conciliation and Arbitration Service (ACAS), in that its representatives have a duty to try to achieve a negotiated settlement between the parties. Thousands of cases are ended this way. Increasingly, the tribunal system has established filter mechanisms so that only cases which have real substance will get to a full hearing. It should be noted that tribunals can now deal with 'ordinary' breach of employment contract claims providing the tribunal is also considering a claim arising out of the dismissal of the employee.

Appeals from industrial tribunals are heard by the Scottish Employment Appeal Tribunal or Employment Appeal Tribunal (SEAT/EAT), presided over by a High Court judge but again with lay members representing both employers and employees. Occasionally, the lawyer Chairperson of both an industrial tribunal and the SEAT/EAT is 'outvoted' by lay members, such has been the emphasis of the tribunal system on the employment 'realities' of workplace disputes.

A further appeal on law can go to the Court of Appeal or Court of Session in Scotland, and should the losing side wish to pursue it, to the House of Lords if the House considers the appeal has legal merit. There is also the possibility of a reference to the European Court of Justice (ECJ) if UK courts consider they need guidance on an area of law which has developed so as to implement European Union law. Examples here are equal pay legislation and the Transfer of Undertakings (Employment Protection) Regulations 1981 (TUPE).

Under UK law tribunals are only able to award compensation to a specified

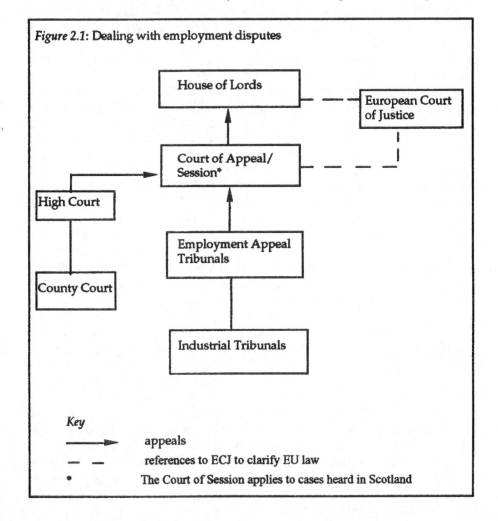

Figure 2.1: Dealing with employment disputes

Key

———▶ appeals

— — references to ECJ to clarify EU law

* The Court of Session applies to cases heard in Scotland

statutory maximum even where the sum arrived at grossly fails to compensate a particular victim for loss. However, where the relevant legal rules are European-derived, there can be no artificial ceiling on compensation.

CAN INDUSTRIAL TRIBUNALS DEAL WITH BREACHES OF CONTRACT?

Many cases going before tribunals do deal with disputes over contract terms. These may include the application of disciplinary rules, or of a contractually agreed redundancy scheme. They are then considered in the context of a claim for unfair dismissal or a redundancy payment. The long- standing problem of UK law has been that in order to test the validity or application of contract terms the employee has either to have been previously dismissed by the employer, or claim constructive dismissal because of a major breach of contract by the employer. The need for an employee to resign in order to establish that the employer had broken the contract has obviously inhibited employees testing their contracts. This has been especially so in times of high unemployment.

There have been some changes in recent times. The Wages Act 1986 provides that employees (but not the self-employed) can make claims in industrial tribunals where the employer has made an unauthorised deduction from pay. Lawful deduction can only be made where the employee consents (for example, to a 'check-off' of trade union dues) or the law allows for it, e.g. PAYE. Although the Wages Act was intended to deal with withholding pay for disciplinary reasons or for stock or cash shortages case law quickly showed that a very wide range of contractual problems and disputes were covered. Cases have been brought and won where employers did not pay agreed wages, holiday pay, bonuses and the like or even where employers felt they were entirely 'justified' in withholding cash so as to offset damage by employees to, say, vehicles or equipment. The number and range of cases has grown such that now around 16,000 claims under the Wages Act are made annually.

This legislation allows contractual terms and rights to be tested and it has emphasised the precise wording, style and management of contracts themselves. Most importantly, it has allowed contracts to be challenged by employees without the necessity of handing in their notice.

Tribunals have also become more familiar with sophisticated and legally complex arguments regarding the nature of contracts of employment themselves. As considered above, TURERA 1993, section 38 extended industrial tribunal jurisdiction for certain breaches of employment contracts. Claims can be brought by either side, providing a claim is already being brought for dismissal or redundancy. This might include cases for unpaid expenses, or for damage caused by the employee. This possible area of legal claims re-inforces the need for clarify and care in the drafting and managing of contracts.

The increased role for industrial tribunals has not taken responsibility for employment contracts away from County/Sheriff Courts or High Courts.

Some employees and employers will have a choice as to where they make a claim. Indeed, some of the remedies of the ordinary courts remain more attractive. Injunctions and public law remedies, e.g. declaration, which allows courts to clarify the legal position affecting contracts, can be very useful. For 'test cases' and complex cases involving the public sector it is unlikely that industrial tribunals will ever provide the necessary expertise. However, there are increased options now for contracts to be legally tested.

ORGANISATIONAL OBJECTIVES AND LEGAL RESTRAINTS: AN ILLUSTRATION

As Chapter 1 explained, employment contracts operate within a changing context, especially employment legislation developed by the EU. Contracts

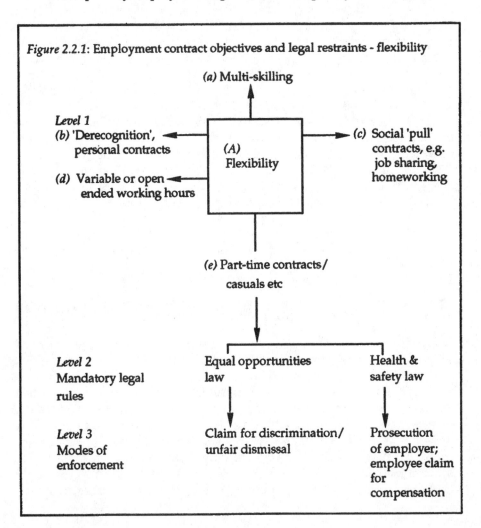

Figure 2.2.1: Employment contract objectives and legal restraints - flexibility

must, of course, comply with legal demands.   They need to also reflect organisational policies.   If, for example, an organisation has a policy to encourage 'flexibility' this will affect both the type and content of contracts and may lead to de-recognition of unions and use of personal contracts.   If an organisation has a strong policy commitment to 'quality', this too will impact on the nature and enforcement of contract terms.

Figures 2.2.1 and 2.2.2 illustrate how these two policies might affect individual contracts (at Level 1) but also how two key areas of law - anti-discrimination and health and safety might respond to or restrain the policies (at Level 2). Level 3 sets out what legal actions might be brought by employees.

Figure 2.2.1 illustrates how the flexibility policy might affect contract types and contract terms.   The organisation might develop 'personal contracts' by de-recognising a trade union because it considers collective bargaining inhibits flexible pay arrangements (2.2.1 (b)).   However, the need to retain key staff also suggests that job sharing as a flexible work pattern could be developed (2.2.1 (c)).   Similarly, the organisation might see the development of part-time or fixed term contracts, use of agency temporary staff and 'casual' contracts as essential to match staffing to business needs (2.2.1(e)).   Fluctuating demand might also lead to increased flexibility in working hours - more overtime, annualised hours etc (2.2.1.d).   They might also require multi-skilling to avoid waste and delays by staff (2.2.1 (a)).

However, as Figure 2.2.1 also illustrates, although the law allows the employer wide discretion it does provide some boundaries to the flexible options available in the form of obligations, especially those derived from the EU.   Not all policies will be legally challengable, even assuming that any changes to contracts have been made lawfully (see Chapter 8).   For example, multi-skilling raises few problems, and only rarely do legal problems surface over job sharing or homeworking.   However, de-recognition of unions has been fraught with difficulty, and the use of atypical workers, especially part-timers, has recently been subject to virtually constant legal intervention via European anti-discrimination legislation.

ANTI-DISCRIMINATION LEGISLATION

Legislation, particularly the Sex Discrimination Act 1975, the Equal Pay Act 1970 and the Race Relations Act 1976, regulates workplace practices which directly or indirectly cause disadvantage.   If, for example, part-timers and temporary staff who are predominately female have lower pro-rata pay than full-timers, and/or are denied access to occupational benefits and training, this will probably be seen as discriminatory and unlawful.   European law, drawing on Article 119 of the Treaty of Rome (equal pay for equal work regardless of sex), has effectively challenged virtually all practices which differentiate between part-time and full-time staff.   In addition, statutory exclusions from job security protections have been held to be discriminatory.

Employment practices which see 'atypicals' as providing a flexible and cheap option now need serious review. The law has relevance not only when recruiting and setting contract terms but also when dealing with downturns in demand. For example, redundancy terms/procedures which allow for the selection of part-timers in Figure 2.2.1(e) for redundancy before full-timers might be challenged if most or all of the part-timers are female.

HEALTH AND SAFETY LAW

Health and safety law can be applied similarly in Figure 2.2.1(d). The employer may wish to insert contract terms which require flexibility in working hours, for example, unlimited overtime and/or evening and weekend working. It might then be argued, first, that such demands are discriminatory against women who have dependent relative responsibilities. This may contravene both UK and EU anti-discrimination legislation. Second, these demands might present a risk to health and safety if hours are excessive and/or specifically contravene EU legislation (the Working Time Directive[6], which places limits on maximum periods of work. This should be fully operative in the UK by late 1996).

Figure 2.2.2 overleaf illustrates how another key organisational policy can be reflected in contract types and terms. This time the emphasis is on quality. The contracts of staff, addressing the need to be aware of customer needs in 2.2.2(b) ,may emphasis interpersonal skills, dress and courtesy. Appraisals (2.2.2(a)) may emphasise employee performance in terms of 'quality' or 'excellence', and the need to achieve or sustain BS5750/ISO 9000.

However, it is particularly important to note the role of health and safety law in a context of the growing incidence of stress at work. Many argue that the push for 'quality' or 'excellence' in Figure 2.2.2 has increased the burden on individual employees to such an extent that their health is suffering. Many lawyers see that such illnesses are well within the legal framework which requires employers to protect health and safety or live with the consequences, especially regarding stress. Claims are now being regularly brought and won by employees who assert that continuous pressure has led to stress-related disorders.[7]

The health and safety agenda now applies not only to the basic protections regarding the workplace, work equipment and work procedures but also has special relevance to particular groups of workers. Important here are pregnant women, night workers, people with disabilities, atypical staff and those working with hazardous substances or who are otherwise vulnerable.

It should also be noted that there are growing concerns for the health and safety of self- employed persons and that the legal 'net' for both health and safety and equal opportunities is increasingly extending to the self-employed.

Equal opportunities legislation might also have relevance to policies to promote quality and excellence if they are not properly developed and man-

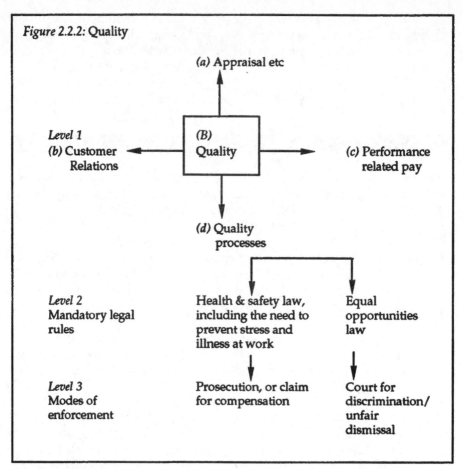

Figure 2.2.2: Quality

(a) Appraisal etc

Level 1
(b) Customer
Relations

(B)
Quality

(c) Performance
related pay

(d) Quality
processes

Level 2
Mandatory legal
rules

Health & safety law,
including the need to
prevent stress and
illness at work

Equal
opportunities
law

Level 3
Modes of
enforcement

Prosecution, or claim
for compensation

Court for
discrimination/
unfair
dismissal

aged. For example, in Figure 2.2.2(c) performance related pay (PRP) has often been developed so as to reward high quality performance by employees. However, the law requires that such schemes apply objective performance criteria, free of gender bids and those who operate schemes do so fairly. Research studies have shown that PRP can be used to the disadvantage of women.

These examples of Level 2 issues are clearly in addition to any legal intervention as a consequence of infringement of the standard employment contract rules. Examples here would be infringement of rules to prevent illegal (e.g. tax evasive,) contract terms (see Chapter 3) and 'phoney' employment relations generally. The Level 3 claims such as for unfair dismissal, breach of contract and discrimination law will follow automatically.

The overall picture is that there are many and varied legal constraints on the way in which employment contracts are devised and managed. Some constraints derive from the 'basics' of employment contracts (Chapter 3), others from the impact of legislation aiming to safeguard employment rights in the broadest sense. Some particular types of constraints are derived from two areas of law (equal opportunities and health and safety) which have considerable and growing potency - not least because they are at the heart of EU law. They must never be underestimated.

REFERENCES

1   Directive 92/85/EEC.
2   Directive 92/56/EEC, amending the EEC Redundancy Consultation Directive 75/129/EEC.
3   Directive 91/553/EEC.
4   Directive 77/187/EEC.
5   The Employment Protection (Part-time Employees) Regulations 1995, SI 1995 No 31.
6   Council Directive 93/104/EEC.
7   *Walker v Northumbria County Council* [1995] IRLR 35. This was the first successful negligence claim for stress. It had been caused by staff cutbacks, increased workload and general work pressures on a senior social worker. For a wider consideration of the way in which European law is affecting UK management, see P Leighton, *Despite the Opt-Out: the Europeanising of UK Employment Practices* (1995), Labour Movement in Europe, UK.

3
Basic Legal Rules When Making Employment Contracts

This chapter is the last in Part I of the book. The two previous chapters have explored why effective employment contract management is vital for employing organisations and have aimed to set employment contracts in their managerial and legal framework. This chapter deals solely with the basics of contracts of employment.

However, although legislative intervention is at a relatively low level, the rules of the common law are vital in establishing the mechanisms whereby *all* contracts must be made. The common law provides the bench marks against which organisational practices are judged through often long-established case decisions. If the parties to a contract are unclear as to its terms, one side is misled or lied to, or the contract's purpose is to circumvent tax law the courts will consider the contract invalid. The fact that law is derived from cases in no way implies that the rules are vague or out of date. Courts can and do respond to the expectations of the parties, the dynamics of employment relationships and the wider economic climate.

This chapter deals with the nature and the application of these basic rules to recruitment of staff and will explore typical problem areas and suggest likely responses by law courts should disputes arise. Each of the six key aspects of contracts will be considered in turn.

As an indication of the type of practical problems which can arise and the legal rules which have relevance three hypothetical examples are set out.

EXAMPLE A

A post as marketing manager for a UK based multi-national was advertised as offering a salary 'which is negotiable', 'opportunities for travel outside the UK' and a 'willingness by the successful candidate to work unsociable hours and to demonstrate complete commitment to the company. Maria is offered and accepts the post at £37k pa, though when her first salary cheque is paid she discovers it represents only £35k. When she questions this she is told: 'We are in a difficult market at present; this is all we can afford'. She has recently been told to work on Sundays from the following weekend. She has two young children at school in Birmingham, her present workplace. She is an active member of her local Methodist church. She questions whether her employer can make these changes.

EXAMPLE B

An employer wished to introduce a smoking policy at work. A policy was negotiated with the trade unions and agreed. The agreed policy was distributed to all employees. An employee, Peter, smoked in contravention of the policy. He was disciplined. Peter questioned whether the smoking policy created legally binding disciplinary rules, and whether the fact that it had been agreed with the trade unions but not with him personally was relevant.

EXAMPLE C

A public sector employer traditionally recognised three trade unions for bargaining purposes. A collective agreement contained agreed procedures for the selection of employees in the event of a redundancy situation. The employer recently decided to 'de-recognise' the unions and to embark on a massive compulsory redundancy programme which used criteria for selection of people for redundancy in contravention of the 'old' collective agreement. Employees affected claimed that the 'new' procedures were in breach of contracts of employment.

The above examples cover a range of legal issues. All the issues turn on the precise detail and enforceability of contract terms. For example in (A) can Maria's employer having apparently agreed a salary of £37k reduce it, albeit for pressing economic reasons? Can she be required to work on a Sunday? It is likely that the answer to both of these questions would be ' no' in law, but clearly much would depend on the precise wording of the contract.

In (B) Peter has been disciplined for smoking at work. Is he bound by the policy? Is it relevant that it was agreed to by the union.? He may well not be bound unless the policy has been properly incorporated into his contract, especially its disciplinary rules.

The last example, (C), raises some highly complex issues, in that the relationship between the terms of an individual's contract and the terms of a collective agreement is fraught with legal difficulties. However, it is probable on current case law that the 'old' redundancy agreement would still apply to employees as it would continue to be a part of individual contracts.

Predicting the likely outcome of such cases is never easy, but fortunately the law does provide some guidance for managers who wish to avoid the type of problems and disputes set out above. The key to understanding and applying law requires analysis of:

- *The processes by which legally binding contracts are created*, and

- *The content of employment contracts*, i.e. how information, rules, procedures etc. establish the detail of the contract and thereby the explicit and implicit rights and duties of employer and employee.

THE PROCESS OF FORMING EMPLOYMENT CONTRACTS

Regardless of the type of contract, UK law sets down some basis legal rules establishing the essential elements of a binding (legally enforceable) contract; these have been considered in outline in Chapter 1. These rules apply broadly to all types of employment relationships. For a contract to be legally binding the following conditions must have been met:

Figure 3.1: The key elements of contracts.

1 There must have been an unambiguous offer of employment, by the employer whereby sufficient information about the contract terms has been provided.

2 There must have been an unambiguous and unconditional acceptance of that offer by the employee

3 There must have been an intention that the agreement should be legally binding.

4 Consideration, i.e. wages, salary, fee, in return for work must be pro vided, (not relevant to Scotland).

5 There has been an avoidance of any terms rendering the contract illegal.

6 There has been certainty about the overall nature and content of the agreement.

---

1. OFFERS OF WORK

A typical problem area might be as follows:

A job is advertised, applicants interviewed and an offer made. If a job offer is made 'subject to satisfactory references' or 'subject to satisfactory medical examination', or it leaves open the precise salary point a successful job applicant will be put on, can this be an 'offer'? Perhaps the offer is made 'subject to verification by the Board, or the Trustees'. In which case what is the impact of 'ratification' and the like?

The law regarding the basics of offers is precise. Job advertisements themselves, do not create any legal obligations; they are merely 'invitations to treat', i.e. invitations to enquire further about a job or consultancy opportunity by writing in or telephoning for particulars. Nonetheless, statements made in adverts or orally about the job should be carefully considered to avoid any misleading statements. Adverts which purport to state 'average salaries' or potential 'earning opportunities' or the business or financial status of the advertiser ('the largest UK consultancy' or 'the company with the highest UK earnings') should be avoided unless they are supportable. The reason is that such statements may be covered by the Misrepresentation Act 1973 which aims to curb misleading statements generally, including those inducing people to take jobs. A job offer made on the back of misleading or deliberately untruthful information can be set aside. Alternatively, the person who was misled is entitled to claim compensation for the expenses associated with job interviews etc.

It is also important to make clear the basis of the offer. If employers wish to make an offer conditional on the verification of certain facts, then the law allows for it. This may relate to previous performance with another employer or academic institution (references), or health record or police enquiries. An offer may, though, be dependent in the outcome of an assessment centre process, psychometric testing or even graphology or biodata from applicants. These processes are becoming commonplace and providing they do not contravene anti-discrimination law, defamation law etc. they are perfectly lawful.

It is important to explain to candidates that decisions will be based on their results. The offer in these situations is *conditional* upon a satisfactory response. The applicant will then appreciate that there are continuing uncertainties about the offer. The law allows employers to make their own judgment about what is 'satisfactory'.

The following is an example from case law:

An applicant for a post with an animal charity was offered the post subject to satisfactory medical references. The reference indicated several days absence due to ill health with the previous employer. The potential employer considered the health record unacceptable and withdrew the job offer. The applicant tried to obtain an injunction forcing the potential employer to confirm the job offer, alleging that as there had been relatively few days' absence in the previous year (21) it was unreasonable to withdraw the job offer. The court rejected this argument; whether a reference is 'satisfactory' is up to the person laying down the conditions. (*Wishart v RSPCA* (1990))[1]

Similarly, these principles apply to offers made subject to enquiries/ references regarding character, behaviour and qualifications. Apart from the law of discrimination, the employer is free to determine the background, qualifications, qualities, health record and attitudes expected of applicants for posts. An offer can only form the basis of a legally binding agreement once those conditions have been met.

Many offers are made subject to 'ratification'/'confirmation' by directors, trustees and the like. If so, despite any assurances made to applicants, such as 'they always act on our recommendation', the law takes the view that the offer remains a conditional one. In some occupations, for example, the education service, the need for formal ratification is built in. The 1988 Education Reform Act, though giving schools with financial delegation the power to appoint staff it leaves LEAs in England and Wales with powers to veto candidates who are not considered 'qualified' on formal, professional or personal grounds.

Managers advertising posts, short listing and interviewing candidates should be unambiguous regarding their own discretions and about the information and 'signals' they give to candidates. If an offer needs ratification or references to be raised this should be made clear and the implications explained.

UNCERTAINTIES ABOUT OFFERS?

How important is that applicants are aware of the contract terms on offer? Can you have a valid offer where the salary or fee rate, hours of work, sick pay arrangements and the like are not specifically drawn to the attention of applicants?

The traditional legal response has been that a general offer can be sufficiently clear providing the applicant is entering a well regulated occupation or industry. In these situations any offers are made on 'the usual terms' (*Sagar v Ridehalgh* (1863)).[2] In traditional industries, often situated in self-contained communities and working to well established and well understood customs, this approach made sense. However, today the variations of types and detail of contract terms has grown dramatically. The introduction of job evaluation, appraisal, a huge range of occupational benefits, complex disciplinary policies and practices, all reflecting occupational and organisational culture has led to increased diversity and complexity. The growth in personal contracts, where there are *no* collective sources of terms has heightened the need for clarification at the negotiation stage.

Can the detail be safely left to an assumed familiarity with the occupation or the employer? The answer must be 'no' for the reasons set out above. As much information as possible should be provided for applicants, along with a clear indication of what issues/topics are negotiable. Although the law has generally been generous to employers in applying the principle that 'ascertainability', rather than precise knowledge of terms is the important thing, it is suggested that the less left to speculation or doubt the better. This is not just because of legal considerations whereby it may be open to an employee who has accepted a job to argue that a particular task or requirement was not part of the 'offer', but because ambiguities and uncertainties are so often the cause of niggling and long running disputes. advertised as offering a salary 'which is negotiable', 'opportunities for travel outside the UK' and a 'willingness by the successful candidate to work unsociable hours and to demonstrate complete commitment to the company.

Another issue to be borne in mind is that offers can be made both orally as well as in writing. Written job particulars and information about a post or a consultancy might well provide background information about the employing organisation as well as some specific material, e.g. about business activities and priorities. However, the selection process itself, especially the interview, will focus on the job offer. Care must be taken. Oral statements at interviews that, for example, 'this job always has a car', 'promotion will be within a year', 'successful completion of this project will lead to a contract for the next phase' *can* form the basis of a legally enforceable contract. Interview panel members may consider such remarks merely inducements or 'off-the-cuff' remarks not intended to be taken seriously but if, viewed objectively, they were plausible and taken seriously by the applicant, legal problems may arise if the car, promotion, etc., is not forthcoming. There will then be a breach of contract.

A particularly important matter, in the context of growing use of recruitment agencies/consultants, is whether the offer made by them to a candidate will be binding on the employer. The recruiter is an agent for the employer and candidates are entitled to rely on statements made by them. Similar observations apply to head-hunting/executive search, though the nature of individual arrangements with the 'head hunters' can vary. The best advice is to be clear regarding the contract with the agency/consultancy and ensure candidates are aware of the arrangements.

Overall, at the interview/selection stage it is vital to be sure of the precise nature of a job offer. It is also vital to ensure that the selection process itself does not unlawfully discriminate on grounds of sex or race. There must be no discrimination against citizens of other EU member states who have a right to seek work in the UK, for example by imposing probationary periods on them not applied to UK candidates, not providing the usual range of occupational benefits or offering only a temporary contract on the basis that they 'might not settle down'.

Asking questions about pregnancy, contraception and other matters particular to women or various racial or ethnic groups could be unlawful.

GUIDELINES ON OFFERS

In a context where law provides only a skeletal framework on job offers employers are well advised to be very clear about their practices. They should:

- Review the possible sources of contract terms - collective agreements, statutes, company rules, policies etc. before the recruitment process begins. This should be done *very* thoroughly.

- Consider carefully how much information is provided for applicants; why is it provided? Is *all* the relevant information included, especially about the job itself?

- Consider what is the intended status of the information - is it general information or intended to form the basis of a possible job offer? Is that clear to candidates? If candidates are to be provided with workplace policies, codes etc. is *their* status clear?

- Analyse carefully what undertakings, promises and the like are made at interviews and in other discussions between candidates and management. Have interview panels been fully prepared? Do individual panel members have authority to make 'binding' statements to candidates?

- Make absolutely clear whether a job offer is unconditional or conditional, and if the latter what the precise conditions are which a candidate must meet.

- Make absolutely clear what are the expectations are of the successful candidate. Are the demands for 'commitment' 'flexibility', mobility etc. explicitly part of the job offer or are they considered merely as establishing the culture of the employing organisation in a less precise way? If someone is not prepared to be mobile, for example, what importance will be attached to it? Is the applicant clear about their situation, i.e. will they feel able 'safely' to refuse a job move? Are they required to move house or be easily able to travel to work?

- Make clear whether candidates can make informal visits to the workplace. If so, what is the role of the visits and any statements or assessments made?

- Ensure that *all* those involved in the recruitment are clear about statements to be made to applicants, about the job itself and about the status of codes and procedures, at the workplace. This is especially important when 'non-employees' are part of the recruitment process, such as trustees, school/college governors, non-executive directors or local government councillors.

All these matters are related to the precise nature of the job offer itself. Clearly, other issues arise such as those concerned with anti-discrimination legislation, so that procedures to ensure that the best candidate is selected will need attention. This is beyond the scope of this book. Similarly, there will be differing practices about de-briefing unsuccessful candidates.

Job applicants are increasingly making fuller enquiries about jobs and job offers and employers need to be prepared for this. As little as possible must be left to chance. There is no place for vagueness or wishful thinking when job offers are made!

2. ACCEPTANCE OF OFFERS

The law requires that the person to whom an offer is made (offeree) accepts it on the same terms. If the offeree introduces new terms, questions the nature of the offer or is otherwise equivocal in their response, the response itself is seen simply as continuing the negotiation process. In some situations, for example a candidate asking for a higher salary, the response will operate as a counter offer. This then leaves the offeror (employer) in a position to accept candidates offer and let the original lapse or insist on the original one. The following example illustrates the point:

> A job offer was made on 'Grade 3'. The offeree wrote back asking that the salary be at Spine Point 16 within Grade 3 (say £15,400 p.a.). The salary for Grade 3 goes from £13,200 to £17,400 but either little attention had been paid to the Spine Point during interview or it had been assumed that the salary be lower. The reply from the successful candidate operated as a counter offer i.e.. that the job was acceptable at £15,400. If the candidate is allowed to start work and nothing is said about the salary, it will be hard to refute the inference that £15,400 was the agreed salary.

TIME OF ACCEPTANCE

There are a few nail-biting situations where the time of acceptance is crucial.

*   An offer is made, but will lapse at 5 p.m. on 12 October. What is the position if an acceptance letter is posted but lost in the post?

*   A fax is sent by the offeree but not received by the key manager or by the specified time.

*   A message is telephoned to the organisations switchboard but not passed on.

Contract law was developed in an era before modern communication systems and has struggled to devise appropriate rules. The basic rule is that an acceptance is effective when actually communicated to the offeror. Leaving messages is inadequate; however, a letter forms valid acceptance of an offer when posted. Clearly 'Special Delivery' 'Recorded Delivery' etc. are more effective as proving time of posting!

The rise of the Telex, FAX and E-Mail have posed new problems but recent case law reveals that if the employer states that successful candidates can FAX a reply the acceptance is only effective when it is received by the employer. Doubts, though, remain over whether the FAX has to be actually handed to the relevant manager to be effective. Wise candidates check that their reply has been received by the relevant manager and that the formalities generally are complied with.

ACCEPTING OFFERS BUT FAILING TO TURN UP?

Another increasingly problematic area concerns people who accept offers, apparently enthusiastically, but then fail to turn up, or say they will come to work only if certain 'conditions' are met. The law is very clear on this matter - they have accepted the offer unconditionally and are then in breach of contract if they don't come. It has become common in some employment sectors for candidates to 'accept' several jobs and then hope to 'play them off'. The only factor inhibiting the employer from taking legal action as consequence of a candidate failing to arrive for work has been the perceived high costs of legal action itself, even though the disruption caused by the non-arrival might have been major.

3. CREATING A 'LEGALLY BINDING RELATIONSHIP'

This is an increasingly important aspect of employment contract law. To set the scene, it is helpful to consider the following hypothetical situation.

Coggo Ltd, a medium sized electronics manufacturer had negotiated with the Union of Electrical Compositors and Allied Trades (UECAT) for many years. A newly recruited director of personnel, Tony, had been keen to develop a more strategic approach to employment relations. He focused on equal opportunities, especially regarding training facilities, but also felt the need to develop a more flexible approach to pending redundancies. The issues were discussed with UECAT and policy documents drawn up. Copies of the policies were available to all employees. Then two events occurred. A female engineer, Julie, who worked part-time and had a young child, but who had never received any training, then expressed an interest in management training. When she claimed a 'right' to training she was told the equal opportunities policy was there to 'establish agendas' and to 'provide a target for the future'. Her manager also added that she could, of course, make a claim for the sex discrimination 'if she felt that badly'.

Economic problems which appeared to have been weathered by Coggo Ltd suddenly got worse. It was decided that 10 long-serving employees would have to go. The redundancy policy devised in 1994 stated that the main criteria for selection for redundancy was skill needs, regardless of age, sex , experience and pay in their respective departments. The workers challenged the selection but were told that the redundancy policy 'was only meant to establish some broad guidelines'. It was not part of anyone's contract so no law had been broken, Tony said.

The union challenged the employer's responses regarding both of the negotiated policies. It argued that as such policies were well within the remit of their collective negotiating rights they should be complied with. The employees affected indicated 'they were going to law' and would argue that the Coggo's decision on redundancy was a breach of their contracts and could not be enforced.

This example raises some of the most important issues of employment contract law. The law distinguishes between matters which are contextua/ background/descriptive and the like and those intended to be legally binding. The acid test for what is legally binding is that if a term which is legally binding is broken the 'victim' can sue for breach of contract or resort to other forms of legal redress (see Chapter 9).

At its simplest level, the law considers that if an invitation is made to dinner at someone's house and the guests do not turn up, this does not entitle the furious chef to sue for breach of contract. If, however, an offer is made to provide sponsorship or a scholarship for someone, but the cash is not forthcoming, the law has more problems in deciding whether there was an intention to create a legally binding contract. Much hinges on whether there was a financial element involved and on the expectations of the parties. It also depends on the context. In an employment situation it is unlikely that an agreement to perform work for another will be rejected as having no legal validity.

However, there are other basic issues. They tend to focus not so much whether the *whole* contract was legally binding but whether particular elements or clauses were. Classic examples have been provision of workplace welfare and social benefits. If a company handbook informs employees that there is an employee car park, or that free dental checks are periodically carried out, or there are discounts on staff purchases and these are withdrawn, courts have very occasionally had to decide whether the employees could sue for breach of contract. What are the key legal rules?

THE LAW

The law often hinges on the way that information is communicated to employees. Language such as 'the employer *intends* to make available', 'the employer *may* provide', or 'x' is provided *'at the discretion* of the manager', or 'employees will *normally* have a Christmas bonus' will counteract any impression of a binding legal obligation. If, however, despite such phrases a particular benefit or facility has always been provided, leading to mutual expectations that it will always be, a different situation may arise. Here, a long established custom and practice may have changed the character of the 'discretionary payment' into a binding legal term.

This approach would be the starting point for the analysis of Coggo Ltd's policies in the case example above on, respectively, training, equal opportunities and selection for redundancy. The wording would be crucial. It is likely that Julie would have difficulties in establishing a 'right' to training derived from the policy. Policies of this nature tend to provide a framework and set organisational targets but are usually not perceived as likely to give rise to claims for breach of contract. Julie might have grounds for a sex discrimination claim if she can establish that she has been treated less favourably than a comparable man.

However, the collective agreement dealing with redundancy selection appears very specific and, providing it has been incorporated in employee's contracts, i.e. had become explicit terms of the contract, could be enforced. If the policy, is clear on the criteria for selection it is likely that there was an intention to create legal relations and it will be enforceable. The facts would need very careful consideration; there would be no certainty that Tony's views would prevail. (A case study of an effective approach to workplace policies appears at the end of this Chapter).

What of job descriptions, work rules etc?

Many employment contracts have job descriptions/specifications etc providing detail of the content and scope of the job. They often comprise a list of perhaps 10 - 15 items, many of which are rarely, if ever, actually performed. Typical of the questions which often arise are:

- Do job descriptions have legal binding status? How important are they?

- What is the legal situation if an employee is called upon to carry out a task which has not ever been requested before?

- What if the employee insists on a legal 'entitlement' to perform all the tasks on the list?

The leading case in this area is as follows:

In *Secretary of State for Employment v ASLEF (No. 2)* (1972)[3] a matter was tested which, although not dealing directly with the above questions, has great relevance. The case arose out of an industrial dispute involving British Rail. Specifically, it was a 'work to rule', i.e. industrial action which caused disruption through employees insisting on following the minutiae of operational and safety rules. Trains did not leave depots if they had dirty windows, or if plugs were missing in washrooms etc. These responses by rail staff were fully in accordance with the Rule Book but, in practice had to be sometimes ignored to ensure the railway system kept moving. Were these rules part of the contract? If so, the rail unions, regardless of their motives, could never be said to be in breach of contract? It was argued that they were merely complying with legally binding contract rules. The court decided that the Rule Book was *not* contractually binding; the rules were merely instructions as to how the job should be done and not part of the contract itself. They could, though, if necessary provide substance for the implied legal obligation on employees to obey lawful orders (see page 62 below).

The implications of this decision are:

• It is likely that job descriptions etc. are not, of themselves, contract terms. However, the contract may clarify the situation by indicating they are.

• The borderline between what courts consider legally binding and those matters which are not, such as works rules, is often a very fine one. The practical implication is that employers should be explicit in constructing documents about the legal status of all items set out in it, especially job descriptions, dress codes, welfare packages etc.

• It is important to be absolutely clear about the status of *all* policy documents at the workplace, such as:
> Equal opportunities
> Smoking and alcohol
> Harassment/dignity/ & violence
> Health and Safety
> Recruitment and training
> Early retirement schemes
> Secondment
> Career breaks
> Job sharing
> Welfare and health policies

Policies can achieve legal force if they are properly incorporated in individual's contracts. When exploring the question of legal status law courts look at the surrounding circumstances, the context and style of the relevant policy document, and the presence or otherwise of cross-references to it in other documents, such as disciplinary rules and procedures.

EXAMPLES OF WORKPLACE POLICIES

The following examples set out different approaches to some typical workplace policies. Policies can usually be made even clearer by adding a phrase such as:

'Nothing in this policy imposes a legally binding duty on X Ltd .... to provide ..... etc'. Or, 'Employees are reminded that this policy merely sets the guidelines for individual managers when exercising discretion when ....'.

'This policy is merely indicative of the organisation's general approach...individual topics would be dealt with individually in accordance with departmental priorities'

'This training policy refers to opportunities only; discussions regarding the nature, content, availability and support for individual training is at the complete discretion of the departmental manager'.

'The company would normally provide financial support for training; the company reserves its right not to provide support at its complete discretion'.

'The Smoking Policy is fully integrated into the organisation's Disciplinary Code. Failure to comply with the Policy will be a breach of discipline and will be dealt with accordingly'.

'As part of its equal opportunities programme the authority undertakes to consider seriously and sympathetically any request to job share by an employee returning after maternity leave. The authority would use its reasonable endeavours to find a suitable job share partner but cannot guarantee to do so'.

WHAT IF A CONTRACT IS FOR AN ILLEGAL PURPOSE?

Infringement of the legal rules can have major and adverse consequences, such as imprisonment.

Consider the following hypothetical case study:

> Three trainees, aged 17, 18 and 20 joined a car hire and vehicle maintenance company. Much of the hire and maintenance work took place outside the UK as the company had subsidiaries in many European states. This required them to travel to continental Europe. Their basic wages were £170 per week. One of the directors of the company offered 'cash performance bonuses' of £40 per journey if they brought specified individuals back as passengers. He told the trainees that such actively was part of his 'international work for refugees'.
>
> The company got into financial difficulties, and full wages were not paid to the trainees. They began a claim before an industrial tribunal under the Wages Act 1986 for unpaid sums. When the case was awaiting hearing the police raided the company offices and confiscated documents indicating that the company had been dealing in illegal immigrants. The trainees were clearly implicated. They claimed their innocence. Aside from the criminal prosecution for complicity in the illegal immigration it now appears that their Wages Act claim will fail as their contracts of employment are open to challenge as being for an illegal purpose and therefore unable to form the basis of a legal claim.

This illustrates another important yet frustratingly imprecise area of law. The apparently simple legal rule is that a contract which is illegal can be declared void and be unenforceable by either side. The law takes this rule very seriously; it considers that no-one should benefit from an illegal contract.

Where there has been collusion it seems appropriate that no-one should be able to benefit from the 'contract'. However, there are two common types of problems in this area, as the hypothetical case above illustrates:

(1) Where the illegal act or dimension of the contract is a relatively small

part of the whole nature of the relationship, or

(2) Where the employee is misled or threatened, or is ignorant of the unlawful nature of the contract.

The position in (1) is that courts generally take the view that if a contract has illegal purpose(s) (to evade tax legislation immigration controls, environmental, or licensing laws etc.) which in some way benefits *both* parties, the illegal element(s) 'taint' the *whole* contract and make it unenforceable. This strict approach is demonstrated by the following industrial tribunal case.

CASE LAW EXAMPLE - 'UNTAXED EXPENSES'

An employee had worked for the company for 16 years, usually in Huddersfield. In 1982, he agreed to work in Barrow In Furness. It was expected that he should have a lodging allowance and other expenses, to be regarded as non-taxable. However, it was also agreed that, in reality, he would travel daily to Barrow in a car provided by the company. He was paid the tax free lodging allowance for 4 weeks. A year later, he was made redundant and claimed a redundancy payment. He lost, because during the 4 week period the year before when, to the employer and employee's mutual benefit, tax had been illegally unpaid, his continuity of employment was broken. His 16 years service, and in comparison, the brief duration of the 'illegal' episode was of no importance. (*Hyland v J H Barker (North West) Ltd* (1985))[4]

Illegality can affect the situation both at the time the contract was originally made as well as when subsequent changes or additional clauses are added. One of the most frequent practises subject to the illegality rules is collusion over the creation 'phoney' contracts of self-employment perhaps to escape tax and other payments (see Chapter 4), especially where individuals were previously employees. Tightening up laws relating to contract documentation (See Chapter 5) also heightens the risk of legal challenge. It is also important to note that the illegality rules apply to all types of employment contract - freelance, consultancy, agency temps as well as employees.

But what if, as in the illustration above, the employer or the employee was either completely innocent of the fraud, deception etc. or, even if they knew about it, they derived no benefit? Here the law shows a little more sympathy as the following case shows:

CASE LAW EXAMPLE - 'THE WAITER AND THE VAT FRAUD'

Two waiters employed by a night club were required to operate a scheme whereby their employer was involved in VAT fraud. The employer was charged with fraud, the waiters provided evidence against him but were subsequently dismissed. The waiters claimed unfair dismissal. Could they claim, it arguably, their employment contracts were tainted with illegality. The Court of Appeal examined the facts of the case carefully and stressed that for the illegality rule to apply, the contract should have been entered into on the basis of an illegal purpose. This purpose should also benefit the employee. It appears that knowledge alone of the illegal act is insufficient to prevent an employee claiming on the contract, so here they won. (*Hewcastle Catering Ltd v Ahmed and Elkemah* (1991))[5]

Applying these legal rules to the hypothetical case involving the trainees and illegal immigration a court may well have some sympathy with the trainees' proclaimed innocence of the real facts. However, the provision of the bonus in that example would be a problem, especially if its size appeared disproportionate to the task it was apparently related to. If it was seen as some sort of inducement it is probable that the contract would be void and their claim unsuccessful.

In concluding, it must be recognised that although most of the case law has concerned tax matters, the increasing impact of European law on basic contract terms, such as working hours, Sunday working, health and safety rules, etc. will probably raise other problems. Agreements between employer and employee to 'opt out' of new legal rules will be subject to this basic principle of UK law. Such 'deals' may well be challengable! Stressing freedom of choice, flexibility, experiment etc. may be popular with many employers and managers, but there may be problems if negotiations aim to circumvent or minimalise the impact of statutory employment requirements on working time, for example. The law's attitude to negotiation is that whatever the intentions of the parties, it is never possible to prevent courts themselves determining the legal realities of a given situation.

The practical implications of 'illegality'
The major circumstances where it has had practical relevance are:

- *employment status*, i.e whether an individual is an employee or a genuine 'freelance', 'consultant' etc., and why a particular 'arrangement may entered into'. 'Phoney' Schedule D arrangements will make the whole contract illegal. (See Chapter 4 generally).

- *fiscal matters* relating to employment contracts, especially agreements to disguise earnings as expenses, as a 'tips' or only declare incomes so as they fall below the relevant earnings thresholds for tax and national insurance purposes; agreements described as 'cash in hand' etc. which are not genuine.

- *agreements to circumvent protective legislation*, such as stating age incorrectly so as to avoid the application of health and safety rules for young workers, or court orders, immigration rules etc.

All the above arrangements can be challenged - it is rash to try to use contracts to avoid tax or other legislative arrangements.

The requirement for 'certainty'
If an employee is asked to carry out a particular task or work overtime or on a particular day; to replace or pay for damage caused to the employer's property, problems can arise. An employee might say 'I didn't know I had to

do/pay for that!', or, 'This is the first I have heard of it'. Refusals might lead
to disciplining or even dismissal and then the issue may well be tested via a
claim for unfair dismissal.

This is the final area of basic contract rules applicable to employment
contracts. The law regards it as essential that at least the key terms of contract
are precise. This has usually meant that they are reasonably ascertainable, e.g.
that they are derived from a specific collective agreement or company rules or
perhaps from well established custom and practice; ideally, they should be
clearly stated in writing.

Case law on the issue is limited and unsatisfactory in laying down clear
guidelines for employers and others. An important case is *NCB v Galley*
(1958).[6] Here a miner refused to work on a Saturday. The employer argued
that the obligation to work on a Saturday came from a collective agreement
containing the following clause relating to working time; 'Employees .....
should work ..... such days ..... in each week as may be reasonably required by
management in order to promote the safety and efficient working of the pit and
to comply with statutory requirement'. The Court of Appeal decided that the
clause was sufficiently certain. Although Saturday was not specified the
wording was adequate to include it.

**Implications for the wording of contacts: can 'flexibility'/open-endedness
be sufficiently certain?**

The decision in *Galley* above has implications for the following 'widely' used
phrases:

> 'You are requested to work such hours necessary to effectively discharge your
> management tasks'
> > *or*
> 'Your duties extend to whatever is required to ensure adequate supply of
> materials/efficient running of the company catering facility'
> > *or*
> 'Your duties are as necessary for effective promotion of company products'
> > *or*
> 'You may be required to work anywhere where the company has commercial
> interests'

They *may* be sufficiently certain, especially if evidence of current practice
and the mutual expectations of the parties is presented. It is better to avoid
doubts, even today when flexibility is so prominent in contracts.

However, courts will not enforce terms which are grossly unreasonable or
oppressive. It is also possible that European employment laws will curb such
open-ended clauses in contracts, especially regarding working hours, and will
anyway require clearer articulation of contract terms. This is as a consequence
of the EU Directive on Employment Documentation (see page 95) now
implemented in UK law by the Trade Union Reform and Employment Rights
Act 1993 (TURERA). Wording which is ambiguous should also be avoided.

The following example, taken from the contract of a temporary English language teacher, illustrates how an imprecise document can give rise to all sorts of problems.

EXAMPLE - THE ENGLISH LANGUAGE SUMMER SCHOOL

The organisation had recruited teachers on the basis that the engagement was expressed to last 'usually....three weeks'. Dates were provided and pay was stated to be:

£190 per week (out of London)

£205 per week (in London)

This was for the period 28.6.199()—18.7.199(). At the end of the engagement, which turned out to be different from that specified, the employer stated that pay was on a daily basis and clearly only for days actually worked. They refused to pay for days within the three week period but during which there were no students. It is arguable that the three week period was the crucial matter; payment was only made at the *end* of the short-term contract and all other matters, such as PAYE and NI contributions were based on that period. This demonstrated the employer's confusion about basic features of the temporary contract and basis of payment.

The employees were very puzzled and annoyed, though did not resort to legal action. This was probably due to the relatively short engagement and small sums of cash involved. (See *New Work Patterns: Putting Policy into Practice*, P. Leighton/M. Syrett, Pitman, 1989).

Process and employment contracts: an overview

The application of basic legal rules is not as clear cut as might be thought. The apparently simple rules relating to offer, acceptance and intention to create legal relations can be problematic when applied to the everyday practicalities of working situations. Although in the vast majority of large, sophisticated and well-managed workplaces effective policies and practices have evolved to reduce disputes and uncertainties, millions of employment contracts are still entered into where even the basics of the relationship are confused or unstated.

The major reason to date why so few problems surface in law courts and tribunals is that in order to test the validity of a contract term an employee has had to resign and claim they have been constructively dismissed (see Chapter 9). Many have been understandably reluctant to do this in times of high unemployment and other uncertainties. However, TURERA 1993 now allows ordinary contract claims to be tested at industrial tribunals in some circumstances; this may well make claims easier and more numerous (see Chapter 2 page 20). The pressures to be clearer will inevitably grow.

THE CONTENT OF EMPLOYMENT CONTRACTS

Employment contracts create rights and duties as a result of the contract terms themselves and because specific statutory duties are applied to them, e.g. regarding job security, maternity, and entitlements to paid time off .

The legal orthodoxy is that the contract/common law system is kept separate from the statutory framework. However the reality is that this is not always possible or even desirable. Statutes define many aspects of working conditions, and employees inevitably view them as a vital source of rights. Employees often consider the contract itself as less important. Managers often see the statutory rights, e.g. regarding maternity , as not only important but as the bench mark from which to develop occupational contractual rights such as extended maternity leave and career breaks.

It is the prime responsibility of the managers to oversee the process of contract-making and to be accurate, fair and comprehensive. They need to not only determine the obvious terms of pay, hours, job content, etc. but anticipate future developments and issues. Most importantly term,s need to reflect organisational needs and policies

All employment contracts contain two types of terms:

(a) *Express terms,* for example, relating to pay, other benefits, notice/ termination periods, restrictions on private business activities etc. These are dealt with in detail in Chapter 7.

(b) *Implied terms,* whereby the law itself adds obligations to the express terms in order to give the contract a workable framework and viability viability. Obligations include those relating to a safe working environment, provision of pay and of mutual trust and support.

The former are the product (in theory at least) of negotiation between the parties. The process will have been initiated by the job advert, which generally contains information about the nature of the work, likely salary/fee range starting date and perhaps job location. Candidates often make further enquiries about the post or receive written information by way of 'particulars'. This might relate to equal opportunities policies, pay policies, information about the management structure at the organisation and possibly to outline information about expected performance standards of employees or freelance staff. At this stage It is likely that the information will be generalised, though providing a firm basis for negotiation. Potential candidates may telephone and/or discuss with a relevant manager how the post would relate to them.

These discussions can occur regardless of sector, level of job, skills, or occupation and are as relevant for an application to a post of check-out operative at a supermarket as to a senior post in a specialised area of international marketing. The information, and subsequent discussions will have moved the parties closer to establishing the express terms of the contract.

Legal theory suggests that all the key terms of contract should have been subject to this rigorous and probing process. The 'right' questions will have been asked and 'correct' answers given, so that the end of the process the key employment terms will be clear. In theory, the following questions will have been asked and answered.

'How much will I be paid?'
'Do I qualify for overtime/bonuses?'
'What paid holidays am I entitled to?'
'What disciplinary rules apply to me?'
'How much notice am I entitled to?'
'How do you define confidential information and how does it affect me?'
'Are there any restrictions on my working part-time for another employer in this type of work?'

The express terms are agreed and clarified such that the parties are able to say 'we have a deal'. All then remains to be done is to confirm the deal in writing (see Chapter 4).

CONTRACT TYPES OR CONTRACT TERMS?

It is increasingly common to hear managers describing employment contracts in very specific ways. Indeed, the phrase 'contract of employment' itself is for many too wide, too general. A discussion between managers about contracts of employment will often be peppered by such comments as:

'But what type of contract is it - surely not a **permanent** one'?

'We give all our home-based staff **nil-hours** contracts'!

'We never employ a manager on anything but a **performance-related**, fixed term contract'

'Haven't you moved to **personal contracts** - we de-recognised all our unions ages ago'!

'Although we have some on staff contracts most are **casuals**'!

'Our **part-timers** are on a separate remuneration package'.

'Because we can never predict demand we have put people on **global** contracts'

'We have our fruit pickers on weekly, **open ended** contracts'

'We have moved recently to **task contracts** for our technical staff'!

These comments merely give an indication of the growing diversity in contract types. Chapter 1 explored some of the reasons for the development of these contract forms, such as the need for increased flexibility. It may be that there are few differences (hours, security, job location etc.) between these types of contracts and a 'standard' contract. However, sometimes these factors are seen as sufficiently important to change the essential characteristic of the employment contract. Workers with contracts having key terms which differentiate them from the normal full-time, office/factory based permanent contracts are, in EU parlance, the atypical workers. These types of relation-ships have evolved to reflect business features or needs, and become more widespread because there are few legal rules inhibiting their development in the UK. Examples are job share contracts, fixed term and fixed task contracts. They are considered more fully in Chapter 6 because some key express terms so completely colour the whole relationship that they are worthy of separate consideration.

Standard contracts contain many different terms. Some, for example those relating to pay and hours of work, need to be specified for all staff.

However, there may also be other specific issues at an organisation which have been identified as needing attention in contracts. Examples might include:

- regular theft of goods/material, probably by staff
- misuse of organisational property/telephones
- 'fiddling' expenses
- high levels of absenteeism
- smoking affecting non-smokers
- suspected drug abuse
- car parking by employees in unsafe or unauthorised places
- allegations of sexual harassment

These types of matters will also need to be considered, and responded to by the terms of the contract.

EXPRESS TERMS: THE SOURCES

It is recognised that the picture of a carefully orchestrated and articulated legal relationship as described at pages 28-42 is not typical of the millions of employment relationships entered into each year in the UK. However, even without careful orchestration there are sources of information from which to define the employment contract. Not all will be appropriate at every workplace. Taken together they enable the detail of the employment contract to build up. Included are:

- Terms agreed between the employer and employee, either orally or in writing - *individually negotiated terms.*

- *Collective agreements*, at national, sector wide or plant level, etc.

- *Standard terms* devised by industry - wide bodies or professional assoc-iations affecting specific occupations and professions.

- *Organisational/company rules,* and the like, especially relating to discipline, occupational benefits.

Individually negotiated terms
Individually negotiated contracts are rare, apart from for senior staff, those in highly specialised occupations or perhaps those working in small organisations. Typically, companies have pay scales, and procedures dealing with matters such as absences. Individual negotiations would then centre around the pay scale, leave entitlement or fringe benefit provisions, for example.

The issues about individually negotiated terms tend to hinge on evidential matters. What precisely was the deal? What was said during negotiation rather then written down? If the memory of one side is that there was a clear oral agreement but that the written information contradicted it there can be major conflicts.

To deal with these problems the basic legal rules are as follows:

- Oral terms can form the basis of a legally binding agreement. In *Lassey v Salterville Nursing Home* (1988)[7] an undertaking was given during an interview for the post of matron at a nursing home that the facilities would be upgraded when she was appointed. This did not happen. Miss Lassey alleged there had been a breach of an express term of the contract. Even though the interview had taken place two years earlier a tribunal decided that the state of the nursing home was sufficiently vital for them to accept Miss Lassey's version of events. The express term was accepted; therefore the contract been broken.

- If there are disputes over what was orally agreed when the contract was made it is simply a question of which version the tribunal/court accepts.

- Where there appears to have been an oral agreement but later and agreed written terms contradict those oral terms, the written terms dominate.

- However, where there was an oral agreement, but later written information is different such document cannot override an oral agreement even if the written information is stated to merely 'confirm' the earlier agreement. Contracts are binding at the time they are made.

Employer and employee can usually mutually determine terms of work. Typical of the terms often subject to individual negotiation (other than pay) are fidelity, confidentiality clauses, restraint of trade clauses, job location (workplace and/or home), flexible hours, cover, arrangements, job content, training and career opportunities.

Employees may also introduce new terms, which will be binding in the same way as those introduced by employers. Care has to be take during negotiation to ensure that terms are not 'slipped in which will create anomalies with contracts of other staff.

Individual employee-driven terms might relate to:

- flexi hours, e.g. to attend to dependent relative or, for child care

- term time hours (school)

- job location, - wholly or partly home based

- career break/sabbatical leave entitlement

- assistance with child care costs.

Care needs to be taken with all of these. For example, 'term time' will need to be defined, as will the length and detail of a career break, the precise amount of child care assistance worked out and the tax situation assessed.

The risk of ambiguity or misunderstandings can be heightened by the different objectives and expectations harboured by each side of the contract. There is no place in employment contracts for imprecision, wishful thinking or viewing certain matters as 'obvious' 'the usual thing' or the like. It is absolutely vital that any terms are thought through, especially if they have not been used before; likely problems must be identified and hypothetical situations posed when drafting terms (for example what happens if a school moves to a four term year?; what if a home-based worker's house is burnt down or repossessed by the building society?; what if there are tax changes affecting child care costs? etc etc).

'Term time contract': examples of difference perceptions

From the *employers point of view* the phrase 'term time' is the totality of the school term, excluding half-terms (which the employee must work) and excluding days for teaching staff development (INSET days) or 'occasional' school holidays. Any public holidays coinciding with breaks from teaching terms would count against holiday entitlement.

From the *employee's point of view*, the essence of the arrangement would be availability for work when their child/children were actually attending school. The problematic issues would be half terms and the INSET which would not be working days; as the contract pay system reflected the longer periodic breaks from work there was no reason they thought, to include the coincidental public holidays which should not count against overall holiday entitlement - holidays in lieu should be provided by the employer.

Neither side here is taking a wholly unreasonable approach. The employer may see the contract as a 'concession' or employee 'opportunity'. It will probably cause some disruption in the organisation. The employee may feel that having such a contract will, at least temporarily, confine her to routine work and loss of promotion prospects - that is the nature of the 'trade-in'.

It will, therefore, be necessary to resolve the following in this type of contract:

- the definition of term time;

- the impact of situations when term dates vary;

- the position of half term and other days when the school is closed;

- holiday entitlement;

- unexpected school closures, e.g. for bad weather;

- the extent, if any, of any negotiated variations to the arrangement;

- ideally, a mechanism for resolving disputes should they arise.

COLLECTIVE AGREEMENTS AS SOURCES OF CONTRACT TERMS

In the UK the role of trade unions and collective agreements in relation to the collective rights of trade union members has become highly contentious. Chapter 2 outlined the changes, and the tensions which are often perceived as a consequence. These arise from the views expressed by many employers and the current government that neither business and public sector competitiveness nor HRM initiatives based on empowerment, quality and flexibility are compatible with active trade unionism and detailed large scale collective agreements.

Despite this, over 30% of the UK work-force are still union members and approximately 40% of employers rely on collective agreements for employee terms of work to some extent.[8] Many employees said to be 'covered' by agreements have never seen them, do not know where to get a copy, and find it difficult to relate their individual work circumstances to the agreement. In addition, the legal analysis of how terms from agreements become a part of individual employee contracts is complex, inconsistent and confusing.

Controversies over collective bargaining and trade unions have put the spotlight on the relationship between agreements and individual employees.

The legal questions

The law asks a deceptively simple question - whether the collective agreement was effectively incorporated into the individual employee's contract of employment. If so, failure to comply with the terms of the collective agreement will be a breach of individual employment contracts.

When determining whether an agreement has been incorporated into a contract of employment, the law:

- **disregards the status of the collective agreement itself,** i.e. it should not matter that the agreement was not legally binding as between the parties to or even that it was expressed to be legally binding.

- attaches no particular significance to the fact that not all the relevant employees are members of the negotiating union(s).

- sees the impact on the **individual contract** as the law's sole concern.

The law then decides whether an agreement or parts of it has met the criteria for incorporation. Incorporation of an agreement will have taken place if:

- its existence and content were **brought to the attention** of the candidate for a job prior to the offer being made and accepted, and

- the terms of the agreement were **appropriate,** i.e. relevant to the employee in question. This means that grades/posts referred to in the agreement must include the relevant employee or at the very least their job location.

- the terms of the agreement are **certain and prescriptive**.

The last point is simply an extension to that made at page 40 concerning the overall requirement that contractual terms must be unambiguous and display an intention to create legal relations in order to be legally binding.

In practice, the law's demands are not particularly rigorous. Collective agreements have been considered incorporated in cases where the information provided for job applicants has been skeletal. Statements for example that 'the usual agreements apply' have been effective provided the information has been contained in a handbook or other document available at the workplace. However, prudent managers will go beyond these fairly minimal legal demands and provide relevant information. The written information for employees set out in TURERA, Schedule 4 now requires employers to tell employees if their employment is covered by collective agreements and if so, which one(s) (see Chapter 5, page 95).

Some practical issues
A number of vitally important questions still arise, despite the apparently straightforward nature of the rules of incorporation. For example:

- What if employees, regardless of membership of a relevant union disagree with the collective agreement negotiated with their employer? Can they insist on their individual rights and opt out or substitute a term that they want?

- What is the situation when an express term of contract is apparently contradicted by a collective agreement? This can easily happen if the collective agreement was negotiated sometime after the recruitment of the relevant employee and the provision of contract documentation.

The answer to the first question depends on how the contract was negotiated. If an employee agreed to be covered by a collective agreement and that agreement was incorporated into the individual's contract, their individual preferences will be overridden. However, if the employer negotiates a change to those terms with the union, unless the individual has *also* agreed to have subsequent terms changed solely with reference to collective agreements the individual is still entitled to insist on the original contract term(s). This is because the original term, as incorporated, became legally binding through individual contracts and can be enforced.

A collective agreement is therefore part of the structure of individual contract and ought to be considered on that basis. However, case law is not always straightforward. Problems may arise because a term is agreed with union(s), the idea is popular with most employees but a handful object. Nonetheless, the individuals may well have a case. Two illustrative case law examples are given below.

EXAMPLE A

British Gas had collective agreements with unions some staff were paid to empty gas meters, their pay depending on the number of meters emptied. British Gas wanted to change to a higher basic pay rate but abandon the bonus scheme which it considered too costly. Two employees Robertson and Jackson, strongly objected to the change which British Gas had made after giving notice to terminate the collective agreement. They won their case; the terms derived from the collective agreement remained a part of their contract until lawfully changed. Even if the change to the payment system had been agreed with unions this would have been irrelevant - it's the individual contract which counts. (*Roberston and Jackson v British Gas* (1983))[9]

EXAMPLE B

Marley had a mobility clause in his contract. A collective agreement regarding a redundancy scheme was incorporated into his contract, which established an employee's right to a six month trial period should a redundancy situation require relocation. Marley was based in Bristol. This office was closed down and he was transferred to the London office. After six months Marley said the job was unsuitable and claimed a redundancy payment. His employers refused, saying they had moved him in accordance with his mobility clause rather than due to redundancy. The case was settled out of court, so the vital question of which term prevailed was never resolved. However, it is important to note that the term derived from the collective agreement had the potential to challenge the mobility clause. (*Marley v Forward Trust* (1986))[10]

De-recognition of unions - what is the impact on individual contracts?
Unions have been recognised for a variety of purposes, the major ones being
as follows:

- pay and other terms of work
- discipline and job security
- health and safety
- training policies
- strategy and development.

For present purposes the first two are clearly the most important, in that
the regular meetings and agreements dealing with both substantive items
(*who*, for example, is selected first for redundancy and by what criteria) and
procedure terms (*how* there is to be provision of information and consultation
over redundancies) will establish the key matters affecting individual employees.

However, due to the considerable numbers of employers who have
withdrawn from such agreements - a relatively simple matter because the
agreements themselves are not legally binding, two major legal questions have
come to the fore.

- How does such de-recognition affect the contract terms of employees
previously covered?

- If individual 'rights' *are* preserved, does this apply to all or just some
rights.

Both these questions have been the subject of European and major case law.
There are also some important provisions in TURERA,1993.

In response to the first question, it is quite clear that de-recognition by itself
does not affect the terms of individual contracts providing the legal rules of
incorporation have been met regarding any agreement with a previously
recognised union. De-recognition does not, therefore, remove any existing
contractual rights to, say, sick pay, holidays or other leave arrangements. Of
course any new employees are not covered, and the employer can offer them
different terms of work, again according to the usual legal rules.

The terms might be more or less attractive than those covering existing
employees. For example, the de-recognition might provide the opportunity
to introduce a formal appraisal scheme which had been successfully resisted
by unions when they were recognised.

On union de-recognition, can the employer take the opportunity to change
the terms of existing employees? The answer to this question is complex: it
hinges on the rules relating to contract variation considered in Chapter 8. It
is also affected by the law relating to unfair dismissal, considered in Chapter
9. However, what is clear is that the de-recognition does not, of itself, provide

a short-cut to make wholesale contract changes, but it cannot be challenged as unlawful regarding 'rights' of trade unionists.[11]

The second question - what parts of the collective agreement are retained in individual contracts - is highly complex and the law is not entirely clear. Most of the relevant case law is recent and has often dealt with the Transfer of Undertakings (Protection of Employees) Regulations 1981 (TUPE).[12] Under these regulations (to be considered more fully in Chapter 8) employees affected by business changes are automatically transferred to a new employer, unless they object. If they do object they lose their job security rights.

The legal issue has centred around which contract terms employees take with them. Where there have been no collective agreements they take their employment contracts, i.e. all terms which are legally binding.   Where collective agreement have been a source of terms, e.g. of pay and hours these are similarly transferred. However, questions have arisen over whether, collectively agreed procedural matters (e.g. redundancy procedures) and workplace policies (e.g. equal opportunities and health and safety) carry over. The answer is probably 'yes' in that some collective/procedural rights are capable of forming a part of an individual's contract, but cannot be definite.

OTHER SOURCES OF CONTRACT TERMS: RULE BOOKS, HANDBOOKS ETC

The increased use of computerised personnel systems, and data accessible on work units as well as in HRM/personnel departments, the development of in-house printing systems and the increasingly bureaucratic nature of employ-ment relations have opened up new issues for employment contracts. Until recently, as considered above, express contract terms were largely drawn from collective agreements combined with works rules and the like, the latter often dealing with matters of discipline and workplace specific issues such as uniforms, fire and health and safety rules and procedures, and rules relating to leave and absence.

In comparison with employers outside the UK, employers here have invested considerable energy and resources in company/organisation hand-books and rule books. Such documents also contain material of general interest, such as information about key personnel, the premises and the activity of the organisation itself. The variation in style and content of these documents is considerable - some are small 'pocket' books, others large and glossy.

Increasingly, these documents contain details of express terms of contract. Contract law simply requires that such documents are effectively incorpo-rated. Attention must be drawn to them by letter of appointment, statement of terms etc., coupled with an explanation whether the relevant documents are legally binding. This is especially important where the handbooks etc. contain workplace policies relating to, for example, smoking, harassment, violence and drug abuse. A breach of any of these is a disciplinary matter.

Unless the policy has been incorporated and it is clear that the rules set out are a part of the disciplinary procedures, disciplining or dismissing an employee for 'breach' of a 'rule' will probably give rise to a successful unfair dismissal claim (although a tribunal would give due heed to the conduct of the employee which had prompted the employer's response).

POLICY DEVELOPMENT: SUGGESTED GUIDELINES

Organisational human resources policies take increasingly diverse forms. Typically, they include:

- smoking
- alcohol
- drug abuse
- violence
- drug abuse
- violence
- harassment/dignity
- equal opportunities
- health and safety
- secondment/assignment

As a starting point the nature and expectations of policies have to be carefully considered. Some, for example, a health and safety policy is required by law (Health and Safety at Work Act, 1974) but may not be considered appropriate to create legal rights or duties. Such a policy will typically state organisational objectives and provide information about personnel responsible for health and safety and be generally descriptive in nature. Other policies, for example, equal opportunities, though not technically required by law are often developed so as to create an equal opportunities culture at the organisation. Views will differ as between organisations as to whether all or parts of the policy are intended to be legally binding. If a policy contains a career break or job share scheme then they may be intended to create legal rights for employees.

The acid test for decisions on the status and role of policies is to ask, 'What happens when the policy is broken?' A sigh and a regret will indicate that the policy simply provides a framework or guidelines. If, though, an employee is caught with illegal drugs in his/her possession or under the influence of drugs this is thought to be serious and warranting a disciplinary response then the situation is different. The policy and its rules ought to be legally binding by being effectively incorporated in contracts.

The questions posed in Figure 3.2 should be considered in the course of policy development. There is no set answer to the questions - much will depend on organisational culture and established workplace procedures -but a robust response to all questions is required. Additionally, policy develop-

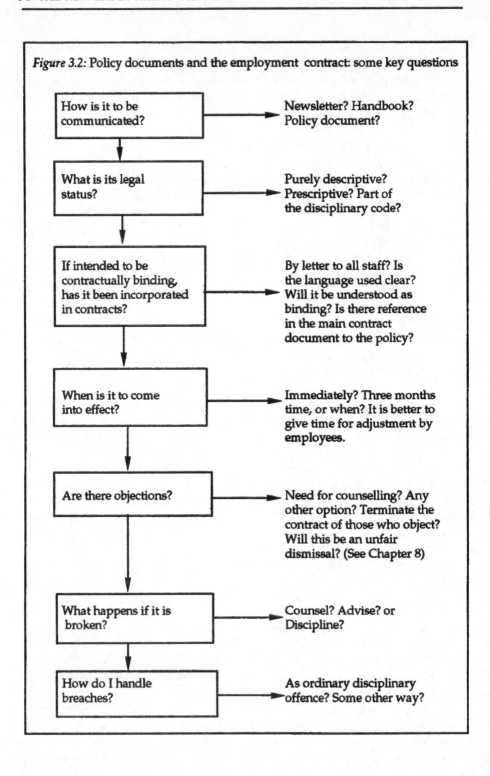

Figure 3.2: Policy documents and the employment contract: some key questions

How is it to be communicated?	Newsletter? Handbook? Policy document?
What is its legal status?	Purely descriptive? Prescriptive? Part of the disciplinary code?
If intended to be contractually binding, has it been incorporated in contracts?	By letter to all staff? Is the language used clear? Will it be understood as binding? Is there reference in the main contract document to the policy?
When is it to come into effect?	Immediately? Three months time, or when? It is better to give time for adjustment by employees.
Are there objections?	Need for counselling? Any other option? Terminate the contract of those who object? Will this be an unfair dismissal? (See Chapter 8)
What happens if it is broken?	Counsel? Advise? or Discipline?
How do I handle breaches?	As ordinary disciplinary offence? Some other way?

ments need to contain mechanisms for amending them in the future. Ideally, the effective incorporation in the contract should include a phrase such as 'the (employer) reserves the right to amend this.... policy from time to time as necessary' This will imply that once the employees have formally accepted that a particular policy is a part of their contract and amendments can be made 'painlessly' provided they are not grossly unreasonable or unreasonably introduced (such as overnight or failing to inform all staff).

POLICY DEVELOPMENT: AN EXAMPLE OF INTRODUCING A SMOKING POLICY

Many employers, often as a consequence of employee pressure and awareness of the impact of health and safety law have developed smoking policies. These may take the form of a total ban on smoking at the workplace or may provide some opportunities for smokers, for example, by setting aside a 'smoking room'. Europants Ltd has decided, after discussion with trade unions to draft a policy as part of its broader 'well-being at work initiative'. Booklets, posters and promotional events have accompanied the initiative. A smoking policy document was drafted and issued to all staff. It declares the whole organisation to be 'smoke free'.

A number of employees, all long term smokers, were very upset at the ban. They formed F.F.S. (Freedom for Smokers) to challenge the policy. One of the group, Tanya, openly flouted the policy by smoking in the reception area. Eventually she was warned as to her conduct but as she continued her protest and was dismissed for breaking the smoking policy. She claimed the dismissal was unfair as the company has no legal grounds for disciplinary, let alone sacking her. She alleged the policy was 'just waffle prompted by fascist ideas.'

In the industrial tribunal a number of key questions were posed by the tribunal's chairman:

1 What was the intended legal status of the policy document?

2 What was the actual legal status of the document?

3 Was the policy a part of the employee's contract?

4 Was there a relationship between the policy document and the disciplinary code at the organisation?

5 Had the correct disciplinary procedures been followed?

6 Was the dismissal fair?

The industrial tribunal sympathised with the company's objectives in aiming to improve health standards but nonetheless had to conclude that the way the matter had been handled was unfair. The organisation had been unclear on question 1 in that they had assumed that everyone would agree with the policy *and* understand that it had to be kept. They had not thought it necessary to either formally incorporate it in employee contracts or align it with the disciplinary code. They had also made no response to those employees who objected to the policy and had generally failed to think matters through. Although the tribunal recognised that the employee herself had behaved in an ill-advised manner the dismissal was held to be unfair as it had not been shown that to smoke was a breach of a legally binding disciplinary rule. The company had also behaved in an over hasty way in dismissing Tanya. She had not had the opportunity to explain her position and the company had made no attempt to provide support for smokers who may have found it hard to stop smoking.

The organisation's Human Resources Director had said in evidence: 'We expected that everyone would see the sense of the policy and simply comply with it. After all, passive smoking is such an important issue and we felt we had an urgent need to respond'.

The case illustrated that however important the issue and however laudable the decision to develop and introduce a smoking policy, the basic contract rules must be kept and policies introduced in a careful and sensitive way. (See further *No Smoke Without Ire: the Complete Guide to a Smoke Free Workplace*, Linda Seymour & Pat Leighton, 1995, Management Books 2000).

IMPLIED CONTRACT TERMS

The express terms of the contract, however defined and from whatever source, concentrate on the 'nuts and bolts' of the relationship. Express terms therefore generally deal with what, when and where, work is to be performed, and what the employee is entitled to e.g. pay, sick pay, PRP, occupational pension etc.

However, there are a wide ranging number of issues concerned with *how* the work is performed and issues of *quality*. Quality can involve the working environment, inter-personal relationships, loyalty and support, and the protection of an organisation's reputation. These issues appear less tangible than the express terms previously considered, but are just as legally significant because the courts themselves have developed a wide range of implied obligations deriving from the nature of the employment relationship itself.

In the nineteenth century, the definition and application of the central obligations of contracts of employment seemed a simple matter. An employment contract was essentially a bargain whereby the employee agreed to perform task(s) for the employer in return for an agreed sum of money. These were the express terms. However, implicit in this was that the employer was responsible for creating and maintaining a safe environment and would pay the employee. The employee for his/her part would perform it capably and not damage the employer's interests. The contract was expressed as the law of 'master and servant', connoting a relationship of dominance and subordination.

However, the law quickly recognised that employment contracts can be more subtle, and that concentrating on purely 'static' legal obligations to work properly and be paid for it was inadequate for many situations. Some occupations require employees to have access to confidential, sensitive or or materials which can claim copyright.

The law devised implied obligations to deal with these situations.

Implied terms: a traditional analysis

Until recently, employment law expressed implied obligations as follows:

The employer's obligations are to:

• pay the agreed wages, or if they had not been agreed, a reasonable wage
• provide a safe workplace
• indemnify the employee against loss or damage, e.g. of their equipment or for bodily injury.

The employee's obligations are to:

• work competently, i.e. in accordance with the skills and qualifications they purported to have
• obey lawful orders given by the employer
• act in accordance with faithful and honest service, eg not to cheat on the employer, abuse the position etc.

Breaches of these obligations can, provide grounds for claims for breach of contract. If the breach was by the employee, and was sufficiently serious, it could lead to an instant dismissal.

Much of the early (and generally still valid) case law was drawn from relatively straightforward workplace situations. Typical breaches of the implied term relating to lawful orders have included lateness, rudeness and the refusal to carry out specified tasks. Stealing from the employer, secretly working for a competitor or disclosing confidential information have been held to be breaches of the obligation of faithful and honest service. Similarly, if an employer has required employees to work in dangerous premises or with defective tools this has been a breach of the obligation to provide a safe workplace.

Employment law has attempted through these implied terms to define and enforce the essential features and expectations of the parties. Chapter 1 considered how managerial practices regarding employment relations have been subject to considerable recent change. Contracts are no longer simply a 'wage-work' bargain. The traditional contract model saw the employer/ employee relationship as self-contained and only slightly related to organisational culture. Terminology, such as 'the parties' and the 'two sides of the contract' reinforced this and did not reflect the common purpose of the relationship. Theories and managerial orthodoxies come and go. 'Corporatimism' and 'worker participation' were the buzz words of the 1970s, just as 'performance', 'quality' and 'flexibility' dominated thinking in the 1980s. Lawyers and law courts are clearly not immune to these trends, which are inevitably reflected in the implied obligations of employment contracts.

THE NEW IMPLIED TERMS

In the 1970s law recognised new implied terms very different in character from those evolved in the nineteenth century. Both terms stress the interdependence of the employment contract and its common purpose, emphasise the integration of the employee in the employing organisation and link directly the demands on employees with corporate/organisational objectives and policies.

CASE LAW EXAMPLE

The starting point of the new line of cases was a case already referred to on page 36 - *Secretary of State for Employment v ASLEF (No 2)*. A work-to-rule by railway staff had led to considerable delays and disruption to rail services. The intention was, by holding to the letter of the BR Rule Book, to achieve maximum effect by means other than strike action. Trains were not driven if there was a minor problem technically specified in the rule book. The disruption was caused, ironically, by a slavish adherence to the rules. This posed a major legal problem. How could such action be considered unlawful, despite its devastating effect, if all the employees were doing was strictly keeping within the rules?

The Court of Appeal solved the dilemma. Whilst accepting that the rule book was relevant, in that it provided the basic instructions on how the job was to be performed, the court held that the employees *were* in breach of their employment contracts. They had broken an implied obligation to *co-operate with* (or at the very least, not thwart) the *legitimate business objectives* of the employer - in this case to keep to the rail timetable and provide other services. Given that the unions' clear intention was to cause disruption they must have been in breach of this implied obligation.

From this case has grown the expectation that employees must **co-operate with a range of organisational objectives.** Employees should be sufficiently flexible to consider business changes aimed at improving productivity or efficiency. A whole range of specific HRM initiatives can have relevance, such as preparation for market testing, appraisal, re-location, changes to working hours, flexible contracts and general restructuring. Failure to consider change or even to go along with it might be seen as a breach of this implied term of co-operation and if the employer dismisses the relevant employees tribunals have sometimes seen such dismissals as fair, being for 'some other substantial reason' (see further Chapter 9).

This implied obligation on an employee has been powerful in ensuring that re-organisation and restructuring has proceeded fairly uneventfully in the UK. It has also helped where a handful of employees have opposed changes supported by the majority. The views of the majority have often been viewed as indicative of a supportive, co-operative attitude and have made the position of those opposed to change more difficult. However, as Chapter 8 shows, the law does not always back the employer and has increasingly curbed attempts to drive through change by demanding workforce co-operation.

A second and even more significant 'new' implied obligation of the employment contract has been that of **'mutual trust and confidence'**. This implied legal obligation affects both the employer and the employee. It has greater impact on the employer because, arguably, the employee's duty of trust and confidence reflects the pre-existing duties of faithful and honest service. However, for the employer it means:

- that employees are not undermined by their employer, especially in front of sub-ordinates or customers/clients etc;

- that the employer is responsive to anxieties and complaints by employees, especially relating to security and safety;

- that the employer does not withhold benefits or opportunities unreasonably or behave unreasonably when 'activating' express terms, such as a mobility clause.

These are merely examples of the type of demands made on employers and their managers. The scope of this legal rule is not entirely clear, depending as it does on an interpretation by a court or tribunal that specified conduct undermined the essential trust between employer and employee. The law recognises that when such events occur it may be hard for the employee to continue working.

The implied term can support organisational innovation. For example, it is possible to speculate that the introduction of Total Quality Management (TQM) or seeking accreditation (BS 5750 or ISO 9000+) requires responses by both managers and their subordinates which the implied contract terms can be applied to. As TQM and related policies are geared to improved standards and service, the conceptual base of the employment contract is entirely consistent with and supportive of it, providing policies are applied sensitively and fairly.

PENSION SCHEMES AND GOOD FAITH

In the wake of the Maxwell scandal concerning the improper use of pension funds attention has turned to the precise nature of the legal obligations of employers and pension fund trustees.[13] A series of cases appears to have clarified some of the issues, and courts have relied on the implied obligation of trust and confidence (sometimes referred to as 'good faith' in this context).

It has been decided recently that:

- where a pension scheme contains a discretion providing for early retirement on health grounds, that discretion should be exercised in accord ance with good faith. Courts can examine the manner of decision-making to check good faith has not been abused. (*Mihienstedt v Barclays Bank* (1991))[14]

• where the trustees propose that a pension fund surplus should be used to increase employee benefits the refusal of the employer to do so can amount to an act of bad faith. (*Imperial Group Pension Ltd v Imperial Tobacco Ltd* (1991))[15]

• employers may be under an obligation to draw the attention of employees to opportunities in a scheme to enhance or extend benefits and to generally keep them fully informed on both changes and what might be in employee interests. (*Scally v Southern Health Board* (1991))[16]

IMPLIED TERMS: SOME DETAIL

In order to focus on the practical application of the legal rules the following are examples of commonplace problems that can arise, some of which have been tested by law courts.

1   Tony, marketing director of an engineering plant is asked to work on a Saturday in order to prepare a vital expert presentation. He does not usually work Saturdays and as he has a golf tournament planned for the day in question; he refuses to work.

2   Mary, an administrator in a building society is asked to take on some of the duties of a colleague who has recently left. She is told that the Society is in some financial difficulties and that she should appreciate the need for extra effort by everyone.

3   Jean, a primary school teacher has composed some songs to help with basic maths appreciation. She has the idea of publishing her material with an education publisher; she has been told that any royalties etc she obtains will belong to her employer. As she spends her weekends doing the composing she questions whether her employer can claim the royalties.

4   Peter, who works in the office of a manufacturer of telecommunications equipment has discovered that some of the recently developed high-tech equipment has been sold to a company called Maylex Ltd. He has also discovered that this company is a probable front organisation for drug traffickers. He speak to a journalist about this but is then sacked. The relevant drug contracts are for an estimated £2.4 million per annum.

5   Joan, a senior civil servant is an active member of a left wing environmental organisation especially concerned with the dumping of toxic waste. It is her judgement that government policy is favouring a number of companies which, she feels, are responsible for the discharge of toxic materials into the English Channel. She provides a statement for the national press suggesting breaches of EU environmental procedures. She is sacked.

6 Winston, a manager in a medium sized computing company has been arrested and charged with indecent assault on a 12 year old girl who lives near to his home. He has strenuously denied the charge but has been suspended from his post, pending the outcome of the legal proceedings.

7   Tracey, a new graduate trainee has been subjected to rude and offensive language and behaviour by Michael, her line manager. He constantly makes comments, often in front of colleagues about her clothes, make-up and likely private life.   After several weeks Tracey speaks to Audrey, the company's director of Human Resources who tells her that Michael's a 'good bloke who means no harm' and she should, 'get used to him'. Tracey has become ill and has had time off work. She believes it is because of Michael. She now feels that the company has not taken her complaints seriously and hands in her notice.

These are merely typical examples of 'classic' situations which have challenged the parameters of implied employment contractual obligations. Some of the examples (1 and 2) raise the question of obedience to an order by the employer; more specifically, the question of whether orders which prima-facie appear to require the employee to undertake duties outside their strict contractual obligations can nevertheless be enforced.

Other examples are built around alleged employee disloyalty to the organisation and its market or other interests, especially its business reputation (example 4). This might be harmed by the private activities of employees outside their working hours. Others, because of publicity, might reflect badly on the employer (examples 4 and 6). Can an employer control or affect the conduct, views, interest or preferences of an employee? Is this not stretching loyalty to the organisations too far?

The question of loyalty is raised by other given examples, even example 7, on harassment. But in this case it is loyalty to what or whom? If the employer is engaged in practices which are dubious, does an employee nonetheless have an obligation (at the very least) to divulge them? (example 5). If not, can the employer still claim that there are 'right' and 'wrong' ways to divulge the information and that, for example, speaking to the press is inappropriate?

There is a borderline between the legitimate interests of the employer and the employee's personal interests in cases where there are no allegations of improper conduct on the part of the employee. Can, for example, the creativity, inventiveness or ideas of employees, which may or may not be marketable, be claimed by the employer to the extent that an employee exploiting the material constitutes a breach of the implied obligation of loyalty as set out in example 3?

Finally, what are the legal protections available to an employee who is arguably being abused by another employee (example 7)?

THE RELEVANT LEGAL RULES

Figure 3.3 sets out the current structure of implied terms. These obligations reflect both the general expectations and practicalities as well as the particular

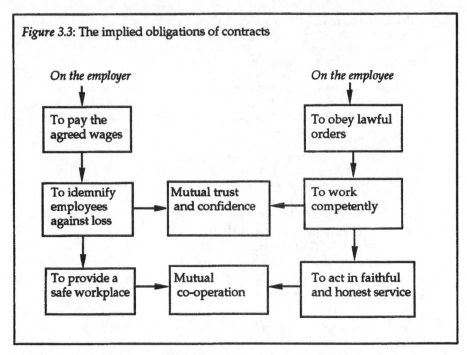

Figure 3.3: The implied obligations of contracts

features of individual occupations or types of employment. The legal rules are flexible and it remains difficult to predict the outcome of a case in a given situation. Dctors and teachers have particular expectations, such as providing a role model for pupils or upholding values relating to the sanctity of life. Conduct relating to an employee's private life or interpersonal relations which would be perfectly acceptable in other occupations can be a breach of implied obligations in these occupations. Doctor/patient relations and teacher/pupil relations are carefully scrutinised and, if considered damaging, will be viewed as breaches of the implied obligation of faithful and honest service, which in these occupations take on a special meaning. Indeed, it is clear from case law that the concepts underpinning implied obligations have not only evolved but expanded.

DUTIES ON THE EMPLOYEE

THE DUTY TO OBEY LAWFUL ORDERS

In most situations there are few problems in applying this obligation. The starting point is to examine the express terms of contract regarding job title etc, hours of work, disciplinary rules and job location. If the order falls within the scope of express employment terms it will, prima facie, be lawful. Clearly, an order which exposes employees to risk, for example, from dangerous machinery, or from attack by clients/customers will not be considered lawful, not least because to do so would contravene the employer obligation to provide a safe workplace.

For example, if an employee is told to work overtime or take extra work home in the evening there would be two questions asked. First, did the contract authorise the demands for overtime etc? The starting point would be the express terms of the contract. If the contract entitled the employer to ask for extra work, in principle the order is lawful and the employee should obey it. Where the contract did not provide for extra work an order is not obviously a lawful one.

However, the courts have sometimes been willing to view such an order as lawful if an employee refusal could be seen as unco-operative towards the organisational objectives. Cases often hinge on the wording of the contract, the degree of flexibility it provides and how the order was given.

What if the contract has not clarified a particular topic - to carry out specific tasks, work on Sundays, wear a uniform or particular style of dress? The courts will ask whether the obligation itself could anyway be implied. It might imply an obligation if such a term was necessary to make sense of the contract. Alternatively, there may be a custom in the industry or occupation that, say, employees usually work irregular Sundays, or wear a white blouse/shirt in contract catering.

In other cases the courts have implied obligation where the employ has willingly performed a task or worked extra hours in the past. This does not always lead to the conclusion that the particular item has become a term of contract simply by being undertaken in the past.

Example: Christmas working

An employee had in the past worked extra hours over Christmas when asked by his employer. His normal weekly hours were forty five. His employer demanded an extra twenty nine hours over Christmas but the employee refused. He was dismissed. The court was unwilling to imply an extra obligation to work overtime during Christmas just because he had done so in the past. He had only worked reluctantly before. His dismissal was unfair. (*Hedger v Davy & Co Ltd* (1974))[17]

Such situations can present difficult problems for managers. The manager's belief that particular tasks or conduct are both necessary, reasonable and obvious is not always adequate to justify an order. The sensible response is to make obligations into unambiguous express terms of contract and not rely on courts to make the best of it should a dispute arise. Customary occupational practices can be more confidently relied on, but not pushed too far.

The outcome of these cases is never easy to predict, even where other employees have gone along with an order. The law still looks at the individual employee's position rather than group trends or what the unions want etc.

DUTY TO WORK COMPETENTLY

This implied obligation is based on a warranty of competence which the employee gives by applying for a particular post. It appears to have most relevance to skilled or craft occupations, and relates back to a time when sophisticated selection procedures were not used. Most employees today outside small or family firms or in casual/seasonal work obtain employment after submitting an application form and being interviewed. The majority of employers require references, and those providing them must take reasonable care in their drafting and their contents or face being held liable in negligence to the recipient. (*Spring v Guardian Assurance Ltd* (1994))[18]

Employers can use aptitude tests, assessment centres and many check out the personal qualities of applicants by psychometric testing, bio data or perhaps graphology. Much less is left to chance, or more significantly to the assertions of applicants.

The common law warranty of competence seems increasingly less relevant. When an employer concludes that an employee lacks the necessary skills and competencies and merits dismissal courts and tribunals will look to evidence of their incapability in their job rather than the so-called warranty of competence. Clearly, if an applicant lies about qualifications or experience this will invalidate the contract not so much because of the lack of competence but because of the breach of good faith and integrity.

DUTY TO ACT IN FAITHFUL AND HONEST SERVICE

This remains an important aspect of the common law's underpinning of the employment contract. Again, it is an implied obligation which sits easily with many HRM policies and practices. In essence, the employee is required to demonstrate loyalty and commitment to the employing organisation. This obligation sees the integration of the individual into the organisation as requiring him/her not to engage in activities which would damage the reputation or business of the organisation. Obvious breaches are stealing from the employer or otherwise behaving dishonestly.

However, much of the case law has hinged on more complex and sometimes controversial matters. If, for example the law demands loyalty from employees what of the 'whistle blower' who believes that the employer is engaged in unlawful activities? Can the implied term of faithful and honest service act as a restraint on the employee contacting the police or other public authorities or to the media?

The law remains uncertain here but, in theory, if an employee who becomes aware of unlawful behaviour by their employer they can divulge information. Such a response will not amount to a breach of the implied obligation or provide grounds to dismiss. However, the employee should take *appropriate* steps - contacting a newspaper prepared to pay large sums of money for the story might not be. Increasingly, contracts of employment prohibit through their express terms the disclosure of sensitive or potentially damaging information to outsiders, stressing the need for the organisation to remain competitive or retrain its image.

Employers may wish to restrain employees from divulging business plans, sales figures, staffing data to outsiders. Case law, often dating from the nineteenth century has, broadly, supported employers' own views of what is market sensitive etc, Thus, disclosure will often be seen as breaches of the implied term, but the law does not support oppressive behaviour or behaviour contrary to the public interest. This is a complex and difficult area; contracts should address the issue through express terms.

A key area of practical importance is where the conduct of an employee outside working time reflects badly on the organisation or arguably affects the performance of duties. Obvious examples are where employees commit criminal acts (or are changed with them), are involved with extreme political or terrorist groups or make damaging and untrue statements to the media. The law has supported employers in broad terms, but some employers go further and use express terms banning smoking, alcohol or drugs not just at work but at any time. The influence of US multi-nationals and American management policies is growing in the UK and affecting even such matters as weight, appearance generally and lifestyle. It is likely that law courts and tribunals would be supportive of employers. Again, the best approach is to make such issues express terms of contracts and ensure that terms are not grossly intrusive or unreasonable.

THE EMPLOYER'S OBLIGATIONS

TO PROVIDE A SAFE AND HEALTHY WORKPLACE

This is an implied obligation of increasing importance. The reason is that both the scope and nature of health and safety law itself have recently changed.

The concept of a safe workplace is primarily defined with reference to the statutory framework. It is developed through the EU, whereby the law now requires the employer to be pro-active with regard to health and safety risks at work. To gain a full understanding of the nature of the implied contract term it is necessary to explore the new statutory health and safety framework in some detail. In 1989 the EU adopted its Framework Directive and subsequently a range of directives from manual handling through to safe work premises and equipment. The directives have led to UK health and safety regulations, which include the following:

- The Framework Directive (89/391/EEC) Adopted 12 June 1989; now the Management of Health and Safety Regulations, 1992. (MOHSOR)

- Workplace Directive (89/6542/EEC) Adopted 30 November 1989; now the Workplace Regulations, 1992.

- Use of Work Equipment Directive (89/655/EEC). Adopted 30 November; now the Work Equipment Regulations; 1992.

- Personal Protective Equipment (89/656/EEC). Adopted 30 November 1989; now the Personal Directive Equipment Regulations 1992.

- Use of Display Screen (VDU) Equipment (90/270/EEC). Adopted 29 May 1990; now the Display Screen Regulations, 1992.

- Manual Handling (90/269/EEC). Adopted 29 May 1990; now the Manual Handling Regulations 1992.

Additionally, there are **instruments or proposals** on:

- Working time;

- Atypical work; directive on temporary and agency work passed; now in Management Regulations, covering responsibility for casual, agency staff etc.

- Temporary and mobile construction sites, covering maintenance, cleaning etc. as well: now the Construction (Design and Management) Regulations 1994

- Carcinogens

- Biological agents, e.g. bacteria, viruses

- Pregnant women, protection from particular risks, e.g. lifting

- Safety signs

- Physical agents, eg noise, vibration

- Chemical agents

- The employment of young workers

- Extractive industries

The effect is that if an employer is in breach of these provisions, not only will that be a breach of the statutory framework but also a breach of contract. The statutory framework is coherent and consistent in its approach to a safe workplace. The employer must, on a continuing basis, undertake assessments of risks to employees (and others), take adequate steps to minimise those risks and establish procedures to monitor health and safety. There must be training, consultation and information on health and safety. Contracts of employment will be affected directly or indirectly by these regulations.

It is important also to note the widening health and safety agenda. Not only are topics such as noise, bacteria and viruses as well as work equipment covered but also, importantly, the need to protect employees from excessive working hours and to provide adequate support for pregnant women and younger workers.

Interestingly, the implied term of providing a safe workplace, sometimes in combination with the implied obligation of mutual trust and confidence has had a wider application than simply requiring the employer to provide safe premises and equipment. Examples of where the law has intervened include situations of employees complaining about unsuitable personal protective equipment but being ignored, expressing concerns about the safety of taking cash to the bank where they believed there was a risk of mugging,[19] or where an employee believed long working hours were affecting his health.

CASE EXAMPLE

Johnstone was employed as a junior doctor. His contract required him to work 40 hours per week but to be 'on call' for a further 48. He could also be required, and frequently was, to work additional hours, sometimes taking his hours to over a 100 per week. He claimed his health had been seriously affected. It was decided by the Court of Appeal, inter alia that the employer was in breach of the implied obligation to provide a safe workplace. (*Johnstone v Bloomsbury Health Authority* (1991))[20]

The case is a very interesting and important one, though debate continues about the real significance of the decision. Specifically, this is because Johnstone had expressly agreed to work long hours; the health authority was under pressure to provide a service and was merely exercising its contractual right to demand extra work. Nonetheless, it was decided that the implied obligation to provide a safe workplace had been breached, and an out-of-court settlement for compensation was reached in 1995.

TO PAY THE AGREED WAGE AND PROTECT FROM LOSS

Neither of these obligations has given rise to important case law, not least because such matters are increasingly subject to detailed express provisions.

Managerial prerogative and implied terms
A current important issue concerns the extent to which the express terms of contract can override the implied obligations set out above.

One of the inevitable consequences of HRM policies geared towards increased organisational flexibility or reductions in waste, overmanning or avoidance of payments for downtime has been the development of express terms which provide for flexibility. Contracts can be drafted with fluctuating hours, incorporating clauses allowing for re-deployment or job content variation, for re-location both within and beyond the UK and the like. In practice many such clauses lie dormant for years and employees come to expect that they will not be activated.

Employees rely on their non-enforcement, such that although in theory, they can be asked to move from South Wales to Newcastle the reality is that they are only ever asked to work within daily travelling distance of their home. When clauses have been activated arguments that they were unfair or unreasonable have often fallen on deaf judicial ears.

However, if the way in which the express term was 'activated' was unreasonable or inhumane the courts may intervene. If, for example, a supervisor in an administration department is told to work in the office canteen, pursuant to an express term in her contract stating she '.... may be required to carry out any other necessary duties', the law may intervene. The intervention may come through a court interpreting the phrase 'necessary duties' as only duties consistent with her skills and current post, or by accepting an argument that such a peremptory act would break the implied obligation of mutual trust and confidence.

The extent to which judges will intervene to curb managers from exercising their strict employment rights goes to the heart of employment contracts. The debate centres around the issue of whether the law has an on-going obligation to ensure fairness and justice according to some generally agreed legal norms or should stay out of such matters, as employees are free to accept work or not. If things turn out differently than the employee hoped (rather than technically negotiated for) it is hard luck. The differing views have given rise to some interesting and hard fought case law. The examples below concern the 'activation' of mobility clauses and illustrate different approaches.

CASE B: THE MOBILITY CLAUSE - LEEDS TO BIRMINGHAM

Mr Akhtar was employed in a bank in Leeds. His contract provided that he could be required to work in any of the bank's UK premises on a temporary or permanent basis. On Tuesday 2nd June he was told to move to Birmingham by 8 June. His wife was not well and he asked for time to sell his house. He was not offered support from the temporary relocation scheme.

He resigned and then claimed he had been constructively dismissed. It was not disputed that he could be required to move. However, it was decided that the implied term of trust and confidence required the employer to handle the contractual issue in a sensitive and not unreasonable way. (*Akhtar v United Bank* (1989))[21]

CASE A: THE MOBILITY CLAUSE - LONDON TO MARLOW

The company was relocating from Central London to Marlow, Buckingham-shire, some 40 miles away. The contracts of secretaries contained a mobility clause - 'The company may require you to transfer to another location'. The secretaries argued that such a move could only be insisted on when it was within reasonable daily travelling distance, ie it did not require moving house. The EAT decided that the clause was unambiguous; it was not unreasonable and the company had not acted in a harsh manner. (*Rank Xerox v Churchill* (1988))[22]

These two cases can be distinguished largely on the basis of the manner in which the mobility clause was activated. There remains debate about how powerful an inhibiting factor the 'reasonableness' test is. Courts are only rarely willing to judge an express term of the contract as unreasonable. The common law judicial view is that contracts are freely entered into and courts should not interfere with that freedom. However, the manner of exercising discretion is still important. In *White v Reflecting Roadstuds* (1989)[23] the EAT decided that it could interfere where the exercise of managerial discretion made it impossible for the employee to perform the contract. Hence, an order, though technically within a job description but well beyond the skills or capability of an employee, might fall within that principle.

The decision in *White* remains contentious. There are still doubts as to the extent to which courts will inhibit managerial discretion. The best advice has to be that decision making must be accompanied by a reasonable approach. If employers are enforcing the express terms of contract they would be well advised to give opportunities for difficulties to be raised by employees, options explored and a generally supportive approach adopted. The applica-tion of the implied contract terms ought not to be underestimated when decisions are being made or contemplated. Furthermore, express terms should not be drafted too widely to cover all eventualities. A realistic expectation of business need should be made, and an appropriate form of words arrived at. Clauses should only be activated following consultation and appropriate support to enable the employee to adapt.

It should be noted that the implied terms set out above apply only to contracts of employment. Self-employed arrangements are not susceptible to the intervention of law to 'flesh-out' the key obligations, which must be determined through effective negotiation in self-employed arrangements to determine the key obligations.

REFERENCES

1   [1990] IRLR 393

2   [1931] 1 Ch 310

3   [1972] 2 QB 455

4   [1985] 1CR 861

5   [1991 IRLR 473 (CA)

6   [1958] 1 WLR 16

7   [1988] IDS Brief 376

8   See 1994, *Workplace Industrial Relations Survey*, R Welch, P Leighton and N Whatley, *Collectivism or Individualism in Employment Contracts: Evidence from a Second   East Anglian Survey*, (1995), Anglia Polytechnic University.

9   [1983] IRLR 302

10 [1986] IRLR 369

11 See House of Lords decision in *Associated Newspapers v Wilson; Associated British Ports v Palmer* [1995] IRLR 258.

12 Transfers of Undertakings (Protection of Employment) Regulations, 1981 SI 1981 No 1794

13 Many recent reforms to occupational pensions arise out of the consequences of the Maxwell scandal. This led to the setting up of the Goode Committee to investigate pensions, the *Goode Report on Pensions Law Reform 1994* and the Pensions Bill 1994-5. See further Sue Ward, *Managing the Pensions Revolution*, 1995, Nicholas Brealey Publishing.

14 [1989] IRLR 522

15 [1991] 1 WLR 589

16 [1991] IRLR 522

17 [1974] IRLR 138

18 [1994] IRLR 460

19 *Keys v Shoe Fayre Ltd* [1978] IRLR 476

20 [1991] IRLR 118

21 [1989] IRLR 507

22 [1988] IRLR 280

23 [1991] IRLR 331

Part II
Effective
Contract
Management

4

Defining Employment Relationships

The trends and policy objectives outlined in Chapter 1 have led to growing diversity in the types of employment relationships, with employers making assessments of their skill and organisational needs.

Many labour use practices are not new; rather, they have been intensified or applied to areas of work or occupation not traditionally subject to consultancy or sub-contracting. What *is* new has been increasing evidence of careful analysis of skill needs and the review of the options available to employers to meet them. There are many options and this process itself has turned the spotlight on the ordinary, open-ended contract of employment. This type of contract, frequently referred to in the UK as a permanent contract to differentiate it from the 'atypical' fixed term, task or casual contract for a limited length has been subject to growing scrutiny. Similarly, the idea of a 'job for life' subject to relatively little variation has been questioned. Change, especially towards increased flexibility has become endemic. The implications of this will be more fully considered in Chapters 7 and 8.

This conscious approach to labour-use strategies might lead an employer to continue using the standard contract of employment albeit specifically designed to implement particular needs, for example, for flexibility. However, other skills needs might be highly specialised, fluctuating or seasonal. Decisions can then be made regarding the appropriate contract type and content. Similarly some occupations may require trainees or other forms of training contract to fulfil organisational development. Many of these specific and practical issues are fully considered in Chapter 6.

CHANGING ROLE OF THE EMPLOYEE

As well as noting trends towards outsourcing for skills or establishing particular types of contracts, the spotlight can be turned on the traditional employee. The trends towards removing tiers of management, the decentralisation/devolution of the management function, and establishing the 'flatter organisation' by pushing decision making to the rim have all dramatically changed the role of the traditional employee in many organisations.

Personal performance is now measured, sometimes against budgetary indicators, requiring employees to display the entrepreneurial skills traditionally the domain of the self-employed. Marketing and financial skills are often demanded of managers in the public service as well as the private sector. Departments/units now often reflect the features of small businesses rather than the bureaucracies they once were.

All this implies that the nature of employment relationships is changing in content and challenging some of the traditional employment boundaries and categories.

Contracts can have various characteristics. They can:

- last for a few hours, or half a century.

- be paid on an hourly, weekly or monthly basis .

- have earnings directly or even completely linked to output (piecework), or partially by, for example, performance related pay, profit related pay.

- be conditioned by traditional or customary practices.

- can be influenced by organisational policies, e.g. to be family friendly or ethically based.

Contracts can also have different labels - manual, white collar, salaried, managerial, trainee, public servant, for example. They can also vary dramatically in detail, and virtually every employer has developed individual policies and practices relating to employment contracts.

All contracts types have particular features and discrete legal implications. However, although an analysis of labour use/skill needs might indicate that, contract type 'A' (freelance) might be the better business option than type 'B' (fixed term), it is crucial to recognise the way in which law regulates the process. Regulation can occur through:

(a) examination of the lawfulness of otherwise of the employment relationship itself;
    or

(b) the terms which can be lawfully inserted and/or enforced.

Figure 4.1 provides an overview of the full range of employment contracts, both traditional and current. Some have a clear organisational role, such as apprenticeships; others, (e.g. those for self-employed consultants) provide skills not available in-house. Sub-contracting might be used for catering, security and construction work and consultants for specialist advice on, say, quality issues, training, marketing or informational technology.

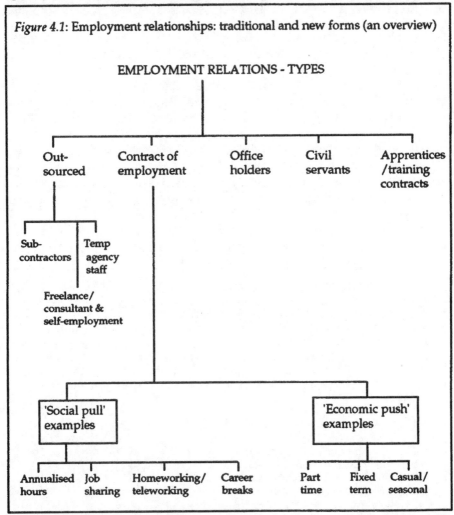

Figure 4.1: Employment relationships: traditional and new forms (an overview)

However, decisions are not always clear cut, for example when deciding between offering an employee a three year fixed term contract rather than on one of indefinite length. There may be clear indicators in some circumstances that a contract should be of limited length, for example where funding, is limited for a specific project or the contract covers the leave of another employee. Other short term or part-time contracts might be used to plug gaps or provide extra cover for peaks demands (e.g. at lunch time in banks) or provide an extra shift on Sunday or late at night.

A particularly important issue is the legal regulation of the important decision to offer an employment contract on a direct employment basis or as a self-employed worker.

THE EMPLOYEE/SELF-EMPLOYED DIVIDE

Self-employed staff are not covered by most employment legislation, especially job security laws, and receive a lower level of protection from other areas of law, such as health and safety and anti-discrimination. If they suffer an accident or injury they are generally unable to claim statutory sick pay (SSP). Conversely, if they inflict damage or injury on others their 'employer' is not vicariously liable for their negligence and 'victims' can claim against them personally.

Self-employment remains attractive to workers, not least due to assumed benefits of Schedule D tax rather than Schedule E and the lower social security contributions of the self-employed. There are also attractions for employers because of the same tax and insurance provisions, reduced obligations under employment law and lower labour costs.

It is unsurprising that this divide has sometimes hit the headlines as well as the law courts, as the following examples illustrate.

EXAMPLE 1: THE DIRECTOR GENERAL OF THE BBC

In the Spring of 1993 a newspaper article alleged that the Director General of the BBC - John Birt, was treated as a self-employed / consultant despite having the senior management role in the Corporation. He had established a private company into which was paid a 'fee' and from which expense claims were made. It was alleged that the consultancy arrangement had been sanctioned by the Inland Revenue and that such arrangements were common in the industry.

As a result of the publicity the BBC announced that Mr Birt's employment status would be changed and he would thereon be considered an employee.

There are several issues arising from the example. It has to be noted, though, that the facts did not give rise to a court case and so the correctness or otherwise of Mr Birts' employment status before or, indeed, after the change by the BBC, has not been determined by law. However, typical of the question being asked at the time were:

How relevant was it that such business arrangements were alleged to be common in the media industry?

How relevant was it that the Inland Revenue appeared to have sanctioned the arrangement?

How relevant was it that the arrangement was clearly the preferred option of both the BBC senior management and Mr Birt?

Was the 'change' to employee status any more convincing?

EXAMPLE 2: THE RIVER BOATMAN

Many companies have tried over the years to make a success of a river bus service on the River Thames linking London City Airport, Greenwich, Docklands and Central London. It has proved a difficult task. Catamaran Cruises operated between Greenwich and London up until 1991 when it ran into serious financial difficulties and was bought by a French Company. This led to proposed changes in working practices and the contract terms of staff so as to make the bus service profitable. Some staff objected to the changes, resigned and claimed they had been unfairly dismissed.

One was a Mr Williams. He had been employed originally as an employee but in 1984 was told that if he wanted to continue working on the pleasure boats he would have to be self-employed. Following difficulties with the Inland Revenue Mr Williams was then told to form a limited company (Unicorn) whereby he and his mother were co-directors. It was argued in the unfair dismissal claims that Mr. Williams, trading as Unicorn, could not be an employee and could not claim.

The EAT decided that despite Unicorn Mr Williams was in fact an employee; he continued to be paid holiday pay and sick pay after Unicorn was formed, and only worked for Catamaran. 'We are not however, prepared in the field of employment law, ...to say that the existence of technical limited company prevents him from being an employee'.

In this situation, unlike the case of the Director General of the BBC the law decided that it was prepared to break through the legal devices to explore the day to day practicalities of the employment relationships.

These examples not only highlight the interest and debate surrounding employment status, but illustrate the perceived attraction of self-employment.

Virtually every legal system in the world has two basic employment categories and struggles to distinguish between them. All try to define the essence of self-employment. For some systems the key feature is autonomy and the ability to work and develop in a more or less unstructured context. For others, self-employment connotes entrepreneurism, flair, creativity but the key remains financial autonomy - and the risk of loss as well as profit. There are many other ways of trying to encapsulate self employment and differentiate it conceptually from being an employee. The difficulties of doing this have led some legal systems to declare the status of certain occupational groups or workers in specific employment sectors by legislation. The UK has left the matter to case law.

A particular issue has been the impact of some traditional occupational classifications and labels. In some occupations, for example, journalism, construction, music, taxis and mini-cabbing there are long traditions of self-employment / freelance status. In others, e.g. teaching, self-employment is rare.

From an organisational perspective the perceived advantages of employing workers on a self employed basis include:

- Some savings on labour costs, especially on National Insurance and the administration of other matters such as PAYE and SSP, as well as on the provision of occupational benefits

- Possibly higher increased productivity and flexibility due to the incentive of higher earnings.

- Less need for close supervision due to the workers' higher skill and experience levels.

- Minimising or avoiding some key employment law responsibilies.

- It is easier to end the arrangement.

However, there are **disadvantages** which include:

- Less control over work and conduct of worker which include the difficulty of enforcing demands for confidentiality, restraint of trade, indemnity, etc.

- Increased demands on management to integrate and harmonise the self-employed worker with the rest of the organisation.

- Lower levels of loyalty, commitment and continuity; possible clashes of interests.

- Possible risks to business reputation through association with 'cowboy' operators and the 'hidden' economy.

Once these matters have been weighed up is it then necessary to more fully explore the law's response and regulation. How does law approach the task?

HOW IMPORTANT IS THE 'DIVIDE'?

It is tempting to see this as a vitally important issue, not least because employment law itself sees these categories as mutually exclusive. Yet is this so? Certainly, self-employed workers are not covered by many of the basic statutory protections such as unfair dismissal or redundancy. However, in making decisions on employment status it is essential to note that law, especially European law is increasingly extending protections to self-employed staff. The major reasons is that European legal protections often apply to 'workers', i.e. both employees and the self-employed. Included are:

- Many health and safety protections, including protection from being 'victimised' because of raising or responding to health and safety concerns

- Anti-discrimination protections if work is 'personally executed'.

Additionally, it should be noted that some recent or planned European laws will cover some self-employed, especially part-time, casual staff, particularly the revised Acquired Rights Directive which provides protections during organisational transfers.

Despite these developments, it is still important to make the decision on employment status correctly, both from a practical as well as a legal standpoint.

The key issues are illustrated by reference to two hypothetical organisations:

EXAMPLE: ORGANISATION A

A cosmetics company is expanding in the UK. It aims to recruit a sales force of at least 200 and to provide an induction and training programme at its Manchester headquarters for one week full time. The company is seeking BS5750/ISO 9000 accreditation and puts emphasis on a 'Quality for Customers' programme. The selection and training of sales staff will be rigorous.

Sales staff will be paid solely by commission, allocated to specific marketing zones and be visited weekly by the relevant Regional Sales Controller. Sales staff falling below a minimum sales volume will have contracts terminated. Sales staff are referred to as 'cosmetics advisors'.

Should the advisors be recruited as employees or self-employed?

EXAMPLE: ORGANISATION B

An employing organisation in the printing industry is prone to fluctuations in work. It frequently obtains contracts which involve large scale meetings and negotiations at its premises. The company has one full time receptionist; another 'specialist' is required but in view of the business uncertainties only on a part-time basis. The receptionist's hours will be 'variable'. She will be described as 'casual' and the intention is that she be telephoned at home when needed for work, with as much notice as possible. The understanding is that when called she will attend work as specified. If she does not, she will be 'dropped' by the company.

The managing director seeks advice as to what type of employment relationship - employment or self-employment is appropriate for the receptionist employed on these terms?

Differentiating between contracts of employment and self-employment

Courts have always struggled hard to find a legal test to differentiate the workers in the type of work situations referred to earlier. Problems in law are compounded by a tendency to inconsistency by judges, so that predicting the outcome of individual cases is very difficult. Contracts exhibiting similar characteristics will be held to be contracts of employment in one court and self-employment in another. It is clear from case law that none of the following is conclusive in determining employment status.

- Hours of work

- How long the contract is for

- Where the work is actually carried out

- The skill level of the worker

- The size or sector of organisation they work for.

Thus, a driving instructor, musician, an architect and a barman have been held to be self-employed in given situations; a market researcher, a mason, travelling sales staff, specialist engineer and a television programme researcher have been adjudged to be employees.

When deciding the matter an industrial tribunal or court will itself determine the *'legal realities'* of the relationship, even if that contravenes what the parties themselves wanted. An agreement cannot, therefore, overrule decisions of the courts. However, the law appears loathe to leave victims of serious injuries caused by a workplace accident uncompensated and will often in those situations veer towards a finding that the victim was an employee, though declared self-employed.

On the other hand, they are sometimes less keen to intervene when the worker whose status is in debate is claiming a protective right, such as time-off with pay or a redundancy payment, especially where they were happy with self employed status until a problem arose. Courts and tribunals are sometimes influenced by the traditions of occupations or employment sectors; they are more likely to find artistic or highly skilled professional people self-employed than routine clerical or administrative staff.

A particular problem when examining the demands of case law is that much of it has dealt with unusual jobs such as church leaders and musicians. There are relatively few cases on builders, mini cab drivers, sales staff, insurance staff and or, indeed, occupations such as cosmetics advisors or even a 'casual' receptionist!

CATEGORISING WORKING PATTERNS: THE LEADING CASES

It may be helpful to reiterate the two most typical situations where employment status is problematic but has been subject to key case law. In the first, the individuals work regularly or have relatively long contracts with an employing organisation (the cosmetics advisors in the illustration above).

Typically, these are professional, highly skilled or artistic staff. The second contains workers with intermittent, irregular patterns of work (typified by the casual receptionist above).

An indication of how the law tackles the problem can be seen from two leading cases on 'regular' workers set out below:

CASE LAW EXAMPLE A : THE MUSICIANS

Three musicians played in a series of concerts, though were not employed directly by an orchestra. They were invited to play from the orchestra's 'index of performers'. It was argued by the DSS that as they played alongside the regular members of the orchestra and played frequently they were employees. The court decided that they were self-employed. They worked for other employers; they taught private pupils and earned income in a variety of ways quite apart from playing in the orchestra; the only significant discipline they had to submit to was the usual musical one of the orchestra's conductor! (*Addison & Others v London Philharmonic Orchestra* (1981))[2]

CASE LAW EXAMPLE B: THE MARKET RESEARCHER

The decision in this case is probably the most important in UK law. The worker in question undertook interviews for a market research company. She was based at home, used her own car to get to contacts and was paid according to the number of interviews she did. However, she was told she was self-employed and was provided with neither sickness nor holiday pay.

The court determined that her correct legal status was that of an employee. She had undertaken a brief induction programme organised by the company, and had carried out the interviews according to the rules set down in the 'Interviewers Guide', a manual provided by the company. She did not work for other employers and was economically dependent upon the company. (*Market Investigators v Min of Social Security* (1969))[3]

In the latter case the court set down the key legal test of employment status. The judge posed the following question:'Was the worker "in business" on her own account?'

To achieve a 'yes' answer, i.e. self-employed status, she would have needed, for example, to provide capital, work for other clients and have the ability to negotiate and determine her 'fee', etc. However, in the case in question she was merely a part-time (and not very well paid) worker and the conclusion was that she was an employee. This approach has become known as the 'business test' of employment status.

THE 'BUSINESS TEST'

This 'business test' has become dominant, and recent case law in the UK continues to apply its approach. *Lee v Chung* (1990)[4] dealt with one of the classic 'problem' occupations in this area of law - the construction industry. The worker in question was a mason who suffered an injury on a construction site. He worked regular hours, used tools provided by the employer, and worked where told to, but thereon had considerable discretion as to how and when he worked. Despite this level of autonomy the court decided he was an employee, and thus entitled to the industrial injury compensation which only employees had access to. He could not be considered 'in business on his own account'; rather he was sufficiently integrated into the employer's business and sufficiently dependent on it to be viewed as an employee.

This legal approach aims to assess the organisational and economic realities of a work relationship. Questions of pay, equipment, working hours, benefits and protections provided by the employer are explored, as is the issue of the extent to which the individual is integrated into the fabric of the employing organisation. For example, do they attend staff meetings, receive company information, attend social events, belong to committees etc.?

The 'business test can be adapted to occupations which have particular customs and traditions, such as publishing and the media. However, courts will not necessarily be persuaded by these traditional labels and practices if the reality is that individuals are able to exercise relatively little discretion and are dependent on the employing organisation for their livelihood. In these situations they will be considered to be employees. Courts do not condone arrangements which leave workers misled and unprotected or which are designed to evade tax or other responsibilities. However, there are many genuine situations which courts are happy to support.

RECENT EXAMPLES

A 'freelance' vision mixer in the television/video industry worked on a series of short-term contracts in studios where he used their equipment. He took bookings and did his paper work from home. He worked regularly and for up to 20 companies per year. Despite not providing equipment, not having the ability to employ or substitute staff it was held that he was, indeed, 'in business on his own account' and thus self employed. (*Hall v Lorimer* (1994))[5]

Managers in a large chain of newsagents were given a choice as to their employment status. Over the chain as a whole roughly half the managers opted for self-employed status. When this was tested it was decided that those declared to be self-employed had a wider autonomy in the recruitment and deployment of staff. This was sufficient for them to be correctly 'labelled' as self-employed.(*Harris v John Menzies* (1994))[4]

Case law on intermittent workers

The second group, contains workers who work for an organisation on an 'as and when required' basis. Their employment patterns are generally irregular and they work in occupations where skill levels are often fairly low. Workers in the hotel and catering industry, agriculture, fishing, homeworking and office work are typical. Case law is less developed for this group of workers, but the following case established the basic approach of law.

CASE EXAMPLE: THE CASUAL WAITER

Mr O'Kelly worked as a casual banqueting wine waiter for specific functions and was on a list of waiters who were used regularly by the owners of some prestigious hotels (Forte). This list contained staff who were given preferential treatment, i.e.. were called first by the employer when staff were needed. In practice, he only worked for the one company. However, it was decided that he was self-employed. The important legal determinant was that, technically, Forte was not obliged to employ him when work was available, and O'Kelly was technically able to refuse it. The relationship was thus re-negotiated each time staff were required; O'Kelly and THF operated 'at arms length'. (*O'Kelly v Trust House Forte* (1983))⁷

Despite being criticised at the time for failing to give due weight to the economic reality of dependence of O'Kelly on Forte, the case has been applied to a number of occupations.

APPLYING THE LEGAL TESTS

Applying these legal principles to the example above of the cosmetics advisors and casual receptionist is not straightforward.

What facts may need to be explored?
It is clear that cosmetics advisors have considerable discretion as to how the work is carried out and the receptionist only works for a limited time. However, in these hypothetical organisations, other facts need clarification. They might include:

- Do the cosmetics advisors have a list of people to contact as likely customers?

- Do the cosmetics advisors have detailed instructions as to how they they carry out selling?

- Do the receptionist and the cosmetics advisors have a clear view of their own employment status; do they consider themselves self-employed?

- Do they have experience of working in their respective occupations so as to form their own views regarding appropriate employment status?

- Is there a tradition of freelance or self-employed work in both occupations?

- Has the employer raised the question of their employment status with the Inland Revenue, or professional body? With what outcome?

However, the cosmetics advisors would probably be classified as employees in view of the level of company control as manifested in a variety of ways, and the integration of individuals into the culture of the organisational generally. The financial arrangements would be considered less central and would probably not counteract the overall impression of employee status.

When applying legal principles to the 'casual' receptionist, emphasis would probably be placed on two issues. One would be the nature of the understanding between the printing company and the receptionist, including the regularity of work and the extent to which the receptionist considered herself 'their' worker and, in essence, felt on 'stand-by' to the company; did she work for others? The second would be how the receptionist was viewed by the company. For example, was the receptionist considered one of the team and integrated into the company?

IMPLICATIONS FOR MANAGERS

It appears that the 'business test' provides the most relevant approach by focusing on the financial basics of the employment relationship and the presence or absence of discretion as to how, when and where work is performed. This approach is favoured by the Inland Revenue and Department of Social Security when they themselves are deciding on the correct employment status (e.g. Schedule D or E for tax purposes) of workers. It is clear that customs and traditions in particular industries and occupations continue to have some relevance while still leaving open a possible legal challenge. It should also be noted that recent initiatives from the EU to 'tighten up' on employment contracts generally (see Chapter 5) will require employers to take more care when recruiting workers. Employment and labour use practices will generally have to be more 'transparent', i.e. capable of objective justification.

SUGGESTED GUIDELINES

When considering the appropriate legal status to provide for a post which is thought to be on the borderline of employee/self-employment, the following should be borne in mind, summed up in Figure 4.2.

* A contract designed to evade tax and other legal liabilities is illegal as being against the public interest and can form the basis of a criminal prosecution. An illegal contract, is unenforceable by both parties, i.e. any money or obligations allegedly owed by one side to the other cannot be claimed for. There is some evidence that tax and other authorities are increasingly willing to institute criminal proceedings. (See the Annual

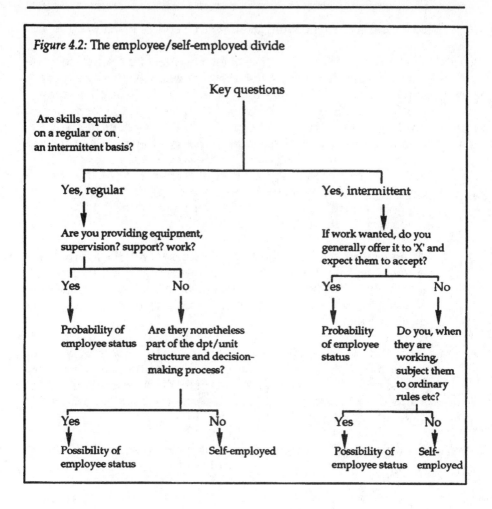

Figure 4.2: The employee/self-employed divide

Key questions

Are skills required
on a regular or on
an intermittent basis?

Yes, regular

Are you providing equipment,
supervision? support? work?

Yes

Probability of
employee status

No

Are they nonetheless
part of the dpt/unit
structure and decision-
making process?

Yes

Possibility of
employee status

No

Self-employed

Yes, intermittent

If work wanted, do you
generally offer it to 'X' and
expect them to accept?

Yes

Probability
of employee
status

No

Do you, when
they are
working,
subject them
to ordinary
rules etc?

Yes

Possibility of
employee status

No

Self-
employed

Reports of the Board of Inland Revenue).

• Regardless of the preference of both parties and of clear documentation to support them, law courts can override their intentions. Courts can and do declare the legal realities of the situation which may well be different from what the parties want. There is, therefore, no way of avoiding the law's impact.

• Managers need to make a careful assessment of the proposed employment relationship to ensure that it is legally robust. The law looks for economic and organisational autonomy on the part of the genuinely self-employed - that skills and facilities are being bought in, rather than the qualities of an individual worker. The law also looks for provision of premises and equipment and for the ability to exercise judgment and control, as well as the ability to offer their services to other employers.

- The two common forms of self-employment identified earlier - the professional/specialist skills, and the 'as and when required' category - require careful preparation and presentation. It is clear that simply providing labels such as 'consultant' (for an accountant/secretary) or 'freelance' (for a clerk, fruit picker, writer) will not of themselves deal with the law's demands, especially if they work alongside employees performing similar tasks in the organisation. The documentation and management procedures must reflect the 'arms length' nature of self-employment. The language of 'instructions', 'discipline', 'salary', 'occupational benefit' must be avoided, along with other indicators of integration and dependence on the organisations.

- Arrangements should be thoroughly discussed with the relevant government departments which will examine and approve the employment status. This is not a watertight guarantee that law courts will not set aside the status should the issue be tested, but can avoid many immediate problems.

- It has to be recognised that job location (working at or from home, or 'on the road') or earnings level (below the threshold for tax and national insurance contributions) are irrelevant to the issue of employment status. A part-time, low paid, home based worker *can* be an employee entitled to employment protection rights.

- Changing employment status of a previous employee will not be convincing if the job itself changes very little.

REFERENCES

1	[1994] IRLR 386
2	[1981] ICR 261
3	[1969] 2 QB 173
4	[1990] IRLR 236
5	[1994] IRLR 171
6	Unreported
7	[1983] IRLR 369

5
Documenting Employment Contracts

In UK employment law the tangible expression of the contractual relationship is through written material. Included are written contracts/statements of contract terms, handbooks, leaflets, policy documents, letters and memoranda. We probably place a higher premium on drafting and the presentation of documents than any other European nation.

Such documents are the first reference point in any court or tribunal hearing. They are also the way in which an employing organisation communicates with staff; they can reveal its priorities and culture. For new employees they are likely to be the first formal contact point with the organisation and can set the standard. They can also be a barrier. Documents can be hostile and negative. They can be slipshod, poorly presented and legally out of date. Therefore, they can give out important messages from the organisation - both good and bad.

Documents are also provided for freelance, consultants etc. Indeed, their provision is especially important as implied terms to make sense of the contract have a lesser role to play than in contracts of employment. The essential nature and obligations of the contract must be spelt out to avoid irritations, misunderstandings and disputes. When a consultant has access to equipment, communication systems, clients and, perhaps, sensitive market or production data, it is essential to protect both the organisation's and the consultant's position by clarifying rights and duties..

This chapter considers:

- the range and nature of material typically provided for employees.

- the basic legal rules of relevance to written information, including the requirements of TURERA, 1993.

- the options available to employers regarding type and content of document to use.

- a case study on adopting a coherent and effective approach to employment contract documentation.

- an approach to documenting self-employment contracts.

THE DOCUMENTS FOR EMPLOYEES

Documentation should cover most or all of the express terms of an individual's contract (see Chapter 3). All the basics should be there and enable the employee to find out what the relevant provisions are regarding pay, job content, working hours, occupational benefits etc. Traditionally, at many workplaces some information has been kept for reference in the personnel/HR office or departmental office but not provided individually for employees. The reason has often been that the cost can be very high to provide individual copies.

It has been thought that so long as relevant information was 'reasonably accessible' to employees that it was a perfectly lawful and acceptable way of providing information. This approach is now less sustainable as, current law demands a more personalised provision of written information so that employees have their own record of employment terms and can refer to it as and when they wish.

Employment documents focus on the express terms, but they can also be used to draw employees' attention to the vitally important implied obligations, e.g. of co-operation and confidentiality.

AN APPROACH TO THE TASK

Most organisations use written contracts or statements of terms of work for employees, supplemented by handbooks, rule books, works rules etc. There are often additional policy statements, memos and documents on notice boards etc.

The typical contract 'package' produced by employers might therefore include;

- a letter of appointment;
- a statement of terms or written contract; (the minimum content of which is required by Sched 4 TURERA, 1993);
- a rule book/handbook or similar;
- notices on notice boards;
- information in staff news letters;
- regular inserts in pay advice/pay packets;

- policy documents;
- pension schemes.

Taken together this can amount to a lot of paper and a lot of words! There may be overlap, repetition or gaps in information, and it may not have been reviewed or analysed for some time. New policies may have been developed, individual benefits introduced, or changes to disciplinary and other procedures made, so that the package has grown like 'topsy'. The fact that so many personnel systems are computerised and materials word processed has eased the process of change and additions. However, individual items in the package may be very diverse, ranging from information about the products and profiles of senior managers of the company, statements of ethical principles, opportunities for discount shopping, subsidised travel, accommodation, meals and dental care through to clauses on fidelity and, restraint of trade and the disciplinary code.

Each of the documents should be examined and each item analysed as to whether it is intended that the item be descriptive, discretionary or prescriptive.

- *Descriptive* items will be those matters set out for information only which it is not intended to be legally binding.

- *Discretionary* items are matters, such as assistance with training costs provided by employers, options for early retirement, secondment etc, where items are potentially legally binding but management has retained the right as to whether they will beapplied or not.

- *Prescriptive* items are those intended to be legally binding, i.e.failure to comply with them is a breach of contract.

This approach can be tested at organisational level by considering one typical item in documents. For example, many employers continue to both require attendance on training programmes and/or provide financial support, e.g. for fees, or provide paid leave to prepare for examinations.

If an employee demands to be allowed to go on a training course and have fees paid. Figure 5.1 overleaf sets out the key legal questions applied to a policy to see if there is an entitlement. The issue is, therefore whether, if training is not provided the employee can claim that the contract has been broken.

When dealing with a specific issue, such as the training one the following are examples of the three types of clause - descriptive (1), discretionary (2), or prescriptive (3) - which might be used:

(1) 'This organisation is keen to support the aspirations of its staff to improve and develop their skills. Employees who have been successful on courses etc. frequently feature in our news letter *Zippo News*'.

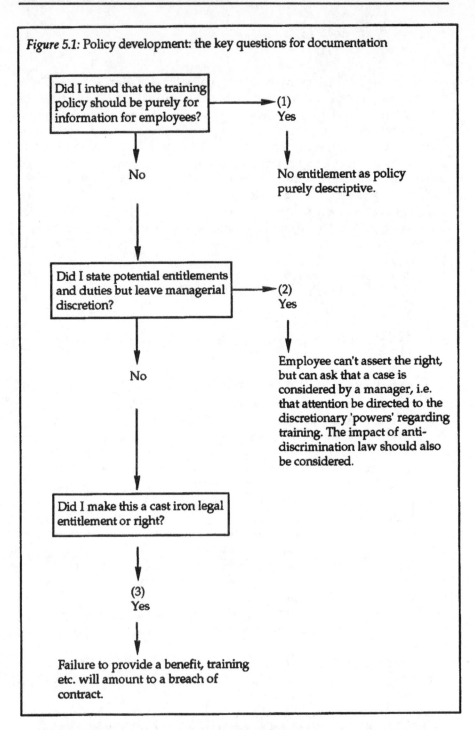

Figure 5.1: Policy development: the key questions for documentation

(2)'This organisation is keen to support skill development by staff. Managers may, at their discretion, provide financial support for individual employees to a maximum of £500 per annum. Managers may also allow a period of up to two weeks paid leave per annum for employees on an award bearing programme for the preparation of assignments, projects or otherwise for course assessment'.

(3)'As part of its commitment to skill development by employees Zippo Ltd agrees to provide up to £500 pa for employees' fees on approved programmes of study. It furthermore undertakes to provide up to two weeks paid leave per annum to facilitate the preparation of assignments, projects or otherwise, as part of course assessments. Employees are reminded that should their manager require participation on a particular training programme they should normally to pursue it. Failure to do so will be viewed as a lack of co-operation with the development initiatives of Zippo Ltd and may lead to disciplinary action being invoked'.

Each of (1), (2) and (3) is a perfectly lawful and valid response to the issue of training support. Managers need to be precise about which approach they are taking to the topic. Failure to comply with (3)by an employer or employee is, prima-facie, a breach of contract; in some extreme situations the failure to provide support in (2) could amount to a breach of the implied term of trust and confidence (see Chapter 3, page 59) but is not a breach of any express term as the wording shows there is no intention that it be legally binding. Clearly, the wording in (1) indicates only a vague interest in training support and is expressed in such a manner as not to be legally binding and is of only minimal legal significance.

LEGAL RULES ON DOCUMENTATION

Until 1963 there was no legislation requiring employers to provide anything in writing for their staff. The 1963 Contracts of Employment Act specified certain items of information which the employee had to receive, or at least have 'reasonable' access to. The items were the basic ones of pay, hours, and holidays, sick pay, pensions (if relevant), and have been added to subsequently.

The confusion for managers has been that the 1963 Act seemed to require a written statement of terms, rather than a written contract itself, though the latter could be one way of the carrying out the statutory duty to provide written information. The intention of Parliament appeared to be that an employee should receive a 'receipt' of their terms of work which would provide them with sufficient information on which to base a legal claim, if necessary.

Legislation allowed an employer to provide a letter of appointment or even a memo which identified the employer and employee but from thereon could refer the employee to handbooks, rulebooks, notices, collective agreements etc. Hence, many employees had limited 'personalised' information about their terms of work. Much was available but still had to be sought out. Furthermore, many part-timers (working less than specified hours a week) and casual staff (on contracts shorter than 3 months) had no legal entitlement to written material. Now virtually all employees now have an entitlement to written information about terms of work.

STATEMENT OR CONTRACT?

Employers in the UK have always had, (and continue to have) a choice as to how they provide written information - a written, legally binding contract, or a statement of terms which merely evidences the terms of work. This is an important distinction and one which is not always fully appreciated.

- A written employment contract is definitive on the terms of the contract and cannot be overruled by orally agreed terms or by custom and practice. The corollary for the employee being bound by the contract terms is that the employer is also bound. Hence, any benefits agreed to be provided by contract must be provided, any opportunities offered must be available etc. Such legally binding contracts can be inhibiting unless they are very carefully drafted so as to provide discretion and flexibility.

- A statement of terms is exactly that; a document which provides basic information on key terms of work but is more in the nature of 'confirmation' or 'receipt'. Statements should not include signatures or other language indicating that the document is legally binding. Statements can be overruled by other information, including that orally agreed, if such information represents the reality of the employment contract. Research indicates that most employers who provide detailed written information believe they are using written contracts, but are often erroneous in that belief.

The following examples are illustrative of typical confusions.

'Statement of Terms'

'The following are your terms of work, pursuant to the Contracts of Employment Act, 1972

Signed_____(employee)

I have read and understood these terms of work'.

This is simply a statement of terms; The title, though, is confusing. The source of law is woefully out of date and the signature is merely to indicate understanding, rather than agreement to contract terms. An employer aiming to rely on the terms of this document might well be hard pressed to do so, especially where the employee's recollection of conversations at interview, or perhaps understanding of customs of the workplace were at variance with the written document.

'Conditions of Employment'
This contract is made between Fizzo Ltd and James Johnson. Work is to commence on 5th January 199... as a carpet fitter.

Pay is at £4.00 per hour, hours are 8.30 - 5.30 Monday to Friday. There is no payment for sickness or absence. There is no pension scheme.

Signed_____for Fizzo Ltd

Signed_____(employee)

Date_____

This is a very simple document (and also one that does not fulfil statutory requirements - see page 95). However, if the employee was ill on 5 January 199... and did not start work until 12 January 199... but then was dismissed in January two years later a tribunal would be bound to ask which was the correct date for determining whether the employee had the required two year period of service to bring a complaint to an industrial tribunal? Is it the written document, or the physical time when work was started? If the document is a written employment contract the earlier date will be the legally significant date; if the document is merely a statement of terms the fact of the later start date will convince a court of law and will override any other statement of terms. It is likely that in the example it is merely a statement of terms.

These matters are not, therefore, of mere academic interest. The law continues to attach importance to distinguishing the two different types of document. In the case of the carpet fitter's document there would still be doubts as to its legal status. The heading of the document does not clearly indicate that it is intended to be a written contract and neither signature is made so as to unambiguously agree to the contract terms. The entire document is imprecise and minimalist.

WHAT IS A WRITTEN CONTRACT?

If it is intended that a written document be a legally binding contract it should have the following features:

- A clear title, indicating that it is a written contract of employment.

- It should ignore any legislation, even TURER Act 1993, as 'authority' for its content. Such laws change too frequently; it is best to remain with the basics of contract law.

- A content which at least covers the statutory minimum; other matters can be added.

- Language appropriate to a legally binding document such as 'shall', 'are required', 'may, at the employer's discretion', 'must ensure', etc.

- References to other documents, such as disciplinary codes and smoking policies (insofar as the law now allows cross referencing) must be unambiguous regarding t he status and impact of those other documents. There must always be a clear distinction between the 'prescriptive' (binding) and material merely 'descriptive' (non binding) .

- Signatures should be made so as to clearly 'accept' the terms and conditions. The signature should be at the end or be made so as incorporate the total content.

- If, however, organisational HRM policy is against using a legally binding contract as and a statement of terms is thought more appropriate the document should then to have the following characteristics.

- A title which makes plain that it is a mere statement of terms, not a written contract.

- If signatures are used they are merely to indicate that the employee has received/read/understood the terms of work.

It is important to weight up the pros and cons of written employment contracts. The new agenda of HRM may indicate that a contract document should be used to re-inforce managerial discretion, remind employees of their legally binding obligations, and reserve the employer's right to extend, amend or otherwise change employee duties, or job location etc.

De-recognition of trade unions and/or the move to personal contracts will almost invariably suggest that a written contract be used. The growing orthodoxy is that using legally binding contracts has advantages in terms of ensuring flexibility as well as tightening up on disciplinary rules etc.

The downside is that inaccuracies or ambiguities cannot be easily resolved; the employing organisation is stuck with them. There is little scope for arguing in a court or tribunal that many managers ignored the strict wording relating to disciplinary rules, did not require mobility of staff in practice, and the employment relationship was 'looser' than appeared. This situation can harm an employer's case by suggesting inconsistency or lack of clarity in their managerial objectives.

The answer is that the form of the contract documentation is a matter which should be considered and periodically reviewed, especially if there is a change to 'on-line' documentation with print-outs. These will not easily be signed and therefore become a written contract!

If the intention is to apply I.T. to contracts, this type of issue must be borne in mind.

LEGAL REQUIREMENTS ON CONTRACT DOCUMENTATION

Employers have been required to provide specified written information for employees for over 30 years. The latest change to legal requirements has been prompted by the 1991 European Directive on Employment Contract Documentation. This directive's objective is to ensure that all employees are clear about their employment status and their key terms of work. This information then enables employees to ensure their agreed terms of work are being kept to. The directive has relatively little to do with the concept of the contract of employment; it is designed to ensure that European and national employment protections are being provided.

Central to this policy is the idea that individual employees should have individual and, broadly, comprehensive documents. They should not have to seek out rule books, handbooks, policies and the like; the onus is on the employer to provide material. The only major exception is where employment rights are derived from public sources, such as labour/employment legislation and are therefore accessible to all.

The directive was implemented in the UK by Schedule 4 TURERA and has been effective in the UK since 30 November 1993. It inserts new sections 1 - 6 of Employment Protection (Consolidation) Act 1978 and requires that a 'written statement of terms must be provided for all new employees and for existing employees if they request it.

Other requirements are:

- Statements must be provided for new employees who work eight or more hours a week, and who have been employed for more than one month.

- The statement must be provided not later than two months after beginning employment. A statement must nonetheless be given to every employee who qualifies, even if they leave the job before the two months are up. Existing employees who request a statement must also be provided with a statement within two months.

- The main particulars (marked below with an asterisk), must be given in a 'principal statement' (i.e. one single document). The rest can be given by instalments, but still within the two-month limit. (Note: the 'principal statement' does not have to come first!)

The statement must contain particulars of the following:

- the *names* of the employer and employee;

- the *date* when the employment began; and

- the date on which the employee's period of *continuous employment* began (taking into account any employment with a previous employer which counts towards that period);

- the scale or rate of *remuneration* or the method of calculating remuneration;

- the *intervals* at which remuneration is paid;

- any terms and conditions relating to *hours of work* (including any terms and conditions relating to normal working hours);

Plus any terms and conditions relating to:

- *holiday* entitlement including public holidays, and holiday pay (with enough detail for the employee's entitlement, including entitlement to accrued holiday pay on termination of employment, to be precisely calculated);

- incapacity for work due to *sickness or injury*, including any sick-pay provision;

- *pensions* and pension schemes;

- the length of *notice* required from either party;

- the *job title* (or a brief description of the employee's work);

- where the employment is *temporary*, the period for which it is expected to continue or, if it is for a fixed term, the date when it is to end;

- the *place of work* or, if the employee is required or permitted to work at various places, an indication of that fact and the employer's address;

- any *collective agreements* which directly affect the terms and conditions of the employment, including, where the employer is not a party, the person by whom they were made; and

- where the employee is required to *work outside the UK for* more than a month;

  the period of work outside the UK,

  the currency in which payment will be made,

any additional pay and benefits to be provided by reason of the work being outside the UK, and

any terms and conditions relating to the employee's return to the UK.

The following should be noted:

1   If there are no particulars to be entered under any of the above headings this must be stated.

2   The statement may refer employees to some other document for particulars of sickness and pension provisions; and the law or a collective agreement for particulars of notice periods. Any such document or collective agreement must, however, be available for the employer to read while at work, or be reasonably accessible in some other way.

3   The statement must also include a note relating to disciplinary rules and grievance procedures, including:

any disciplinary rules applicable to the employee, or a reference to a reasonably accessible document which specifies those rules;

details of appeal and grievance procedures, namely: a person to whom employees can apply if they are dissatisfied with any disciplinary decision and a person to whom employees can apply to seek redress over grievances; and the manner in which such applications should be made; where there are further steps consequent on any such application, details explaining those steps or a reference to a reasonably accessible document which explains them; and

4   A statement as to whether a contracting-out certificate is in force for the employment must be made.
(*Note*: Written information about health and safety rules does not have to be provided. And employers of less than 20 employees only need provide details of who deals with grievances rather than full details of procedures).

5   Notice of any changes to the particulars must be given individually to employees at the earliest opportunity, and in any event no later than one month after the change. A statement of change may refer to documents or collective agreements — but only to the extent allowed in the original statement.

6 Enforcement of the above rights will be by making a complaint to an an industrial tribunal complaint under section 11 of the EP(C)A. The tribunal can declare the terms of work, i.e. specify what written informiation should have been provided. There is however no entitlement to compensation for not being provided with a statement. This may be tightened up in the future.

PRACTICAL POINTS TO NOTE

The 1993 Act opens up the possibility of existing and typically long serving employees seeking a new document. If the employer does not provide it, or the employee considers that the information available is not accurate or comprehensive they are entitled to make a claim in an industrial tribunal for the tribunal to 'declare' (identify) their contract terms. This may well be a prelude to a claims for breach of contract - some of which can also be heard by tribunals.

- With regard to particulars of applicable collective agreements, there is no need to spell out which parts of the collective agreement are incorporated into the contract of employment, and it would appear there is no need to make the whole agreement accessible to the employee. Much still needs clarification by case law.

- The law requires careful preparation of documents for part-timers and those on short term contracts. Very few employees are now excluded from legislation relating to contract documentation and there will be increasing merit in establishing effective computerised information systems which can double-up by providing the written statements. It is clear that each time a contract is entered into, even if referred to as a renewal or a re-engagement, information must be provided, even if to re-affirm existing documents. However, the law is not entirely clear; if in doubt the fail-safe approach would be to re-issue document on each re-engagement.

- Contracts for self-employed workers do not need to comply with the requirements regarding documentation from TURERA. However, the approach of the legislation in requiring clear statements of the key central terms could be followed (see below). Where consultants, freelancers and the like are regularly used use of computerised documents is often helpful if only as a basis for discussion.

CONCLUSION

The opportunity should be taken at regular intervals to formally review policies and practices regarding contract documentation to ensure that:

the documents continue to comply with both common law and statutory demands;

- any reviews take the opportunity to integrate other organisational policies affecting say, disciplinary rules, occupational health procedures, equal opportunities initiatives, and new policy development such as smoking, child care etc;

- so far as possible, the language used should be precise but also sufficiently flexible so as to allow changes to be added or new circumstances responded to as painlessly as possible;

- contract documents be as readable and attractively presented as possible so that documents are accessible and routinely used. Use of colour, design and language should not only reflect organisational culture but ideally express the interdependence of the employment contract and the value of the employee. Documents should never alienate employees, for example, by referring to them as 'servants', 'operatives', or 'hands'. This issue is especially important with part-time or fixed term staff who, through their limited involvement with the employing organisation, will deduce a great deal from the documents' style as well as content;

- all the documents used or referred to are consistent in content and style. In particular, care must be taken to ensure that an item which is prescriptive in one document is not merely descriptive in another.

To illustrate how an employing organisation can approach the review and analysis of contract documentation practices, a case study from a leading UK employer is set out. It describes the priorities, forces and criteria used to develop new contract documents. The process was both lengthy and detailed but resulted in coherent and comprehensive documents which themselves are the vehicle for future organisational policy development. The case study reflects the increasing demand for employers to adopt an international, especially European, approach to contracts, as well as the need to respond to and anticipate legal change.

CASE STUDY: UNITED BISCUITS PLC

UB is a leading international snackfoods group and has operations in 24 countries. It has an excellent reputation for creating and developing household-name brands internationally in its core business sectors, biscuits and savoury snacks; and in the UK, in chilled and frozen foods.

UB comprises four divisions: McVitie's Group (biscuits), KP Foods Group (savoury snacks), Ross Young's (chilled and frozen foods) and - in the USA -

Keebler Company (cookies and salty snacks). Each division has its own boards and profit targets; UB Group provides strategic direction, financial, R&D and other services support.

Over the past three years, UB has built on its success in its home markets by developing a strong international preference. It has a participatory, 'partnership' operating style which is based on respect for its people, understanding markets, respecting and utilising the special knowledge of own-country managers, and developing synergies and co-operation. Its growth has therefore come from a combination of organic growth and the development of its acquired companies.

UB decided to adopt a strategic approach to the management of these particular changes. In order to identify the key issues needing to be addressed in the light of anticipated Directives and UK legislation, an audit of its European HR practice was conducted on behalf of UB by Professor Patricia Leighton in early 1992. This audit covered UB's then practices relating to contract documentation, along with other related policies and practices.

Getting started

In view of the pace of change within European employment law it was suggested and accepted that the review of contract and changes should have the four following characteristics:

- durability
- robustness
- flexibility
- economy of effort

Any programme of change had to have durability, in that future European developments could be accommodated relatively easily because the basic contract and other procedures had an overall cohesion whereby amendments and additions could be absorbed without the need for wholesale review.

Secondly, the resulting contract package needed to be robust, ie. legally watertight not only regarding content but also in terms of the interdependence of the documents themselves. For example, it was checked whether there were adequate cross references and that all the parts of documents were intended to be legally binding or were intended to be merely descriptive.

Thirdly, the contract package needed to have sufficient flexibility by, for example, adopting generic categories, e.g. grouping 'leave' entitlements in such a way that other situations such as parental leave could be added. The core documentation provided clear guidance whilst allowing sufficient flexibility for divisions to reflect and express specific terms and conditions.

The changes needed an economy of effort and expense. To this end, the experience of other employing organisations both in the UK and outside were drawn on, and any reviews/changes within UB divisions taking place at the same were as the opportunity to effect changes to accommodate EU law.

Document analysis

It was possible to analyse documents from all UB companies in the UK, giving a good indication of UB practice. This revealed considerable diversity in the style, content and approach of companies/divisions to contract documentation and some variations between different staff grades/categories regarding style, content and approach.

There was also diversity regarding document headings ('contract of employment', written statement of terms', 'statement of main terms and conditions of employment') and the role and nature of signatures; the titles of secondary documents also varied greatly - 'company rules', 'notes for guidance', 'employee handbook', etc.,

However, the analysis also revealed considerable care and attention to detail in the documents especially regarding disciplinary matters and health and safety. The material was also up to date. The main outcome of the analysis was the need to separate out the 'prescriptive' (binding) and the 'descriptive' (for information only). This required several lengthy discussions at UB's Personnel Director's Forum.

Outcomes

Following these discussions it was agreed that the opportunity be taken to recast and attractively present documents so as to reflect both changes in law and wider policy objectives. A 'head' document, was devised having the title 'Written Particulars of Terms & Conditions of Employment'.

This document contained the statutory minimum, incorporating the changes required by the employment law. The head document contained *solely* prescriptive material such as discipline, requirements for health surveillance, safety rules and, equal opportunities/dignity codes, and requirements for co-operation and flexibility.

All other material went into an information booklet for employees on 'non-prescriptive' general interest matters. The suggested model did not preclude house-style or company/division culture continuing, but had to be agreed to by all in the group.

It emerged that typical items requiring review were;

> information on job location and job title; collective agreements (if relevant)
> several aspects of paid leave (maternity, parental, etc.)
> disciplinary rules to cover harassment, etc.
> health and safety rules, to include health surveillance/medical checks
> retirement ages for men and women
> defining hours of work for *all* staff (looking ahead to the
> European Working Time Directive as well)

Attention was paid to devising a form of words which would ensure flexibility. For example, health checks, should not just be related to the operation of the sick pay scheme, but become more general yet central so as to meet the considerable demands of the health surveillance provision of various European directives and UK regulations. Clearly, in the light of UB's business activities, (mainly food production, health and safety matters had always been at the heart of workplace policies and practices. It was essential that such matters were fully reflected in the contract documentation, and were not marginal or 'bolted on'.

Development of revised material and approval

Drafts were discussed with the legal department, the policy review group and the industrial relations committee to ensure that a legally defensible document emerged - but also one that was practical in terms of usage and professional in approach. Both committees include senior personnel practitioners from across UB. The final draft was approved early 1993, and issued to new employees from November 1993 and available for existing staff. It has been kept on disk and amendments have already been added. This has been especially noticeable regarding senior staff contracts.

The exercise was challenging, but interesting, and it was very much hoped that by combining the skills and experience of personnel professionals with an employment lawyer not only could problems be anticipated but also effectively resolved.

The next steps
After the review was completed, thoughts turned to wider issues, in particular the development of international policies relating to employment contracts, and to consider practice in companies outside the UK. Data was then collected with a view to coherent and consistent approach to employment contracts across companies.

DOCUMENTS FOR SELF-EMPLOYED STAFF

The major groups here are consultants, freelance and casual workers, who have a direct contractual relationship with employers but on a self-employed basis. There is no obligation to provide specific contract documentation. But the same professional approach is always desirable. Contracts should be in writing. Many self-employed staff will be working alongside your employees and there will be a general need to harmonise aspects of contractual arrangements, such as disciplinary standards and safety procedures. However where the worker is performing a self-contained task, perhaps off-site, this need will be less pressing.

With the exception of self employed casual staff, it is likely that many contract terms will have been previously negotiated. This strategy should have eliminated uncertainties and likely flash points. It should have established:

- The objectives of the contract

- Basis of payment

- Criteria to determine successful completion

- Procedures for monitoring

- Procedures for handling disputes.

Other matters may have to be considered, though much will depend on the types of work. Many derive from the fact that the consultant/freelancer (be it management consultant, computing staff, trainer or 'session musician') will be integrated in the organisation to a greater or lesser extent.

Issues to consider

- What is the contractual position when the consultant, etc. is ill or unable to work? Do they lose pay, can the time be made up or can they provide a substitute?

- Can the consultant delegate some or all of the work?

- Where and with what facilities, including secretarial support, is the work to be carried out?

- Are there to be any restrictions on the consultant taking on other work during the continuation of the contract?

- What is the label or title to be attached to the consultant? Is the employer to be able to 'exploit' their name, and vice versa?

- Whose is the copyright or other rights in materials produced by the consultant, especially when done jointly with in-house staff?

- What are to be the arrangements for expenses, use of facilities, etc?

- Who has the responsibility for insurance?

- Is the employer to provide any indemnity for the consultant, and vice-versa?

- What are the precise provisions for dealing with complaints about work and conduct of the consultant? Can the contract be terminated immediately or can cash deductions be made? Are there to be provisions for arbitration to resolve disputes? Contracts should also deal with mode and time of payment and similar details. so often minor issues can cause major disputes.

EXAMPLE: THE TRAINING ORGANISATION

This organisation had used consultant trainers for a number of years, most on a regular and long-standing basis. Goodwill had built up. But with the expansion of the organisation's training and advice service, previously informal and unwritten arrangements needed to be 'tightened up'. Specific problems had emerged. For example, if a consultant was recruited, but then the training course did not run, what was the position? Similarly, if the course ran but the trainer could not attend, what happened then? The objective was to be fair to both sides, but also reflect the sometimes variable and imprecise nature of engagements. The following document aimed to deal with these issues, and took the form of a letter with a tear-off slip to signify agreement to the terms.

'Dear...

We are pleased to offer you appointment as a trainer for a course concerned with... on...at a fee of £... This will cover provision of training materials, but reasonable travel expenses will be provided, plus subsistence and accommodation where this has been previously agreed.

Should the course not run for whatever reason we undertake to provide as much notice as possible. Expenses reasonably and necessarily incurred in connection with the course will be reimbursed.

Save in an emergency, if you are unable to participate in the course you will undertake to provide a substitute trainer who is acceptable to the organisation. Materials provided for the course remain your copyright and should be your own or acknowledged work. Information provided by ourselves or which becomes available during training should not be used by you without our express permission....

Consultancy contracts rarely reserve the right to withhold payment if the consultant's work is of a very low standard. However, insofar as the consultancy contract impliedly carries with it a warranty of competence, payment can be withheld for breach of contract on normal legal principles.

Although consultancy arrangements require goodwill and trust in order to thrive, frequent disputes arise over abuse of information gleaned during the consultancy. Lack of clarity about individual responsibilities and over satisfactory completion of the work.

EXAMPLE: THE FINANCIAL ADVISER

A.S. Associates entered a consultancy contract with a large commercial undertaking. They became aware of serious financial irregularities which subsequently became the subject of police investigations. They, too, became involved in the legal proceedings. There was nothing in the consultancy contract to provide indemnity or immunity or to cover legal costs. Although in the event they did not face court action they did suffer losses and criticisms which probably affected their reputation.

Where contracts involve access to sensitive confidential matters, the contract should clarify the situation and deal with indemnities and costs. Overall, because self-employed arrangements are at 'arms-length' it is even more vital that documents anticipate and deal with likely problem areas. As usual, the expectations of the parties do not always avoid with reality. It is vital to identify and express the realities.

6

Special Types of Employment Contracts

Chapters 1 and 2 set out some of the key trends in policy, law and HRM itself which increased pressure to review both the nature and content of employment relationships. Organisational change focusing on restructuring, de-layering, decentralisation and, say outsourcing clearly have employment and employment contract implications. However, employment relationships are also affected on by a wide range of issues other than those of organisational policy development. For example:

- technological change

- fluctuating demand for services/skills

- seasonal demand for services/skills

- fixed costs, especially for premises

- labour costs, especially those relating to occupational benefits and

105

statutory protections

• recruitment/retention problems

• traditional patterns of employment in a particular sector or locality

These factors may require contracts with distinctive features which create a special type of employment relationship. For example, seasonal fluctuations in agriculture, the retail trade or hotel and catering may lead to short term/fixed term contracts. Some workers have fixed term contracts which have labels particular to an occupation - 'Christmas Post staff' 'Outdoor clerk' etc. Technological change, especially in computing, may suggest outsourcing/sub-contracting rather than investing in expensive in-house equipment and high costs for training and retraining of staff. Similarly, high premises costs cause relocation; however, contracts for home-based work might be the preferred solution.

This chapter considers how different contract types can be developed effectively and sets down the key legal framework.

Business needs and priorities directly affect the type of contracts offered to staff. However, in recent years some types of contract - fixed term for example - have become more widely used, though the precise reasons for their popularity are not always clear. Effective contracts can only be made and managed where the employer and the employee are both sure about the reason for and role of the contract. If they are, much of the contract's detail follows on automatically. Identifying the 'right' kind of contract is a vital precedent to establishing its detail. It has to be 'right' for the organisation, the worker and colleagues and clients/customers.

A very important factor to bear in mind is the role of employment law, which is wider than simply that of the law of contract. Certain contract types (part-time, casual, agency temps, some home-working) are typically undertaken more by women than men. The question of anti-discrimination law referred to in Chapter 2, especially from EU law is particularly important. The European Union itself has been concerned about certain contract types for many years, considering that, for example, part-timers and fixed term and other 'atypical' workers are prone to exploitation and disadvantage in the labour market. Hence, since 1983 there has been a series of draft directives which have sought to provide atypical workers with pro-rata benefits of full time, permanent staff.

However, UK law has itself moved dramatically to extend statutory protections to employees, regardless of weekly working hours by the Employment Protection (Part-time Employees) Regulations, 1995. The implications are that it is less important to categorise workers according to hours worked and there are mounting reasons for adopting an holistic approach to contracts.

An EU Directive requiring adequate health and safety protection was adopted in 1990 for fixed term and agency staff and has passed into UK health and safety law (the Management of Health and Safety at Work Regulations 1992). Directives dealing with other terms of work have not yet been adopted, though the intention is still there. If adopted they would, for example, prohibit the constant re-newal of fixed term contracts. The possible relevance of EU laws and proposals will be considered in connection with individual contract types.

TYPES OF CONTRACT

This chapter deals with contract types under the following broad categories:

Contracts characterised by time
    part-time
    job share
    annual hours
    variable hours
Contracts characterised by length
    fixed term
    casual
Contracts characterised by where work is performed
    homeworking
    secondment/postings
Contracts characterised by their legal status
    self-employment
    office holder
    trainees and apprentices
    self employed/consultants/freelance workers.

This chapter addresses three basic questions in relation to contract types:

1   How to decide on the most effective contract type for the employing organisation.

2   What are the legal rules which have particular relevance for the contract type.

3   How to make the detail of the contract reflect its essential purpose(s) and to avoid legal and practical pitfalls.

IDENTIFYING THE APPROPRIATE CONTRACT TYPE

This process will inevitably require data from the employing organisation (and probably beyond it) and thorough and careful analysis, including of the following areas:

LEVEL AND NATURE OF DEMAND

- What demands are made of the organisation?

- What are the human resource implications in terms of skills required and working hours?

- What fluctuations in demand is the organisation subject to?

- Does it vary according to the time of day, month or year?

- Is fluctuation consistent or unpredictable?

LABOUR COSTS

- Compared to other organisations, are overall labour costs high or low?

- In each category of staff, what components of labour costs are made up from:

  basic salary?
  statutory payments (NI contributions, etc.)?
  holidays, sickness, injury and maternity?
  voluntary social welfare benefits (inc. pensions)?
  subsidised services, benefits in kind, training?
  personnel administration?
  office accommodation and facilities?
  transactional management costs, e.g. regarding the employment
  of agency staff, consultants?

PRODUCTION OR SERVICE CAPACITY

- Is the organisation making maximum use of capital equipment, production capacity, office facilities and/or business premises to meet organisational goals?

CENTRALITY OF FUNCTION

For each category of staff, for example, maintenance, security, secretarial, marketing, personnel:

- how central is their work to the principal objectives and functions of the organisation?

- how much discretion do they have in performing their responsibilities?

- what impact does the function have on the organisation?

- is the function relatively autonomous or closely integrated with the work of other employees?

- is the function performed primarily on-site or off-site? Has it the capacity to be performed off-site using office technology?

- what reporting and communication systems are involved?

LABOUR MARKET FACTORS

- Does the local labour market supply most of the organisation's skill needs?

- What skills are particularly difficult to recruit and retain?

- Are the organisation's skill needs drawn from sectors of the labour market with a growing proportion of women or other minority groups likely to be attracted to particular types of work.

- Are some contract types, e.g. 'casual', seasonal work well developed and popular in the local labour market?

HRM FACTORS

- What policies have been or are planned for the organisational that have relevance for labour use? This might include pay, devolution of recruittment and pay determination to line managers, adoption of a 'core/periphery' employment model etc.

- Are there likely to be problems in the application of existing HRM policies to particular categories of work, e.g. applying appraisal or profit sharing to part-timers/job sharers?

- Will the use of certain employment types conflict with both the objectives as well as operational matters, for example with 'Investors in People', 'Opportunity 2000', or Total Quality initiatives?

- Will practices regarding contract types give out the 'wrong messages' to customers, clients, potential qualified staff?

INDUSTRIAL RELATIONS CONSTRAINTS

- Do existing agreements with trade unions constrain certain working practices or patterns? Or has the organisation moved or does it intend to move to personal contracts?

- What arrangements are there beyond union recognition for employee representation and involvement?

- How supportive and involved are unions in personnel issues generally?

- What is the attitude of local officials to labour use strategies?

EXTERNAL POLICY CONSTRAINTS

What are the external policy constraints affecting human resource options within the organisation? Do they, for example, relate to:

- Government policy or guidelines (for example, those influencing the use of contract services in local government and equal opportunities in the Civil Service)?

- Multinational corporate policy (for example, affecting human resource policies of a UK subsidiary) or policies to harmonise HR strategies in European companies?

- legal constraints, both national and international, especially anti-discrimination law; these would include EU laws and are factors of growing importance.

These questions reflect the desirability of not only carefully analysing organisational needs so that workers can be most effectively employed but to also be aware of the needs and preferences of workers themselves. The wishes of women employees to job share after return from maternity leave or work at or from home are examples. These types of contracts which are designed to respond to employee needs are typically the most complex and require very careful drafting.

CONTRACTS CHARACTERISED BY TIME

The major types here are:

- **part-time**

- **job share**

- **annual hours**

- **variable/flexi-hours**

PART-TIME WORK

There is no definition of part-time work in terms of actual hours. For UK statistical purposes a part-timer is anyone who works less than 30 hours per week; for the EU it is working less than the normal weekly hours of full-timers. Patterns of part-time working are mixed, with 'school hours', 'twilight shifts' 'Sunday working' and 'lunch time cover' being examples of the way in which part-timers are used. Part-timers can therefore fill gaps, help with peak demand, ensure equipment is fully utilised and provide skills where they are not needed over the whole normal working week.

Part-time work is attractive to many workers, especially those with child care responsibilities, dependent relatives or health problems or the nearly/recently retired.

Advantages and disadvantages of part-time work

Many, though by no means all part-timers tend to be towards the bottom of pay scales; part-time working in senior posts is still rare. Weighing up the relative merits or other use of using part-timers, the following are the commonly considered advantages:

- working hours can more precisely match work demands;

- savings on wage costs; likely saving on labour costs;

- lower training and recruitment costs;

- likely higher productivity levels;

- often easier to recruit to or retain.

These factors have led to considerable and continuing growth in part-time work. However, using part-timers may not always be a good idea and managers need to be aware of some of the recognised disadvantages of using part-timers:

- less enthusiasm, commitment and energy for the organisation ('it's just a job');

• slightly higher turnover and absence rates;

• relatively higher administrative and management costs;

• possible lack of continuity in senior/professional posts.

• legal obligations broadly in line with those applying to full-timers.

Among the relatively higher administration and management costs are the costs associated with employment contracts themselves and their documentation. Similarly, induction, training, especially in health and safety and skills updating can be more difficult to organise and relatively costly.

Overall, part-time work is attractive to both employer and employee. However, it is not necessarily a cheap option when the legal management and administrative costs are assessed.

Relevant legal issues : occupational

Legal intervention to provide occupational legal protections for a part-timers has come mainly through anti sex discrimination legislation concentrating on pay and occupational benefits. Law has developed rapidly because most part-timers are women.

Case law indicates the following:

• Paying part-timers less on hourly/shift/premium rates than full-timers will probably be unlawful unless there is some objective, genuine reason for the part-timers getting less (over-productivity, poorer quality work etc). Offering lower pay contravenes Article 119 of the Treaty of Rome, which requires equal pay for men and women. (*Clothing Jenkins v Kingsgate* (1981))[1]

• Part-timers should have access to and equal treatment by occupational pension schemes. (*Fissher* (1994))[2]

• Part-timers can usually require access to all occupational, fringe and ex-gratia payments on a comparable basis to full-timers. Again, it is only where there is a genuine business reason that access can be denied. (*Kowalska v Hamburg* (1990))[3]

• Failing to offer training, promotion or other career opportunities to part-timers can also constitute unlawful discrimination. (*Botel* (1992))[4]

It should be noted that all contractual provisions and benefits should, in principle, applied to part-timers. Excluding then is increasingly difficult to justify. The terms of contracts affected include:

- pay, premium rates; applications of PRP; project related pay etc.

- access to overtime (though it is still lawful to limit overtime rates to only those hours beyond the normal full-timers . (*Helmig* (1995))[5]

- training requirements and financial support;

- occupational benefits;

- contractual severance, redeployment and related clauses;

- occupational maternity, sickness and sick leave provisions.

All should be checked for explicit or implicit discrimination against part-timers.

Relevant legal issues: statutory protections
As a result of the decision of the House of Lords in *R v Secretary of State for Employment ex parte EOC* (1994))[6], the 16 hour rule regarding claims for redundancy and unfair dismissal led to the Employment Protection (Part-timer Employees) Regulations 1995. There are now no minimum hours thresholds for the basic statutory rights.

At the time of writing there are still a number of legal issues to be resolved about part-timers and job security legislation, including whether retrospective claims can be made. It should also be borne in mind that other aspects of job security law, such as claims for wrongful dismissal in the County or High Court, or public law remedies apply regardless of hours worked (see Chapter 9).

Part-time contracts
In many organisations, part-time contracts have been devised and applied separately from full-time contracts. As differences in law between the treatment of full and part-timers are being eroded, there is merit in developing contracts which have the same basic structure, look similar and where the number of hours worked is the only major distinctive feature. In terms of anti-discrimination law this approach can be attractive, as it will minimise the risk of part-timers feeling 'second class' employees.

General questions to address

- Is there to be a *separate part-time contract* or can the documentation just contain a section allowing managers to delete, say, full-time/part-time /0..5/etc. as appropriate? If a separate document is to be used what are the precise organisational reasons?

- How to define access to occupational benefits and policies in equal or pro-rata terms. This has particular relevance to holiday's sickness and pensions.

- How to define and express access to training and career opportunities.

- Whether and how to apply contractual provisions relating to perform-ance, flexibility, confidentiality, restrain of trade etc.

- How to make the contract itself absolutely clear about working time, both regarding the number of hours (or equivalent) and when they are to be performed? Are there to be paid breaks? Is there to be any flex-ibility and if so, how is the flexibility to be exercised? What about public holidays; are they to be paid for?

The following are usable contract terms, especially to deal with the last point above:

'You are required to work 18 hours per week in total. The actual hours will be Monday 9am - 1pm, Tuesday 9am - 1p,. Wednesday 9am - 1pm, Thursday 10am to 2pm and Friday 10am to 12pm'.

'Hours of work: Your hours of work are expressed on an annual basis. Each year, commencing on the 1st of April your hours of work will be specified. Currently, your annual hours are _____ excluding public and annual holidays. Each week you will work no fewer than 10 hours and no more than 18'.

'The precise hours will be specified for each 28 day work cycle'.

'Your departmental manager will notify you normally 14 days in advance of the commencement of the 28 day work cycle'.

'You are not entitled to any paid breaks during working hours', *or*
'You are entitled to a paid break of 20 mins during each daily work session'.

'You have been appointed to a 0.5 post. The full time hours are 35 per week. Your working hours are....'

'Your weekly hours are 20. Management reserves the right to require you to work up to 4 more hours a week (or any other specific or unspecific time) should organisational needs require it'.

'Your weekly hours are 16. The actual hours you work will be determined by the departmental manager who will provide as much notice of hours to be worked as possible. He/She will normally notify you the previous Friday, at the latest, of the hours to be worked during the following week'.

'You will be normally required to work 20 hours per week. It may be possible from time to time to vary the hours and when they are worked, providing the departmental manager agrees in writing'.

'You will work from 8am to 4pm, with 45 minutes break for lunch, on Mondays and Tuesdays. Payment will (will not) be made for Mondays which are public holidays'.
'You are paid hourly. Your current hourly rate is £4.70. You qualify for shift pay but do not qualify for overtime rates', *or*

'...you do qualify for overtime rates but only after completion of the equivalent full timer'.

Occupational benefits

'As a part-timer you are entitled to use all XLtd's social, sporting and health care facilities. You qualify for the company's sick pay scheme (see details in Handbook) and its pension scheme (see details in Handbook). You do not qualify for the company's health care scheme until you have completed two years continuous service'.

It is absolutely vital to note developments in law, especially anti-discrimination law which may affect the validity of clauses such as set out above.

JOB-SHARING CONTRACTS

Job sharing is essentially a work arrangement whereby two or more employees share the responsibilities and benefits of, usually, one full-time post, and the practice has grown considerably in the UK over the past few years. Frequently, the arrangement has been on a Monday - Wednesday morning for one sharer and Wednesday - Friday afternoon for the other. Others work on week-on-week off basis or one sharer doing mornings and the other afternoons. However, some of the most successful job shares have resulted from a more careful analysis of the precise demands the 'peaks and troughs' of work and what working hours would most effectively discharge the job tasks.

The analysis sometimes results in job sharers working together for a day or half a day and neither attending for some part of the week where there are no operational reasons for attendance. Job sharing can be more or less static, i.e. the hours remain, broadly, constant. It can be performed on a more flexible basis as long as the sharers are co-operative.

Job sharing has become strongly established in the public sector and has recently made inroads into the private and professional services sectors. For some time it has been thought that job sharing was appropriate for middle to lower level white-collar work where job tasks and working could be easily divided. Secretarial, administrative, medical and para-medical work were dominant. However, research has shown that job sharing is effective for managers in a range of high level, policy-oriented and creative posts. It has broken through into senior posts in central government, the media and the caring and other professions such as town planning, law and engineering.

However, research has also identified the likely problems as well as the advantages of job sharing. The culture of an organisation, especially its labour market position and its attitude to equal opportunities matters, can exert great influence.

Key issues regarding the employment of job sharers

The major advantages of employing job shares are considered to be[8]:

- Increased work output by the sharers - the 'sum' of the two sharers in the job often adds up to more than the 'whole post'. Job sharers are conscious that full-timers suspect they are onto a 'cosy number' and they work harder to refute this.

- As an aid to recruitment and retention of employees. The retention of staff who might not return full-time after maternity leave or would take early retirement from a full-time post due to domestic pressures etc. are typical reasons for supporting job sharers.

- 'Two heads are better than one.' Many jobs are enhanced by the presence of two employees, especially where sharers have complementary or contrasting skills. Policy and creative areas especially benefit, as they often require a very wide range of skills hard to obtain in one employee.

- Increased flexibility, for example, through the willingness of sharers to cover the whole post for short periods, or to deputise occasionally for the other on occasions, such as during holidays or illness.

- Less time off work. Most job-sharers make medical and similar appointments on their days off. Labour cost savings can be considerable.

There are possible disadvantages. These include:

- There can be a loss of continuity in a post - (the 'two Mondays syndrome'). Where post-holders need to relate to a particularly narrow range of clients/customers etc. this can be disruptive.

- Some job sharers can be unresponsive to crises or peak demands, when compared to full-timers. This may be because of the inflexibility of out-of-work demands or that the structure of job share contracts was too rigid. Some of these problems can be avoided by careful design and management.

- Increased personnel and administrative costs. These largely derive from the need to effectively plan and implement a job share, and additional communication facilities; national insurance and other labour costs are only marginally higher.

- Increased investment of time by managers, for example to set up, communicate with, train and develop job sharers.

Relevant legal issues

Job share contracts remain part-time contracts in law.   As part-timers job sharers qualify for most job security and other statutory rights.

A particular legal issue has sometimes arisen over whether an employer is acting lawfully when refusing a request to job share, by a returner from maternity leave who previously worked full-time. It is hard to be precise on this. However, case law indicates that if the line manager is supportive and job sharing is viable from a practical perspective a refusal is likely to be unlawful sex discrimination.

It is unlawful to hold one job sharer responsible for any errors or misconduct of the other although failure to co-operate or communicate between sharers could provide potential grounds for a fair dismissal. The following legal rules also have relevance:

- Job sharers, in common with other part-timers should not be excluded from occupational benefits, including training, and other human resources initiatives and opportunities at the workplace.

- Job sharers should not be dismissed, or 'forced' into full time employment should one job sharer leave or the organisation embark on restructuring and the like. Anti-discrimination law could again be infringed.

Because job sharing is essentially a 'new' way of working and is perhaps the prime example of 'social pull' initiatives it has generally developed in a more carefully prepared and articulated way than 'ordinary' part-time work. Organisations are advised to have job share policies which will set out the aims and role of job sharing as well as some administrative and detailed matters. This enables a coherent approach and has helped to overcome likely problem areas as well as publicising the scheme. It can help to deal with the resistance of some groups of staff, especially line managers who sometimes expect job sharing to be burdensome and complex and do not see the reason for its introduction.

A policy document, if well prepared and presented, can lessen fears as well as providing focus for job sharing itself. Indeed, there is no reason why other contract types - fixed term, annual hours, homeworking etc. - should not also have a policy document which clarifies thinking and practice on the topic.

If a job share policy is devised it will be vital to decide on the legal status of the policy document itself in relation to the employment contracts of job sharers. If it is seen as providing contract terms then it must be lawfully incorporated into the contract and care taken with the detail of the policy (see Chapter 3 generally). Most will have direct relevance for job share contracts themselves.

The following issues should be addressed:

- General statements regarding the motivation(s) for the scheme.

- The scope of the scheme: which jobs are available/excluded from the scheme.

- Procedures for recruitment to job sharing: advertising, selection, the distinction, if any, between procedures affecting applications from in-house staff and outsiders.

- A general statement regarding the position of job sharers and occupational benefits, especially pensions.

- Any special rules regarding supervision, discipline, grievance procedures and the like.

- Any special rules regarding training, appraisal and promotion.

- Clarification of the situation when one or both job sharers leave. Is the vacancy to be advertised, the remaining sharer to be offered a full-time post, re-deployed or dealt with in some other way? Are there to be time limits or vetoes to any of these procedures?

The question of the position when one job sharer leaves is crucial. A policy may contain a clause committing the employer to find a replacement when one sharer leaves. If the employer then decides to 'freeze' the 'half post' for reasons of financial cutbacks or operational matters, this amounts to a breach of contract. It is possible to justify the decision legally (see Chapter 9). Nonetheless, it may be desirable to consider the position carefully before putting pen to paper. Of all the legal and managerial issues affecting job sharing, this is the one which has caused most controversy and must therefore be given adequate attention (see below for suggested clauses).

Job share contracts
It is usually advisable to devise a specific job share contract rather than adapt a part-time or full-time contract. Whatever documentation is used it should be compatible with other policy and contract documents at the workplace. It is helpful to reflect the particular features of job sharing in the contract documents, such as the need for sharers to communicate between themselves and others and perhaps the obligation to provide cover if one sharer is ill or

on holiday.

When devising the job share contract the following should be addressed:

- Are there going to be any contractual limitations on job shares under-taking other paid employment outside the enterprise, or on job sharing another post at the same enterprise, or working there part-time? If so, a clause would operate as a restraint of trade clause and be subjected to the usual legal rules of reasonableness.

- Is the contract going to define precisely the hours of work or leave matters to individual/joint negotiation of managerial discretion?

- Is the contract going to define the work to be carried out by the job-sharer? Are specific *individual* responsibilities going to be spelt out?

- How are job performance targets (if any) to be applied to the job share? Is the appraisal scheme to be applied?

- How is the job share to be affected by any in-house arrangements regar-rding matters such as bonuses, merit payments, performance related pay? Are the schemes to apply and, if so, do they apply to the job or the individuals? How are increments to apply?

- How are any in-house arrangements regarding overtime and other special payment, such as those for unsocial hours, to apply to job shar-ers?

- Are the job sharers to be under any obligation to cover the absent sharer? If so, to what extent? If one sharer is absent, does the other sharer have first refusal to cover the whole post?

- How is the organisation's job evaluation scheme going to apply (if one exists)? Are the sharers to be treated individually, or as a team? Do you need to specify that an element of the evaluation will be the ability to work together as a team?

- Will promotion arrangements allow promotion together as a 'team' or will promotion be made solely on the basis of their individual qualities and promote them, in effect, out of the job share as an individual?

- Will the contract incorporate details of training opportunities? Is the training to apply to the post and the sharers or is the line manager to decide on how training is done; or is training to be on a purely individual basis?

- How will occupational benefits, especially sick pay and pension rights, apply to job sharers? How will fringe or other benefits, such as cars, financial assistance for moving, and health care support apply?

- What will be the contractual position where one sharer leaves? Will the post be re-advertised as a job share? Will the remaining sharer have the option of full-time employment?

Any job share contract has to comply with Schedule 4 TURERA, 1993, though its content will almost certainly go way beyond the statutory minimum of written information. Given that the thorniest issue of job share contracts has been the position when one sharer leaves is promoted etc the following is a suggested clause:

'When one job share partner leaves or wishes to move to full-time employment or is promoted within the organisation the remaining job share partner will be offered the post on a full-time basis. Should the remaining partner not wish to work full-time the organisation will use its best (or reasonable?) endeavours to find a replacement partner.
'Should this fail the remaining partner will be offered a suitable alternative part-time post'.

Problems can arise when a sharer refuses alternative work. If disciplinary action or even dismissal follows the legal situation is unclear. However, there is always the need to be wary of anti-discrimination legislation.
Replacing one sharer can also cause problems with the one remaining. The following clause could be helpful.

'When one job share partner leaves .... etc. etc. the company will recruit a replacement job share partner. Should the remaining partner express dissatisfaction with either the procedure or the replacement employee they shall have available the company's grievance procedure. The company undertakes to deal with such matters in a sympathetic and supportive manner. However, it must reiterate that the continuing efficiency of the organisation has to be its primary objectives and that all employees are expected to be co-operative'.

When dealing with organisational change, which could be anything from re-location to market testing and contracting out of work it is vital to keep in mind the position of job sharers. The following might be inserted:

'The company undertakes to inform and consult with job sharers in the normal way should re-organisation or other changes become necessary. Whilst the company aims to provide continuing support for job sharing this cannot be guaranteed. However, the company will discuss with both job share partners the possible options prior to any decisions being taken and will endeavour to retain a job share where possible or provide a suitable alternative work arrangement'.

Clearly, selecting job sharers first or having a policy of 'breaking up' job sharing as a first step in re-organising would run the severe risk of contravening anti-discrimination legislation or, more likely, infringing the implied contract term of mutual trust and confidence (see Chap 3). Overall, job share contracts have become well established and there is much experience to draw on. Many organisations offer advice and information, especially 'New Ways to Work' based in London.

CASE STUDY: THE NATIONWIDE BUILDING SOCIETY

A Nationwide Building Society Area Manager was approached by an experienced Branch Manager who wished to reduce her hours of work. she was working very effectively but personal circumstances dictated a need to change her working pattern. The Society was happy to suggest job share as a way of meeting her requirements and retaining an effective staff member. The Area Manager in conjunction with the Human Resources Department therefore identified a suitable partner to enable the project to progress.

It was the first example of job share at this level in the Society and three areas were identified to be of particular concern, these were - management of staff, liaison with customers and responsibility for security.

At this stage the above areas of concern were examined by a number of people within the organisation to decide whether there would by any barriers to the job share. It was felt that a key to resolving any potential problems would be the make-up of the contracted hours. Staff need to see continuity in the management of the branch in order that operations are co-ordinated and customer service is given the priority which ensures the success of the branch. Identifying responsibility for security at any one time is also essential as this is a key part of the Branch Manager's role. For these reasons a handover period was seen as vital.

The two potential job sharers put together a proposal as to how these issues could be resolved and then together with their line manager and Human Resources a contract was agreed whereby each would work a week beginning at lunch time Wednesdays. A handover period was built in. Each of the job sharing branch managers now works a 19 hour week, either Monday 9.00am to 5.00pm, Tuesday, 9.00am to 5.00pm, Wednesday 9.00am to 2.30pm (including 1/2 hour lunch) or Wednesday 11.30am to 5.00pm (including 1/2 hour lunch), Thursday 9.00am to 5.00pm, Friday 9.00am to 5.00pm. The contract was written so that both branch managers would work each pattern or alternate weeks, therefore each now has 5 working days in succession. Responsibility for working alternate Saturdays is clearly identified.

As a result of this flexible approach Nationwide has been able to retain two valuable staff members and has gained the benefit of two different personalities' insights into the management of one branch.

ANNUAL HOURS CONTRACTS

These types of contracts have become more widely used in the UK and across Europe, particularly where there are seasonal or business fluctuations. Fluctuations have caused under-utilisation of staff and then heavy use of overtime at premium rates.

The policy reasons for developing such contracts, whereby at the end of a specific year or other reference period a certain number of hours should have been worked are often specific to a particular employer or sector of work. Reducing overtime, though is the most common reason for change. Frequently, although expressed in annual terms the contract requires a minimum number of core hours to have been performed each week.

There are two basic contract forms. The first, driven by the employer, establishes the annual hours to be performed by employees. It then establishes work cycles, whereby employees perform 'X' number of hours for say, four weeks and 'X+3' for the next four weeks and then 'X-10' for the next period.

The second contract form is driven by the employee and offers annual hours but with considerable discretion as to when they ares performed. The contract may provide an overall framework or establish criteria to guide employee performance. Such an arrangement is clearly only suitable for specialised work, especially in the creative or developmental area, and requires careful monitoring and management.

The advantage to the employee is a constant rate of pay, regardless of working hours. This enables employees to plan their finances more effectively and it is generally thought that annual hours contracts are very popular. Employers report increased productivity, lower waste and reduced wage costs.

Legal issues

Under UK employment law the parties are, in principle, able to negotiate their working hours. However, it will be essential soon to regulate daily and weekly (as well as yearly) working time to ensure that the employee falls within the provisions of the EU Working Time Directive by 1997 through UK legislation implementing it. The employee must have adequate breaks so that his/her health is not jeopardised, and hours must not regularly exceed a 48 hour week. The employer needs to ensure that weekend breaks and holidays are safeguarded. Although there are derogations in the Directive for particular industries and occupations it is clear that working time cannot be left to the preferences of the employee, or the demand of the employer. The employer will have to devise structures to regulate hours, as appropriate. It should also be borne in mind that requiring - (or allowing?) extremely long and unbroken working hours can be a breach of the implied obligation of trust and support (see Chapter 3).

Annual hours contracts can have a supporting policy document setting out the aims and structure of such contracts. Given that the essence of these contracts is their flexibility the contractual issues centre as much on the precise terms regarding how, when and by whom decisions are made as the hours themselves. Some key preliminary questions are:

- How and by whom will be the total number of hours determined?

- What weekly, monthly or even daily maxima and minima will be applied, if any?

- Will there be work cycles prescribed by contract, i.e. blocks of time when working hours will be set. Or will discretion be left entirely to the employer (or employee)? If so, will time need to be recorded and if so, how?

- Are there any opportunities for individual employee negotiation or variation?

- How is pay determined? Will it remain stable or be variable depending on hours worked?

- What are the arrangements for breaks/holidays? Are public holidays to receive particular attention?

- Is there still to be the opportunity for overtime?

- Is there a procedure for dealing with tensions or disputes?

- How are appraisal, if appropriate, and other organisational quality control mechanisms or initiatives to apply?

Usable clauses where the arrangement is driven by the employer include:

'You are required to work .... hours per annum. This averages at 37 hours per week allowing for 25 days annual leave and 8 public holidays per annum'.

'Working time is organised on four week cycles, detail of which is available in your departmental managers office. You will be notified at least one week in advance of the weekly hours to be performed in the subsequent four week cycle'.

'Your pay, regardless of hours worked, will be £x per week/per month'.

Where the contract is driven by the employee, the following clauses may be helpful.

'Although this contract provides flexibility regarding working time you should not allow a situation to arise whereby to meet your contract targets you have to average 48 or more hours a week over any three month period'.

'You are required to ensure that over any seven day period you have at least 35 consecutive hours break'.

'At no time should you work such hours as will cause fatigue. You are required, as part of this contract, to have regular breaks and to record in the documents provided your actual working hours'.

'Your daily hours should not exceed 10; they should be worked between 7am and 8pm. Any period of 6 hours week should include a break of at least 30 minutes approximately after 4 hours work at the longest'.

NEGOTIATED CORE AND VARIABLE HOURS CONTRACTS

These are similar to annual hours and gaining support in the UK, especially in occupations with fluctuating or seasonal demand. Many areas have allowed for increased or decreased hours of work on an informal basis, depending on time of year, weather and demand. Occupations as disparate as teaching, leisure and mail-order businesses have introduced written contract terms to this effect.

Again, the legal formalities are not complex. The need is to express the base or minimum hours, to establish maximum hours and to identify any relevant circumstances which will set the parameters or trigger change. Some examples from employment contracts are:

EXAMPLE: CONTRACT IN THE LEISURE INDUSTRY

'Your average weekly hours of work are 37..5. During the months of October to March they will be 35 hours per week, to be worked between the hours of 9am and 5pm with one hour for lunch. During April to September, they will be 40 hours per week, to be worked between 9am and 6pm with one hour for lunch'.

EXAMPLE: ORGANISATION IN THE CATERING INDUSTRY

'Your weekly hours of work shall be normally 37. Although a rota will be posted one week in advance, management reserves the right to amend this by giving as much notice as possible. You can be required to work such extra hours as are reasonable. Time off in lieu will be given. In no event shall the weekly hours exceed 45'.

Other contracts allow for evening or weekend working, depending on season, demand, etc. Practices are becoming more varied, though for very diverse reasons. A move towards time off in lieu of 'extra' hours is desirable. Sectors such as higher education, where course delivery methods and course structures tend now to concentrate teaching in blocks, are moving to these type of arrangements.

CONTRACTS CHARACTERISED BY LENGTH

The major contract types here are:

- **Fixed term, including fixed task contracts**

- **Casual**

- **Nil/zero hours**

- **Temporary agency contracts**

This is the most complex area of employment contracts. The only common feature as between these different kinds of contracts is that they are all contracts of definite length.

This does not necessarily mean that the precise end of the contract can be foreseen at its outset - simply that an event, date or situation will cause it to end.

Fixed term contracts, (FTCs in EU parlance) is the generic name to cover all contracts of definite length. The reasons why such contracts are used vary enormously but overall the shift to definite length contracts has been rapid in recent years not only in the UK but across Europe. Most EU member states have legislation restricting the use of fixed term contracts in some way.

Many legal systems require procedures to be followed before a contract is offered on a fixed term basis, defining the maximum length of contract and, most commonly, the number of renewals before the employee has to be offered an 'indefinite length' contract or be dismissed.

Some laws require fixed term staff to be offered comparable wages and other terms of work as 'permanent' employees. Many member states have recently relaxed rules so as to encourage job creation and greater flexibility. It is estimated that around 60% of workers on fixed term contracts in the UK are women.

It is commonly thought that the following are the main advantages of using fixed term contracts of various sorts.

- Fixed-term contracts can be tied in more effectively to specific corporate objectives and can be especially helpful when demand is uncertain or for newly established organisations.

- Generally lower wage costs and other wage-related expenses in terms of occupational benefits.

- Relative lack of legal regulation so that workers can be employed more informally (but see page 127 below).

- Contracts can be terminated more easily. Periods of notice required by law are short and temporary workers are rarely protected under job security law - those contracts are for a specific task (fixed-job contracts) are the least protected by statutory provisions.

- Collective agreements are less likely to provide for detailed terms for temporary staff, leaving individual management considerable discretion.

- Generally lower recruitment costs.

However, there are some disadvantages and some dilemmas posed for managers by the use of fixed term contracts. These include:

- Often higher levels of absenteeism than with permanent staff.

- Lower levels of commitment and loyalty

- Their use can be inconsistent with some HRM initiatives such as team briefing/team working, quality circles, Investor in People etc. which stress participation and training and development.

- Increased management time to recruit, train, document contracts etc.

- Risks of disruption and possible impact on quality of work or service.

These contrasting factors often present managers with some dilemmas:

- How to recruit and manage fixed term staff economically and yet achieve effective quality and screening, as well as retaining the integrity and conviction of human resources initiatives.

- How to keep overheads and wage costs relatively low yet motivate workers.

- How to maximise the efficiency of workers who are working for short periods.

- How to retain the fixed term concept of the relationship yet build up sufficient loyalty.

Overall, fixed term work is most effective where professional and occupational loyalty is marked and therefore provides a powerful motivator in overcoming ambiguous feelings of loyalty to the firm. Occupational commitment is a feature of work at the highest skill levels, and also the lowest. Skilled engineers or doctors will have professional standards which guide their work regardless of the contractual arrangement. Experienced bar and banqueting staff will probably have less marketable skills but often considerable experience and an unwritten code of loyalty. Both of these categories of staff have strong traditions of working under such contracts.

More problematic are categories of workers where there is a strong tradition of permanent work. Professions in the public sector, increasingly subject to fixed term engagements are the ones where insecurities and resentment have tended to develop.

Relevent legal issues

A fixed term contract is precisely what it implies - a contract scheduled to last for a prescribed period. That period may be a day or five years, or linked with a project or funding. Nonetheless, should either side end it without cause during that period the other side is entitled to sue for breach of contract (*Laverack v Woods of Colchester*) (1966)[9]. In theory, damages could be high - loss of earnings from the unexpired portion for the employee, costs of finding a replacement for the employer. In reality, it is only contracts relating to particular occupations - e.g. football managers, performing artists - where claims are made if the contract is ended prematurely. For most employers and employees the costs of going to law do not usually warrant making a claim.

The fact that a fixed term contract contains a clause allowing either side to end it with notice or for a specific reason will not prevent it being a fixed term contract in law.

Other important legal rules are:

* Any FTC, scheduled to last for a month or more is covered by the full provisions of TURERA, Schedule 4. Hence, the rules about the type of information and the form in which it must be provided apply to many FTCS. This can be quite costly. Even if the contract is terminated before the end of the month the information must be provided.

* When an FTC is used the employee must be told in writing its likely length and key details - maternity, sickness cover, specific project etc. This requires employers to more clearly consider the precise reasons and use of contracts of a definite length.

* Where a contract is to cover maternity leave or the suspension of a pregnant woman on maternity grounds (or the suspension of any employee on medical grounds) the employee with the FTC must be told in writing the reason and that the contract will end on the return of the suspended or absent employee.

* Problems over ending or not reviewing FTCs. There are special legal rules relating to unfair dismissal and redundancy, particularly those relating to whether intermittent periods of work can together provide necessary continuity of employment of two years which, at time of writing, is required for the major statutory rights. If such periods can be joined together by viewing the non-work periods as 'temporary

cessation of work', continuity will be established. (EPC(A) Sched 13)

- There is the possibility of two or more contracts being joined together to create a so-called 'global' contract which may then be sufficient for statutory protection purposes. (*Atkinson v Hellyer Brothers* (1994))[10]

- Some legal rights are not dependent on length of contract. These include anti-discrimination legislation, trade union rights, maternity and health and safety, including 'victimisation' rights. (TURERA, Sched 5)

- The EU has created draft directives covering atypical workers (part-time, temporary (agency) and FTCs). They would require pro-rata occupational and statutory protections for those on FTCs and prevent unlimited renewals. Although these directives have not yet been adopted, the prudent manager will note the intentions of the EU to ensure that FTCs are not abused so as to lead to increasingly precarious and poor working conditions. Continuous renewal of FTCs (the 'permanent temporary' syndrome!) may well be an ill-advised policy and in future be legally difficult to sustain.

FIXED TERM CONTRACTS

It is important to ensure that the essential purpose and basis of the contract is clearly expressed. Just because the contract may be relatively short lived there is no excuse for not to developing a viable and managerially effective document. Many employers, especially in the retail and hotel and catering industries, have developed effective FTCs over many years. Indeed, given that the essence of an FTC is that the employee's relationship with the employer is short term and employees may not have the time to become familiar with the culture and structure of the organisation it is even more vital to develop well crafted documents.

The typical problem areas of FTCs are:

- The employment status of the worker (see Chapter 5);

- Uncertainties about the circumstances ending the contract;

- Uncertainties about the precise basis of payment;

- Uncertainties about access to occupational benefits, especially sick pay and paid holidays;

- Confusions over extension/renewal of the original period and whether, if the contract is extended whether the original terms automatically carry over.

• Whether the language used in the contract can affect the legal issue of continuity of employment for the purposes of statutory protections.

FTCs: basic approach to effective contract documentation
The two basic reasons why FTCs are used are:

(a) to cover a specific, short-term circumstance or task, *or*

(b) to respond to fluctuating demands, or business uncertainties

Effective contracts can only be devised if the factors creating either the short-term need or uncertainties are carefully analysed. Imprecise or woolly thinking will not ensure effective contracts and will communicate uncertainty and even mistrust to employees ('They don't know what they want, do they?'). It is quite clear from research that employees fully understand genuine short-term needs but do not sympathise with 'back to back' contracts which look very much like lengthy and uncertain probationary periods!

The first task is to make a realistic assessment of skill needs and identify the factors which might condition the length of the contract. Sometimes, the employer can control this (the summer sales, a computing system turnkey project etc.), but sometimes not (because of the weather, public demand, the size and quality of the apple/pea/hop harvest etc).

The second is to choose the correct contract type. Traditionally, in the UK casual/temporary/fixed term contracts have had distinctive meanings. Given the law's current approach there is a growing argument for heading documents 'fixed term contract' and then allowing the content to flesh out these particular features.

The third task is to ensure that the content meets both the statutory requirements of TURERA, is clear and deals with the typical problem areas set out previously.

SUGGESTED CLAUSES

'Your contract with ... Ltd is for a fixed term. It commences on ... 19.. and will end on ... 19....'.

'Your contract with .... Ltd is a fixed term contract to cover maternity leave of Mrs............ It will terminate when she exercises her legal right to return to work.

'You will receive at least two weeks notice of your contract terminating'.

Your contract is a fixed task contract. It will terminate at such time as the project on which you are employed is completed'.

'Your contract is a fixed term contract. It will automatically operate on a weekly basis. It may be renewed by ... Ltd on the Friday of each week. If there is an offer of renewal and you accept it in writing the contract will continue on the same terms as previously'.

Particular clause: pay

Questions of pay have sometimes given rise to problems - it is important to clarify what, precisely, determines whether the employee is entitled to full or partial payment. Is the trigger for pay being provided with work and carrying it out or simply being available for work? Examples of usable clauses are:

'Your contract is a fixed term contract of .... weeks. Pay is at the hourly rate of £4.50. Normal working hours are 8am to 4.30pm with an unpaid break for lunch 12.-1pm'.

'Because of uncertainties regarding demand for the company's services pay is only due when work is actually carried out; a part of an hour shall count as a full hour providing at least 15 mins were actually worked'.

'The company does not guarantee to provide you with a minimum number of hours work each week'.

EXAMPLE: TYPICAL CONTRACT FOR SUMMER SALES STAFF

'You are employed on a fixed term contract as a sales assistant from ...199.. to ....199...'

'Your current weekly pay is £114-75p'

'The company does not provide occupational sick pay during illness nor paid holidays other than public holidays. You are not entitled to join the company's pension scheme'.

'You are entitled to membership of the staff preferential shopping scheme. Details are in the Staff Handbook'.

EXAMPLE: TYPICAL CONTRACT FOR PROMOTIONAL WORK ASSISTANT

'You are employed for a fixed period of three weeks commencing ...199... as a promotional work assistant. Your place of work is the National Exhibition Centre, Birmingham, UK'.

'Your pay is based on £185 per week, payable at the completion of the fixed period of three weeks Failure to present yourself for work for any day or part of day entitles Ltd to deduct the appropriate sum from final payment on *a pro-rata basis*'.

Waiver clauses

Unfair dismissal legislation which normally views the non-renewal of an FTC as a dismissal provides for employee waiver of rights in some circumstances. If a contract is for at least one year a waiver clause relating to potential unfair dismissal rights in the event of non-renewal should it not be renewed can be signed by the employee at any time during the contracts lifetime. The waiver clause can only relate to non-renewal and will not affect any other potential claims if the contact is ended during its fixed term.

Some difficult case law has built up on this point. Simply allowing the contract to run on after its expiry date will not necessarily carry over the waiver clause. The law also sees a distinction between an extension, a renewal and a re-engagement. Where the relevant period of time is an extension of the first the clause will carry over. Where it is a renewal for at least one year, it probably does, but it is best to clarify the point: where it is a re-engagement for at least a year a new contract has been made and the waiver clause must be explicitly re-negotiated and signed. It is possible that employees who have served under 'back to back' contracts will become gradually more resistant to signing rights away.

CASE LAW EXAMPLE

An employee had been employed on a fixed term contract for .....years. In August it was extended for three months to December. The original contract contained a waiver clause. It was decided that as this way, in effect, a new contract the waiver clause had to be inserted again and agreed to in writing to be effective. (*Mulrine v University of Ulster* (1993))[11]

If a contract simply states it is for a set period and when that expires an offer for continuation is made, the assumption would be that any subsequent period would probably be a re-engagement. A prudent manager would explicitly re-negotiate and insert the clause.

The following are some usable clauses:

'The employment contracts is for a fixed term. It will comment on ...199... and terminate on 31...199.... (2 years later)'.

'The contract may be extended for a further 12 months. If so, it will continue on the same terms as before'.

NIL/ZERO HOURS CONTRACTS

Such contracts have become more popular in occupations subject to high levels of fluctuating demand. The intention is to formalise and manage more effectively the so-called 'regular casual'. Catering, building, computing, nursing and recreation are typical of the occupations. The legal status of such workers has often been the subject of case law where the intermittent, open-ended nature of the employment relationship had sometimes led courts to deciding such workers are self-employed. (*O'Kelly v Trusthouse Forte* (1983)).[12]

Many wish to attract and retain a committed 'pool' of workers by providing some benefits in return for the employee giving priority to the needs of the employer. An on-going contractual relationship is created (called, variously, nil hours zero hours etc.) which establishes a contract but does not guarantee either work or pay. The employee does not have to work when called on.

A contract can be formed, including clauses as set out below:

1   'Nil hours contract'...

2   'Work will be offered as and when it becomes available. If offered you should attend the Company's premises at the appropriate time'.

3   'The Company does not guarantee to provide a minimum number of hours in any week; payment is only due when work is performed'.

4   'The Company undertakes to give you priority in offering work as being covered by this contract'.

5   'The Company reserves the right to terminate the arrange ment should you reject offers of work on two or more consecutive occasions other than for sound and compelling reasons'.

This is a workable contract but a few legal issues remain. The most significant is the legal status of the periods when the contract applies but no work is being done it is likely that this will be viewed as a period of continuous employment, or alternatively a 'temporary cessation'. In either case continuity will be preserved. With the ending of minimum hours for statutory rights this issue becomes even more important.

CASE STUDY EXAMPLE: THE REGULAR CASUALS

Forte Crest is one of largest employers of hotel and catering staff in the UK and a major multi-national. It has recently appointed a number of senior HR staff and has undertaken a review of HRM more generally and has set up improved management information systems.

The particular issue for this company was that the review had highlighted the fact that there was a large group of 'regular casual', often bar and restaurant staff who were not included for headcount purposes as they were only notionally used for peaks of work, to cover for regular staff etc. In reality, this group included many extremely loyal and long serving staff (one 'casual' could have been eligible to receive a watch for 20 years service!) and made up around 15% - 20% of staff employed at any given time. The background to the review of employment contract practice and introduction of new contracts for regular casuals (and some other groups) was prompted by:

the recession at the end of the 1980s which had led to downsizing, with the casuals in the front line. This had caused concerns within the company and would have generated some bad publicity.

the imminent abolition of wages councils which, in their view, had been inflexible regarding both pay and working hours.

the reorganisation of the Hotels Division into five brands/collec tions with a devolved and explicit HR role, including for employ ment contracts and their management. This implied that individual managers would need clear guidance on contracts.

the need to have a clearer view and control of both labour costs and the particular featuring of a group of 'regular casuals' and how they relate to the deployment and working conditions of employees more generally.

the need to provide an effective contract package for attracting and retaining good 'casuals' and being seen to provide a fair but effective response to fluctuating work demands.

changes in the UK legal and industrial relations culture.

The 'zero hours' contract

The objective of these contracts is to have an on-going contractual relationship with a group of vital, yet intermittent staff which does not guarantee any set number of hours worked and pays for actual hours worked.

They are called in with at least 24 hours notice, and if the request to work is subsequently withdrawn within 24 hours prior to the expected started time they are guaranteed four hours pay. They qualify for SSP and are provided by full contract documentation and are subject to the usual discipli-nary and grievance procedures. They are included in attitude surveys and other aspects of employee relations, including opportunities for prizes, incentives and other benefits in kind when on offer.

A number of related developments influenced this approach to employ-ment contracts. The first was tightening up labour use strategies to check that casuals of all sorts were only used in their 'correct' way, e.g. agency staff only used when all else had failed. Secondly, working time rules had changed with the abolition of overtime for all staff and the consequent need to have effective working time structures.

Thirdly, and perhaps most significant was a move to 4-weekly cycles of work where the hours of all types of staff are planned and budgeted for in advance. At the heart of the review were ideas for forward planning, coupled with individual 'zero hours' staff negotiating and committing themselves to specified working hours.

Legally, zero hours contracts are interesting devices which, in this case, have aimed to provide a fair and balanced outcome for one of the perennial problems of employment contracts.

Task contracts

These remain rare. They are FTCs, where the essence of the contract is its ending by completion of a specific task rather than a particular date. Their ending is not considered as a dismissal in law and there are no possible unfair dismissal or redundancy claims.

From an employer perspective such contracts are attractive because if the contract and its ending were properly handled it is highly unlikely any unfair dismissal and redundancy claims could be made. In order for contracts to be considered task contracts it is necessary for them to be genuine and convincing, not a device used to circumvent employment rights.

EXAMPLE: CONTRACT FOR A FIXED TASK - PARTICULARS OF EMPLOYMENT

'You are employed as a project manager for the company's development project in ....'.

'Your employment will continue during the length of the project and will end on its completion but may be terminated by either side on two weeks notice during its continuation'.

'Should funding and support for the project be withdrawn your contract will automatically terminate'.

CONTRACTS CHARACTERISED BY LOCATION

Many organisations reviewing labour use strategies in the 1980s, as well as the impact of new technology and organisational restructuring more generally, began to see the prospect of employees working at or from home as an increasingly attractive option. Information technology has meant that proximity between employer and employee is no longer necessary for some types of work and there is a growing literature on the growth of 'teleworking' or 'outreach' networking or remote working, as it is variously called.

Work across continents is feasible and is rapidly developing. However, the move to homebased work has occurred not only through technological change but because employees have sometimes expressed a preference for working wholly or mainly at home. The costs of commuting are one reason, as well as the ability to vary when job tasks are performed to fit in with domestic responsibilities. Another popular reason for formalising work at/from home has been where travel to clients, customers etc is required so that work involving inspection or monitoring, selling, or investigation have typically been seen as having the potential for homework.

In some cases employees spend virtually all their time at home, entering data or perhaps undertaking secretarial or assembly work. In other cases home is a base but much time is spent working on other premises. Clearly contracts for homebased work have to anticipate and respond to a wide variety of issues. Some employers have invested much time and energy to ensure that contractual arrangements are effective.

THE EMPLOYMENT OF HOMEWORKERS

Homeworking is not easy to manage and marks a radical departure from the usual employment relationship. Many of the matters taken for granted (supervision, social contact, structured working hours etc) in an 'ordinary' contract are more complex in a homework contract. It is vital that the full implications of employees being based outside the usual work premises are fully taken on board. The most successful schemes have been preceded by detailed and lengthy preparation - moving staff to work from home without this preparation will probably cause problems.

Among the advantages of homeworking are:

• Reduced office/workplace costs, including those linked to working space and regular travel;

• Homeworking enables employees to dovetail their work and domestic responsibilities; it also provides a middle option between on-site and self-management, enabling them to achieve a greater degree of control over their working hours or techniques without sacrificing financial security.

• Homeworking is usually attractive to workers; this can make recruit ment easier.

Homeworking, however, may have disadvantages:

• Some homeworkers reportedly feel cut off from the social mainstream of the organisation; they may need regular access to workplace facilities and data; and their work will have to be based on regular briefings and appraisal. For all these reasons, regular or occasional visits to the organ- isation's main premises - with the consequent costs this entails - may be necessary.

• Additional training may be needed:
    for homeworkers, to enable them to regulate their own work and and use new equipment;
    for line managers, who may require greater teamworking and pro- ject management skills

• A legally robust decision needs to be made on the employment status of homeworkers; recruitment selection may be lengthy and detailed.

• Management and communication systems, performance appraisal, reporting systems and selection criteria will need to be redesigned or improved to allow for a more sophisticated form of off-site supervision and control.

• Particular attention may need to be paid to occupational benefits - sick pay, pensions etc. - as well as to the basic contract documentation.

• Human resources initiatives need careful application to homeworkers.

• The application of health and safety legislation can be problematic. Homes and work equipment have to comply with UK health and safety regulations. This is particularly important regarding:

> safe premises
> work equipment
> display screen equipment and work stations
> working time
> training on health and safety matters
> consultation

Legal issues

Relatively few legal issues have, as yet, surfaced in courts and tribunals relating to the employment of homeworkers. The factor which has determined many decisions has been the degree of control by the provider of work.

If clear standards are laid down, quality control is rigorously applied and there is an expectation that work, if offered, should be accepted case law has tended to view homeworkers as employees. (*Gardiner and Taverna v Nethermere Ltd* (1983)[12]

Looking ahead, it will be important to keep in mind the health and safety demands and the possibility that the EU will legislate to provide minimum employment protection for homeworkers.

Homework contracts

The following areas will need consideration:

• *Hours of work:* Strict monitoring of hours of work is unlikely to be possible, or even desirable. Hours might be expressed broadly, in monthly or annual terms, or, as has often been the case, pay related directly to output. In any case, many homeworkers are paid by task. Where work requires availability for visits or phone calls or other mechanical communication systems, it might be necessary to specify those hours.

- *The method and level of payment* will need clarification, especially where work is not based on task or piecework. If employees are using their own equipment as well as their own premises, it is vital to reflect this in pay scales, and to consider the loss and liability insurance aspects. If the employer's equipment and materials are being used, questions of proper care and insurance arise. The responsibility and costs of transportation of goods and materials must also be specified. Travel expenses must be considered, especially to headquarters, as should telephone costs.

- *Sick pay and procedures* must be considered and specified to facilitate proper monitoring.

- *Requirements, if any, for attendance* at an office or headquarters to be set out.

- *Disciplinary rules and grievance procedures* may need adaptation, especially regarding line management. Disciplinary need to reflect the primary concern of quality of work rather than personal behaviour, with clear criteria indicated.

- *Access to occupational benefits* must be clarified and appropriately modified, perhaps to compensate the homeworkers for the inaccessibility of traditional in-house benefits, such as canteen and social club facilities. This might be balanced by more direct help with the homeworker's own premises, such as a redecoration allowance or help with council taxes and other outgoings.

- *Where the organisation has a formal appraisal system,* this will have to be modified and specified for the homeworkers, especially if homeworking is an option on a temporary basis for in-house staff.

- *Some contractual matters dealt with informally for in-house staff* may have to be spelt out for homeworkers. This covers confidential information, fidelity, and restraint of trade terms. Where the homeworker has a franchise to sell or repair a product, the responsibilities will need to be specified and monitored. The contract may need to clarify the situation regarding working for another organisation.

More generally, the contract documentation needs to be informative and comprehensive on communication procedures and for personnel matters. If so it can help prevent the isolation felt by many homeworkers.

It will be important to differentiate prescriptive from descriptive matters (see generally Chapter 3).

CASE STUDY EXAMPLE: THE REMOTE WORKERS

The contract documents here were devised for an entirely new situation and a new company. The decision was made to employ, as employees, a large number of homeworkers (always referred to by the company as 'remote' workers) primarily concerned in production for secondary publishers of major databases on home terminals or at small regional work centres.

Crossaig Ltd is based in Scotland and was established in 1990. Its parent company is a US organisation which acquired Crossaig in 1992 and is part of the Thomson Corporation. The type of work operates in a highly competitive environment with many third world rivals. It employs around 60 staff, only 9 of whom in the main office. Remote workers are clustered around Helensburgh and on the Isle of Sky, Tayside, Perthshire and Grampian.

Devising appropriate contracts was predicated on a number of key factors. The first was the need to approach contracts in a highly professional manner. Linked to this was a clear decision to provide employment contracts which were fair to the employees but which did not jeopardise the company's competitive position. Remote workers were to be treated as 'our people' so as to retain quality, enthusiasm but also control for the company. Thirdly, there was a clear commitment to establishing a formulae giving employees 'rights' and which fully reflected current and likely employment law demands.

Crossaig identified a number of key issues relating to contracts:

- how to treat remote workers in a comparable though distinctive manner as the 'ordinary' office staff;
- how to allow flexibility and autonomy for the worker and yet retain control and efficiency for the employer;
- how to reflect the key and necessary features of the remote working arrangement in the documents;
- how to ensure legal demands, e.g. for equal opportunities, were fully met.

The company sought the advice of their regular consultants who were given the brief of devising contracts which met the above objectives but which also dealt with the practical issues of both the business itself and remote working. Examples were how to define contract terms to deal with times when the system was 'down' or when the employees were ill and how to establish effective health and safety procedures and rules.

Although some consideration was given to the literature and to the experience of other employers of homeworkers the approach was essentially open minded, flexible and contained few assumptions. The aim throughout was to provide comparable documentation to the office based staff and avoid any hint of 'second class citizenship'.

In essence the remote workers contracted to do a specified number of hours per week, though due to fluctuating work demands Crossaig did not guarantee the hours worked. When they were actually performed was not usually relevant. Mostly, they worked exclusively for Crossaig. Their basic pay was based on items of work with a significant pay element to reflect good quality work. Earnings can be quite high. Other occupational benefits such as maternity, pensions, holiday pay and sick pay were considered, there being an expectation that they would be provided if at all possible. In the event, some benefits, eg holidays were not provided, as it was considered that the relatively high pay contained a holiday pay element. There was considerable discussion of a wide range of practical issues mainly relating to the fact that the employee worked in their own home, away from their line manager but were using equipment provided and maintained by Crossaig. The potential for abuse (e.g. taking in other work, using telephones for private calls) was an important factor in deciding to go for a fairly detailed, clearly expressed series of contract documents which highlighted the practical issues of remote working and the need to anticipate and respond to potential dispute topics.

Secondment contracts

These contracts - variously referred to as assignment or expatriate contracts - are becoming increasingly important because of growing employee mobility across the EU and wider. The EU itself has a draft Directive to regulate cross border 'postings' within the EU. The essence of secondment, from a legal perspective, is that an employee's contract remains with the employer but its day to day management rests elsewhere. Aside from issues of management and supervision there are often real problems of appropriate pay levels and structures and the application of important legal rules, especially those relating to health and safety.

Some of the major advantages of secondment are:

• It fits well with corporate social responsibility: secondment sometimes plays a key role in many organisations' community support policies. It is seen as being 'good value' for money since an experienced secondee worth up to £25,000 p.a. is more valuable to the host body than a similar cash grant.

• It is useful career development for key managers: A growing number of companies regard secondment as a means of giving valued or key staff the opportunity to acquire new skills and experience.

• It can help cement relations across borders and across multi-national companies, especially those which put a high premium on corporate identity.

It may ease other staffing problems, for example:

• Pre-retirement secondment as a means of preparing older workers or easing them out;

• Surplus employees: secondment as a means of dealing without placement (for example, in the case of a merger, internal re-organisation, or plant closure);

• Avoiding conflict: to ease personality clashes;

• Assessing individuals: this reason often being linked to systematic career development (see above).

- Career break: to re-motivate employees who have peaked in their careers or been in one job too long.

The main disadvantage of secondment is its intrinsic complexity and the need to anticipate problem areas. Secondment has been growing steadily over the past 15 years. Difficulties can arise when there is over-use to solve 'difficult' staff problems. Secondment can then become associated solely with 'failures'.

It is vital to define a comparable and acceptable contract package when working, especially, for an unconnected organisation and to establish precise arrangements for repatriation on return.

Some key legal issues

As set out above, from a legal perspective secondment/posting of employees, often across national borders is complex. Among the major legal issues are:

- applying the contract provisions of the seconding organisation to the work situation at the host organisation;

- compliance with TURERA, Schedule 4 where employers are seconded abroad;

- compatibility of contractual, especially disciplinary rules;

- health and safety laws, both statutory and by common law whereby injuries and statutory duties remain the primary responsibility of the seconding organisation, rather than the 'host' organisation;

- effective procedures to deal with disputes;

- determining which legal system applies to the contract when an employee is employed by a company registered in country A, but regularly works in country B. (Case law suggests that unless the contract specifies it the place of regular work is the relevant one - see page 142).

Where a secondment involves a period of at least one month outside the UK the following written information must be provided (TURERA).

1   The period of work outside the UK;

2   The currency in which remuneration is to be paid;

3   Any additional remuneration payable, and any benefits to be provided

to or in respect of him, of being required to work outside the UK and, the UK; and

4   Any terms and condition relating to return to the UK.

These are fairly routine matters; it is the practical day to day issues which so often present problems and which the contracts needs addressing.

EXAMPLE: ILLUSTRATION OF LIKELY PROBLEM AREAS

John Wilson, a marketing manager, was posted to Hungary in 1994 and while working was injured by an employee of the 'host' organisation. It is then discovered that the employee was not covered by insurance in the host organisation. The seconded worker's employer's insurance also refuses to pay out on that policy because it had not been informed of the posting - it was to a country (Hungary) that it still considered 'unstable'?

The arrangement for payment while he was working for a development organisation in Gyor was that he should be paid in forints, the Hungarian currency, and the UK company should make up shortfalls of up to 10% in any three month period should, there be currency fluctuations. The forint then devalued by 35%. John was also disciplined for failing to comply with company requirements before travelling on a short break to the Ukraine. He had been demoted to a routine administrative post by the host employer, a disciplinary measure popular in Hungary but alien to John's employer.

The legal requirements, along with the case illustration, imply that for some secondments managers will need to draft the contract terms very carefully. Attention is often paid (as in this example) to matters of pay and social security provisions. However, compatibility of working conditions, performance management and questions of insurance were not adequately considered.

Employees embarking on secondment need to be well briefed and pre-pared for the experience. There must also be close liaison between the employer and the host. There are many opportunities for misunderstandings which, while it cannot necessarily resolve them, the contract will help to resolve by focusing the parties' minds.

Other matters requiring attention will be whether the seconded worker will return to the post they left or to another; whether pay/benefits rises given to other staff will be payable; and whether there is a requirement for re-training. For example, if during the secondment period the employer de-recognised a union and moved to personally negotiated contracts, what will be the effect? Can the 'secondee' still return their original contract terms if they so wish? Will refusal lead to a claim for constructive dismissal? It is likely that the secondee will not be covered unless they agree to change.

The consequences of accidents and injuries are especially important. UK law usually considers any harm inflicted by the seconded worker as the responsibility of the seconding employer. Similarly, in contractual terms, losses suffered by the seconded worker remain generally the responsibility of the original employer.

The other especially important issue is the application of rules regarding performance and discipline. Company A (the employer) may operate a performance-related pay scheme, Company B (the host company) not. Company B might have a rigorous appraisal system, and a poor performance there lead to invoking discipline procedures. Company B might have an excellent Wellness policy, whereby emphasis is placed on health issues in the broadest sense and infringement of which is viewed very seriously. Perhaps in Company A, overtime might be negotiable and voluntary but at B mandatory, as is a strict dress code at B.

The list is endless and all indicates that the planning for secondment needs real attention to detail. The detail might cover disciplinary matters but also the essential culture of the organisation (how informal are staff relationships, how involved are staff in decision making, has accreditation for BS5750 been sought or obtained?) Problems are frequent; they need addressing and documents need to be especially unambiguous and comprehensive.

The secondment contract should address the following issues:

- Comply with the requirements of TURERA, if the employee will work outside the UK; even if not, the formulae set out in the legislation is helpful.

- Arrangements for pay, increments, pension and related matters.

- Length of agreement, option for renewal or permanent transfer, if appropriate.

- Procedures if secondment is unsatisfactory, both to employee and to the host organisation.

- Grounds and procedures for termination and, if appropriate compensation.

- Determination of which countries legal system will apply to disputes.

An increasingly important practical problem is deciding which legal system applies when a seconded employee is dismissed.

EXAMPLE: AN ILLUSTRATIVE CASE

Hendrick Geels, a Dutch national living in Aix les Bains, France was appointed by Mulox, registered in the UK as its agent for Europe. He was dismissed in May 1990. He applied to French courts for compensation and won. Mulox appealed on the basis that Geels worked throughout Europe (not just France) and Mulox was registered in the UK, whose law covered the employment contract.

The ECJ decided that its role was to avoid duplication of potential legal claims and to ensure that the 'socially weaker party' (the employee) was not disadvantaged. The most sensible approach was to give jurisdiction to courts in the country where the employee performed the relevant contractual duties. A seconded employee domiciled in an EU member state should normally sue in those courts. However, for non EU states the contracting parties themselves (employer, employee as well as the host 'employer') should agree on where cases are heard should disputes arise. (*Mulox IVC Ltd v Geels* (1994))[13]

EMPLOYMENT RELATIONSHIPS BASED ON STATUS

More and more employers in the UK are outsourcing for skills. Self-employment has grown steadily since 1979 and within that broad category are highly specialised consultants, freelance journalists, artists, construction workers and some 'casuals'. The question of legal status, i.e. what differentiates the employee from the self-employed has been considered previously in Chapter 4. This section deals with some of the legal and managerial issues relating to effective contracts for self-employed staff.

CONTRACTS OF SELF-EMPLOYMENT AND CONSULTANCY

Devising contracts for self-employed workers requires at least as much care as contracts for employees. The reason is that if self-employed workers work alongside employees as a freelance or a consultant most of the legal mechanisms which are automatically parts of employee contracts are unavailable, especially the implied terms of fidelity and competence. Similarly, disciplinary rules cannot apply, along with the implied obligation of co-operation.

It is vital that contracts with non-employees not only address the pay and the task to be performed clearly and unambiguously, but that performance quality as well as other necessary protections for the employing organisation are analysed and articulated.

Contracts can be made orally. Indeed, many short-term or one-off contracts - e.g. to clean windows, carrying out minor building or vehicle repairs - are often entered into this way. However, a longer contract, one which gives access to sensitive business information, or one where complex tasks are undertaken need to be put in writing and deal with some important concerns.

Some of the key contractual issues which will need to be addressed are:

- definition of the precise task/activity to be performed and the extent to which the work will require the involvement or support of the employer.

- whether equipment and materials will be supplied by the self-employed worker or by the employer.

- how long the contract will last, or what will determine its length; how prescribed or how flexible will the working hours be?

- how payment is to be made - staged, or on completion?

- what quality standards are to be applied and how and by whom they are to be judged?

- what restrictions are to be imposed regarding the self-employed worker working for others, or soliciting for business?

- what provisions, if any, apply to confidential or market sensitive material?

- what provisions apply where there is a dispute between the parties; how, ideally, are they resolved?

- what provisions, if any, apply regarding liquidated damages, for example where the self-employed person walks out, or otherwise breaks the contract?

- what organisational rules or policies are self-employed workers subject to, for example, a smoking or alcohol policy? What if they are broken?

- what are the rules relating to health and safety which must be adhered to, for example, relating to training, adhering to procedures and co-operation with policies generally? What part will self employed workers play in risk assessments, what information are they required to provide, (e.g. a hazardous substances or work procedures?)

There are a number of other employment relationships which have particular characteristics and particular significance. Included here are:

- public/civil servants

- apprentices

- trainees, especially publicly sponsored trainees (YTS etc)

- workers with tenure

In addition, but beyond the scope of this book are members of the armed forces who until recently have been outside most employment law structures.

Managers in sectors where these special groups are employed are faced with a number of discrete issues, not least that special rules can apply if there are disputes about performance or conduct. Some key questions arise, for example:

- Do such workers have applied to them the usual rules of contract?

- Can they claim the usual employment statutory protections such as maternity rights?

- If they are disciplined or dismissed, do the usual statutory or contractual provisions apply?

- Are there legal claims available to them which ordinary employees cannot make use of?

These are important questions because managers need to be aware of the special approach, rules and procedures which may be available to these groups.

In the UK approximately 35% of the workforce is still employed in the public sector, including central and local government and other organisations such as the BBC and the many 'quangos' (quasi-governmental organisations). It is thought that the UK National Health Service, with almost 1.5 million employees, is the largest employer in the EU.

PUBLIC SECTOR EMPLOYMENT: THE BACKGROUND

Until fairly recently, many, public sector workers, especially senior ones such as Chief Constables, registrars of various sorts, prison officers, and general practitioners (GPs) were not categorised as employees at all. Because of the public nature of their work and frequently traditional job titles they were considered by law to be office holders or Crown servants and not subject to the ordinary rules of employment contract law.

Disputes over terms of work and job security fell within public law rules where the key legal questions were directed at the process of any decision making (rather than the decision itself) by superiors/managers. For example, were the procedures had been laid down by statute, charter, governmental rules etc. strictly adhered to? Was there evidence of bias or malice? Were all the relevant factors considered and given adequate attention? If a decision to dismiss a prison governor was flawed and thus unsupportable, the decision itself would be set aside and be null and void. The dismissal decision would be ineffective.

During the last few decades, employment law has developed its legal protections, especially relating to the application of disciplinary procedures and job security to those with 'ordinary' contracts of employment. Hence civil servants and ordinary employees have moved closer together through having comparable, though distinctive legal protections.[14]

One recent issue has been whether workers categorised as civil servants or office holders can make use of the new statutory employment protections such as unfair dismissal? If a civil servant, say, in the Inland Revenue refuses an order at work and is disciplined and then dismissed, can he/she claim the protection of public law (i.e. that the prescribed procedures had been improperly applied) and/or could they submit the usual claim for unfair dismissal? Can a claim for wrongful dismissal also be mounted? (see Chapter 9).

The situation is complex but the following provides some guidance:

- Employment by a public authority does not necessarily mean that the individuals can use the public law procedures to assert rights. For example, a deputy police surgeon employed by a police authority could not use public law because the nature of the employment relationship with the authority was, in reality, solely a contract for services (self-employment) and had no public law elements. (*R v Derby CC ex parte Noble* (1990))[15]

- Having a public law element sufficient to bring a public law claim does not inevitably prevent an ordinary employment contract claim being brought. A GP, covered by the National Health Service Act 1977 and subject to NHS (General Medical and Pharmaceutical Services) Regulations 1974, asserted that he had not been paid the appropriate practice allowance (pay). Despite the statutory framework, it was decided that the relationship between GP and the Family Practitioner Committee (FPC) was contractual and an ordinary contractual claim could be brought (*Roy v Kensington and Chelsea FPC* (1992)).[16] There are, therefore, some situations where a choice of legal remedies does exist.

- Many civil servants are able to use ordinary contractual remedies. Whether they can will turn on whether there is a contractual element to their employment relationship.

CASE LAW EXAMPLE : THE PRISON OFFICERS

Prison officers at Wandsworth Prison, London, objected to a new shift system introduced as part of the so-called Fresh Start Agreement. This had been negotiated and agreed according to the unusual negotiation procedures in the service. It was decided that the terms of the agreement had been incorporated into an officers' Terms of Service. This was sufficient for a prison officer to mount a claim in contract law. It was decided that he had an arguable case. However, the decision did *not conclude*, that prison officers definitely have contracts of employment; they may have special contracts. (*McLaren v Home Office* (1990)).[17]

It cannot therefore be assumed that civil servants and office holders are 'outside the frame' of usual employment law. Recent legal developments suggest that decision-making by managers, especially the application of disciplinary procedures should be subject to especial care in the public sector (see Chapter 7). The strict demarcation between the public and private sector has been blurred, but overall legal rights for workers have been expanded rather than reduced.

Documentation of employment relationships

Public sector contracts have traditionally been the most highly structured and centrally determined, whether by Whitley Councils or increasingly by pay review bodies and the like. However, changes in the public sector, devolved management and decentralisation have meant that most of the contract issues discussed elsewhere in this book now have relevance to public servants. Many public servants sign the Official Secrets Act, and obligations of loyalty and integrity are taken especially seriously and disciplinary rules rigorously employed. At the same time flexible employment contracts have taken a strong hold and Chapter 6 has increasing relevance to the public sector.

WORKERS WITH TENURE

Tenure has become a controversial topic, not least because the idea of a 'job for life' has been so seriously challenged in virtually every occupation in recent years. A case which highlighted tenure as an issue concerned a northern university which had undergone much change and financial pressures. A long established lecturer, popular with colleagues and students and against whom there were no allegations of incompetence or misconduct was declared redundant due to lack of demand for his subject. Posters, media interest and controversy raged. He was a 'tenured' lecturer and should not lose his job.

It was asserted that they could only be dismissed for misconduct and not for redundancy, or economic or organisational reasons. It was argued that if lecturers could be easily got rid of, academic freedom to express radical or unpopular views would be at risk (*Page v Hull University* (1993)).[18] Broadly, the court accepted there were risks if tenure was abolished, and he won.

However, with educational institutions under increasing financial pressure, the 1988 Education Reform Act section 203 provides for the dismissal of academic staff for redundancy as well as 'good cause'. Nonetheless, the nature of academic contracts is recognised in that University Commissioners are charged with the duty to ensure that 'academic staff have freedom within the law to question and test received wisdom, and to put forward new ideas and controversial or unpopular opinions...' (s 202(2)).

Academics' employment relationships will continue to be special. Their conduct and views are supervised and protected by a specific statutory body - the University Commission - and where there are disputes over the application of disciplinary and other rules derived from university statutes and charters, academics have redress to academic 'visitors', who are individuals with exclusive powers to hear complaints (*Thomas v University of Bradford*

(1986)).[19] Should the visitor not conform to the rules of natural justice, public law remedies remain available.

A related, though distinctive issue, concerns the employment status of ministers, priests and the like in various churches and religious groups. Do they have contracts of employment and if they are removed from their post, perhaps because of unpopular views expressed in the pulpit, can they claim protection from employment law?

It appears that they cannot. Case law has determined that ministers of God (and presumably, in other religions) do not have contracts in the ordinary sense. Although their working relationship is part spiritual and part secular, they are special and do not allow ministers, priests, etc. to bring claims for unfair dismissal and the like. (*Davies v Presbyterian Church of Wales* (1986))[20]

TRAINING CONTRACTS

This is an increasingly complex area. Many contracts have a training element, but in some training is the central purpose of the relationship and contracts frequently require records of attendance at colleges and the acquisition of NVQs of varying sorts. Obvious examples are contracts of apprenticeship ranging through hairdressing, mechanical engineering, and journalism to the legal profession. These often have formal documents applied to them and make frequent reference to employment legislation, collective agreements and, until 1993, wages council orders. For many the ordinary statutory protection apply, i.e. unfair dismissal, discrimination laws, and health and safety laws.

Traineeships, cadets and other training relationships not covered by formal apprenticeship contracts are in a more difficult situation. If the training element dominates or is the sole reason for the relationship employment contract protections are not available. However, the law treats trainees as if they were employees, especially for health and safety purposes.

Even though they do not have an employment contract, documents for trainees should be clear, realistic and well prepared so as to avoid misunderstandings.

REFERENCES

1   [1981] IRLR 228
2   [1994] IRLR 666
3   [1990] IRLR 447
4   [1992]
5   *Stadt Lengerich v Helmig* [1995] IRLR 216
6   [1994] IRLR 176
7   *Barrett v Newport BC* [1992] Case No 34096/91 (but see *Clymo v Wandsworth LBC* [1989] IRLR 241; *Carey v Greater Glasgow Health Board* [1987] IRLR 484.

8   See generally P Leighton, *Does Job Sharing Work?*, 1988, Industrial Society/
        Anglia University
9   [1967] 1 QB 278
10   *Parkinson v Hellyer Bros* [1994] IRLR
11   [1993] IRLR 545
12   [1983] IRLR 369
13   [1994] IRLR 240
14   See, for example, the discussion in *R v East Berkshire Health Authority ex parte*
        Walsh [1984] IRLR 278
15   (1988), *Times*, 21 November
16   [1992] IRLR 233
17   [1990] IRLR 338
18   [1993] AC 682
19   [1987] AC 795
20   [1986] IRLR 194

7
Contract Terms

Chapter 6 considered the objectives and forms of some of the major and emerging contract types. This chapter considers the key terms, such as those concerned wit, remuneration, working time, job location, performance management, discipline and notice periods. Such terms will almost invariably form parts of all employment contracts. However, the range of issues employers will want to include generally goes far wider.

Defining and expressing contract terms has become increasingly demanding and complex. Although many contracts in manual work or administration, for example, are capable of expression through relatively few key terms, this is not usual. Contract documents have become more diverse, priority topics vary from organisation to organisation and the style and manner of presentation of material varies enormously.

Managers who attach importance to employee communication and mission statements need to set employment contracts in those contexts. A company priding itself on team working, employee involvement and devolved management will find it hard to sustain these policies if the company disciplinary code is couched in draconian language, rules are totally inflexible, constantly refer to staff as 'sub-ordinates' or assume they are likely to be dishonest by featuring 'theft of company property' on virtually every page in the relevant documents!

Finding the 'right' words in the 'right' sequence to express key terms is no easy task. Clearly, the range of possible items for inclusion is vast. Some items are required by TURERA 1993 (See Chapter 5, page 95), but nonetheless the law leaves to the employer considerable choice of how to express the prescribed items.

To bring some structure to the consideration of the major contract items, the chapter is divided into the following six sub-sections, which cover terms dealing with:

1   *Remuneration,* to include basic pay, enhanced pay, deferred pay (pensions, organisational and individual performance related pay, maintenance of pay through interruptions to work and employee illness or absence.

2   *Working time,* to include flexibility, shifts, overtime, breaks, holidays and time-off arrangements, and Sunday working.

3   *Place of work,* to include mobility clauses, multi-site operations, working outside the UK.

4   *Occupational benefits,* (excluding remuneration-related ones) including health care, social facilities, shopping and travel facilities, claw back clauses.

5   *Performance,* to include discipline, co-operation appraisal, quality measures and illness/stress matters, training, etc.

6   *Loyalty and commitment,* to include restraint of trade, exclusivity, confidential items, intellectual property, fidelity bonds.

Some important clauses will be covered at a stage when they become of major practical importance. For example, notice clauses and 'garden leave' will be dealt with in Chapter 9. There will be references to some key health and safety requirements which are increasingly affecting contracts and specific contract terms.

Each of these sub-sections will be preceded by consideration of some of the important HRM and other developments of relevance. It will then outline the legal rules relating to contract terms, including EU initiatives as well as UK law. This enables managers to plan ahead rather than be faced with a constant need for up-dating.

ADOPTING A STRATEGIC APPROACH

Despite differing organisational priorities there are a number of key issues to address in order to adopt a strategic approach to contract documents generally and the expression of individual terms within it. Among the important issues are the following:

TECHNICAL ISSUES

•   Terms on contractual requirements/obligations must be clearly and unambiguously expressed. It is essential that the language used differerentiates clearly between prescriptive, descriptive and discretionary matters. These matters have been considered generally in Chapter 3 but need to be kept constantly in mind. Terms must not be vague or too open-ended; they may then contravene the law's requirement for certainty. They should be concisely expressed and not require explanation or expansion - they should be free-standing and conclusive.

- Terms must keep within the law. This has particular relevance regarding the need to keep strictly within the provisions of TURERA 1993, Schedule 4. Terms must not contravene anti-discrimination legislation, tax legislation or, for example, the Unfair Contract Terms Act 1974 whereby terms which unreasonably exonerate the employer from liability when loss/damage occurs to the employee will be ineffective.

- Terms should be expressed in a manner and form consistent with both organisational culture and existing human resources policy documents. Contract documents should, ideally, be part of the seamless web of HRM policies and use language, lay-out and examples consistently. If a very elitist, negative or divisive style is adopted, the employment contract document will be an ineffective or even a negative managerial tool.

Management issues

It will be important to ask:

- Is the energy and effort devoted to defining and expressing contract terms adequate in the light of the priority given to HRM generally within the organisation?

- Is the style and presentation of documents and their individual terms giving out messages that the employing organisation would like?

- Are the priority areas of corporate/organisational HRM policies fully and appropriately reflected in the contract terms? Do they express adequately commitments to ethical concerns, to quality, flexibility and individual performance? It is worth asking whether commitments to the quality of the working environment, support for team work, appreciation of loyalty etc. are clearly expressed through the documents?

- Are the human resources policies reflected in the contract terms of all employees? Are part-timers, fixed term workers etc. treated correctly for example, regarding training and benefits?

PRESENTATIONAL ISSUES

This concerns the type and style of documents to use. Many of the core terms of contracts can be presented by using a standard form contract available from the basic law stationers. Such documents cover the statutory minimum of terms (TURERA), and highlight topics such as bonuses, paid holidays etc. which can be included or left out. Most organisations use these statutory terms as a base but add much more so as to fully reflect the needs of both their own organisations and the post in question. Some of these issues have been considered in Chapter 5 but must nonetheless be borne in mind where considering specific contractual terms.

Other organisations have adopted documents which have a series of boxes as options and allow the employer to tick the appropriate one. For example, the manager would be instructed to complete the following:

Please tick as appropriate

☐ You are entitled to paid public holidays.
☐ You are not entitled to paid public holidays.
☐ You are entitled to join our occupational pension scheme
☐ You are not entitled to membership of our occupational pension scheme until you have completed one year's continuous and satisfactory employment.
☐ You are not entitled to join our occupational pension scheme.

This approach can be clumsy and wasteful, but where employers have many atypical staff it can be helpful to adopt an approach which requires inclusion or deletion of certain provisions. This 'either/or' approach is useful when coupled with a document which allows gaps/boxes to be filled in to fit the individual employee. For example:

'You are entitled to one months/two months/one weeks notice by the employer' (delete as appropriate).

'You are/are not entitled to paid public holidays'

'You can be required to work anywhere within daily travelling distance of your home/anywhere in the UK/anywhere we (X Ltd) have premises'.

'Your job title is......................The key tasks of this job are........................'.

It is important to decide whether terms should be set out in the main/ principle contract document or whether (assuming the law allows it) they can be set out in a supporting document such as a handbook, rule book etc? This is an important question when dealing with matters such as confidentiality, restraint of trade, intellectual property rights etc (not covered by TURERA). The answer will hinge on how important the matter is; how much prominence it is to be given; how detailed it is and the costs of providing individual documents.

It must be decided how 'user friendly' the documents ought to be. Contract documents are frequently read once and then consigned to a filing cabinet or bottom drawer. Is there merit in making them more accessible? Are the documents to be regularly referred to, discussed and perhaps amended? Are they to be regularly and formally reviewed - say at the time of appraisal or staff development interviews? Are they formally re-considered at time of promotion or upgrading? Answers to these questions might suggest attention to readability, clear presentation and ease of amendment.

Are documents and their terms attractively presented, indicating a professional and caring organisation? Has lay-out, colour and type-face been effectively used and checked for its appropriateness and consistency with other organisational documents? Has there been a systematic survey on employee responses to current contract documentation - do staff like or dislike documents? Is contract documentation included in any appropriate in-house attitude surveys?

Are individual terms, regardless of topic, legally robust? It is always important to go through contract terms with individual employees to check that they understand a term or clause and that the employee's understanding matches that of the employer. This is especially important when more general phrases are used such as, 'Employees should not engage in activities which will prejudice the reputation of the company'. Is it clear what is meant by 'prejudice', as well as the type of activities the employee might engage in which would put the company's reputation at risk? Are they business activities or personal activities? These issues must be explored so as to avoid later problems.

Similarly, 'overtime will be available from time to time'. It will need to be clear what and who conditions the availability of overtime, whether the employee can refuse to do it etc. It is absolutely vital that both parties fully understand the meaning and practical implications of that clause. If it is unclear, confusing or open to regular dispute it will simply need to be re-drafted. There is no point whatsoever in managers defending clauses or insisting on their enforcement when there is the likelihood of genuine confusion over meaning. The law takes a simple approach - if you meant a term to have a particular effect make sure you express it to do so; the law is not there to bale out employers who could not bother to get the wording right!

Do the terms fully reflect organisational priorities and seriousness of intent, as well as simply complying with law? The acid test is whether, if terms were not complied with, the innocent party would be entitled to claim for breach of contract. It is bad practice and legally problematic to say: 'I know that is what has been written down but we did not really mean it' or 'Yes, we did include that clause, indeed, we always have done but we never enforce it'. It is vital to state clearly what intentions are and not anticipate that problems or disputes can be easily resolved informally or that one particular interpretation will necessarily dominate.

Think the worst! Hence, documents must be always devised with a view to dispute avoidance: energies and efforts are best employed at the planning and implementation rather than litigation stage!

TERMS RELATING TO REMUNERATION

Drafting employment contracts to fully and precisely reflect the major changes and complexity of most organisational pay policies can only be undertaken if its understood what they are aiming to achieve. Often, the total reward package has a complex set of inter-connecting elements, some reflecting local factors (London weighting, dislocation allowances, housing/subsistence payment, overseas compensation etc.), and others reflecting skills scarcity, and individual or organisational performance (bonuses, profit sharing, PRP etc). It is unsurprising that the pay and benefits section of any personnel/HRM department or function is typically the largest.

Recent changes in pay policies have major implications for employment contracts, not only regarding contract terms but who decides on pay and the criteria applying to pay awards.

However, for the purposes of employment contracts there are some important messages from those who have also evaluated the impact of organisational change, including de-centralisation. Most agree that for decentralised organisations to be effective remuneration policies need to be linked with performance management. It is no use, many argue, giving line managers decision-making powers over remuneration if they do not have performance measures in place and the ability to regulate and check performance.

This has important implications for employment contracts. In particular, contract terms relating to remuneration must not be insulated from terms relating to supervision, discipline and the like. If the introduction of new remuneration policies means that many old contract documents such as detailed handbooks/works rules etc have to be dramatically revised or even thrown away, a similar radical approach might be needed for codes of discipline! Even small organisations adopting an improved reward package - more bonuses or commission payments for example - will be affected by this principle. All contract terms need to inter-relate and be consistent with one another.

Although most UK employers (though not to the same extent in other parts of Europe,) have moved decision-making on remuneration 'down the line', other employers are revising this policy and are moving decisions the other way - back to the 'centre'. The motivators have been the avoidance of pay 'leap-frogging' and inconsistent approaches by individual managers. Central co-ordination of remuneration decision making is required, which implies that if other aspects of employment contract management remains 'down the line' a clear framework and effective communication needs to be devised so that individual employment contracts are also co-ordinated and consistent.

Central co-ordination by a well informed HR professional will also ensure that some of the 'banana skins' of equal pay legislation can be avoided. This issue was highlighted in 1992 in a study of performance related pay, especially in de-centralised organisations, which found that 'individualised' decision-making - predominantly by[1] male managers - was intensifying the differential between male and female pay rates. European case law, for example *Enderby v Frenchay HA* (1993)[2], illustrates how thing can go wrong if attention is not paid to equal pay/equal value issues.

WHAT OF SMALLER FIRMS?

If the personnel/HR literature has been dominated by the themes of decentralisation, performance management and the alleged benefits of performance related pay it is important to bear in mind the vast numbers of employees, often in small and medium sized enterprises (SMEs) whose remuneration is a simple matter of an hourly or weekly rate but who sometimes have the opportunity for more pay, e.g. through overtime, bonuses or tips. Collective bargaining is less likely to be a feature.

It can be easier to negotiate and express such terms when free of union involvement. However, although the task for the employment contract manager is mainly to determine the right pay and premium pay rates the basic principles of contract remain valid. Terms must be unambiguously expressed, entitlement to pay itself (e.g. on public holidays) defined, the circumstances relating to overtime, night rates etc set out, decision making powers located and terms checked for consistency against other relevant terms, (e.g. those relating to performance).

These rules relating to contract terms apply regardless of organisation size and sector. ACAS annual reports relating to industrial tribunal (ITs) claims show that small firms are the 'growth' area, in complaints. The Wages Act 1986 (see below) is the fastest growing topic for claims (30% increase 1992-3).[3] These trends may well be intensified by the move to ITs of contract claims generally (see Chapter 2, page 20).

LEGAL ISSUES FOR TERMS RELATING TO PAY

UK law has a tradition of non-intervention in pay matters, and there is scope for considerable flexibility regarding the remuneration/reward package. The one statutory intervention on pay was the Wages Councils legislation from 1911, which in 1993 still applied to over 2.5 million workers in the UK despite being watered down by the 1986 Wages Act. It was abolished by TURERA, 1993.

European law has aimed to provide a EU-wide minimum pay rate but has only achieved a low-key intervention to date. This is the 1993 Opinion on an Equitable Wage[4], which requires governments to explore ways of ensuring that especially vulnerable groups are not exploited. Governments must report the steps they have taken by 1996. For UK employers the Opinion has little practical effect (although 'emanations of the state' may be subject to more EU scrutiny (see Chapter 2). Broadly, pay remains subject to no statutory provisions, other than the ones set out below and the need to provide correct written information as a consequence of TURERA, 1993 (see Chapter 5).

KEY LEGISLATIVE REQUIREMENTS

Equal pay legislation - and the legislation and case law interpreting and applying it - has become of crucial importance. It is heavily influenced by EU law and decisions of the ECJ.

EQUAL PAY ACT 1970

This Act was passed in 1970 and come into effect in 1975 when the Sex Discrimination Act, 1975 was passed. The aim of the Equal Pay Act is to 'ensure that every term in a woman's contract is not less favourable than in a man's contract in respect of pay and other conditions'.

This covers situations where a woman is paid less than a male colleague doing the same job, but extends beyond this to treat any term in her contract that is less favourable as contrary to the Act. Examples would be where a male employee receive a company car, a season ticket, has professional fees paid etc., while a comparable female employee's contract makes no mention of such benefits.

Like the Sex Discrimination Acts the legislation is framed with reference to women. It does of course apply to men as well. By the time the Equal Pay Act came into force it had already been amended by the Sex Discrimination Act 1975 which also aimed at eliminating discrimination in non-pay matters such as selection, training, promotion and dismissal. The Sex Discrimination Act works on different principles to the Equal Pay Act but they are designed to be complimentary and provide a single statutory framework for the avoidance and eventual elimination of discrimination.

The Act was amended from 1 January 1984 by the Equal Pay (Amendment) Regulations 1983 following the decisions of the European Court of Justice in *European Commission v United Kingdom* (1982)[5] that the Equal Pay Act did not allow adequately for equal pay claims to be brought. Legislation had to include doing 'work of equal value' (not just the same or similar work) to that done by a male employee. This was required by Article 119 and as clarified by the Equal Pay Directive of 10 February 1975.

Article 119 of the Treaty of Rome states that: 'Each member state shall... ensure and subsequently maintain the application of the principle that men and women should receive equal pay for equal work'. Because Article 119 is both directly applicable and has direct effect it is enforceable in domestic courts and allows an individual employee claiming equal pay under both United Kingdom and European Community legislation.

A LONG-ESTABLISHED CASE LAW EXAMPLE

A woman discovered that she was paid less than her male predecessor. Her claim for equal pay failed because the UK court held that the UK legislation only allowed for comparisons to be made with men employed contemporaneously. The European Court of Justice however said that under Article 119 this was not the case. She was entitled to base her claim for equal pay on a comparison with the pay of a previous post holder. (*McCarthys Ltd v Smith* (1980))[6]

Terms on pay cannot be re-designed when the opportunity arises by a man leaving and a woman being employed. If the job is the same she cannot be employed more 'cheaply'!

How is 'pay' defined for the legislation?

Under Article 119 of the Treaty of Rome pay is defined as: 'the ordinary basic or minimum wage or salary or any other consideration, whether in cash or kind, which the worker receives, directly or indirectly in respect of his employment from his employer'.

Pay has been held to include:

• basic pay, enchanced pay, incremental procedures, bonuses, share options etc;

• post retirement travel facilities;

• pay outs; survivor's rights pensions contributions;

• statutory sick pay and occupational sick pay;

• ex gratia payments including severance arrangements.

• statutory and occupational redundancy payments and compensation for unfair dismissal.

It is essential therefore that all the above (at least) are in contemplation when any job specification etc. is drawn up and the contract devised.

Scope of the Equal Pay Act

The Act applies to all who are 'employed', defined as covering not only employees but also many self-employed workers. Not all self-employment situations are covered, but those where consultants, freelance and similar staff work closely with employees or the employer will be.

CASE EXAMPLE: THE SALES DEMONSTRATOR

A self- employed salesman who had been hired to demonstrate pens for sale in a department store. He discovered that two of the other demonstrators (who were women) were being paid more. The tribunal held that it was competent for his claim for equal pay could go forward, as he was 'personally executing' a service and the working relationship was sufficiently close for the strict employee/self employed divide to be irrelevant. (*Quinnen v Hovells* (1984))[7]

The mechanism of equal pay legislation
The Act works by implying an equality clause into every contract. The effect of this equality clause is to give a woman the same pay and conditions as a man when:

• the woman is employed on like work with that of a man in the same employment.

• the woman is employed on work rated as equivalent, i.e. following a job evaluation with that of a man in the same employment; or

• the woman is employed on work which is of equal value to that performed by a man in the same employment where a job evaluation has not been done.

Care must be taken with all aspects of pay and benefits because successful claims are now being made across traditional or bargaining occupational groups. If neither 'like work' or 'work rated' as equivalent apply, the woman may claim on the basis that her work is of equal value to a male comparator in terms of effort, skill, and physical and mental demands., thus giving her practical access to a job evaluation scheme. This is not an automatic right.

A woman who is in any of the above situations and discovers a term in her contract which is less favourable than a man's is entitled to have her contract modified accordingly.

ILLUSTRATIVE CASE EXAMPLES

Mrs Lawton worked as a cook in the directors dining room preparing between 10-20 lunches daily. She sought equal pay with two assistant chefs who worked in the factory canteen where they prepared over 350 meals daily. It was held that she was entitled to equal pay. What was important was the skill and knowledge needed for the job. There was no need to examine in minute detail the work done. (*Capper Pass Ltd v Lawton* (1976))[8]

Mrs Shields was employed as a counterhand in a betting shop. She was paid 62p an hour. Men employed alongside her doing the same work were paid 106p an hour. The alleged reason for the discrepancy was that the men were paid more because they were expected to eject troublesome customers. It emerged that not only had there been no trouble but the men were not trained to deal with it in any case. Shields was entitled to equal pay. In his inimitable style Lord Denning said that women had their own way of dealing with difficult customers and (of Mrs. Shields 'she may have been as fierce and formidable as a battle axe' (while the men) 'may have been small or nervous who would not say boo to a goose'. The employer in this case would obviously be faced with a substantially higher salary bill than he had anticipated. *(Shields v Coomes (Holdings) Ltd (1978))*[9]

Employers should be aware that if a woman presents a claim based on any of the above scenarios and they refuse to modify her contract then she is entitled to present an equal pay claim to an Industrial Tribunal. She must do this either while she is still employed or within six months of leaving.

To succeed in her claim the woman must satisfy the tribunal that one of the three options above applies to her. It is of no consequence that she has no contractual entitlement to pay; a tribunal will 'read in' equal pay.

Work 'rated as equivalent'

What is involved here is the employer carrying out a job evaluation scheme to establish if the woman's work is equivalent to a mans. The outcome of a job evaluation and consequent grading will usually contribute a term of the contract.

The comparator

In order to decide if a term in a woman's contract is less favourable, a comparison must be made between the woman in question and a man employed by the same or an associated employer. She can choose a comparator who works at a different location from herself provided that they enjoy broadly similar terms and conditions. She need not name her comparator and may choose a predecessor in the role. The fact that the man and the woman have separate, even statutory, wage setting arrangements is irrelevant. *(Enderby v Frenchay HA (1994)*[10]

DEFENCES TO AN EQUAL PAY CLAIM

A woman can be optimistic about defending a potential claim if she is employed on like work, work rated as equivalent, or work of equal value, and the reason she is paid less is genuinely due to a material factor or reasons other than her sex. The employer may argue that at the recruitment stage the male comparator has some unique personal quality which is deserving of extra pay, or that he was paid more in a previous job and that 'market forces' dictate the need to pay people.

ILLUSTRATIVE CASE: THE LIMB FITTERS

Greater Glasgow Health Board set up its own limb fitting service, after years of using subcontractors. They already employed a small number of prosthetists who were paid on NHS scales. To get the new service established quickly the Board offered above NHS salaries to prosthetists transferring from the private sector. There was a difference of £2,800. Ms Rainey was newly qualified and was recruited onto the NHS scale. She claimed equality with the transferees (who were all men). Her claim failed; the House of Lords was satisfied that the reason for the difference in pay was a genuine material factor which had nothing to do with sex but everything to do with objectively justifiable economic and administrative reasons. *Rainey v Greater Glasgow Health Board* (1987))[11]

However, when recruiting, settling on pay, other benefits etc. care must be taken to check that the system is not operating to the detriment of women or men. Assumptions that a married women will not 'need' a large car, as is provided for her colleagues, or that a man will never accept lower pay when changing jobs etc. must be avoided. Similarly, the design and operation of appraisal schemes to directly or indirectly set pay must be scrutinised to see that the criteria applied do not discriminate, even unintentionally. For example, awarding high 'marks' for 'strong leadership' 'forceful negotiating skills' and low 'marks' for reliability, thoroughness, integrity, strong inter-personal skills etc might be problematic.

It has to be appreciated that case law is challenging a vast range of discriminatory practices relating to pay, including policy of part-timers, FTCs and other work patterns typically dominated by women. It would seem from Rainey (and some later case law) that market forces and administrative reasons can act as defences to equal pay claims.

THE WAGES ACT 1986

The Wages Act 1986 requires that all deductions from pay, other than those statutorily required (PAYE, N.I. etc.) are only lawful if the employee has given written consent prior to the deduction being made (s1(1)(b)) or by 'any relevant provision of the workers' contract (s1(1)(a)).

A deduction for these purposes is when the 'total amount... paid... is less than the total amount... properly payable'. (s8(3)). Even if an employer feels justified in withholding cash - e.g. if the employee damaged the employer's property, or was not entitled to a bonus, or had not given the correct period of notice when leaving - the Wages Act will have been broken unless the requirements of section1 have been complied with. The employee has a right to recover the amount deducted.

The only major exception to the rules requiring contractual authorisation or express consent in writing to a deduction is where a deduction is made for taking industrial action. This is especially appropriate for 'go slow', 'refusal to co-operate' and 'work to rule' situations. Deducting pay then will be lawful, but it should be in proportion to the time/production lost as a consequence. Even if the employer feels fully justified in withholding pay, a short cut cannot be adopted if the contract does not authorise it.

As mentioned earlier, employees are resorting to this legislation in ever-increasing numbers and yet the message appears not to have got through to managers. It is vital that the contract authorises deductions, as this is an easier way to respond to problems rather than getting the employee to sign their agreement after the 'incident'.

Recovering pay from employees has always been a problematic area of law, so the easiest way is to anticipate likely areas/topics in the contract itself. Terms relating to discipline, remuneration and notice will need to be considered. In 1992-3, 16,000 cases were taken to ITs, clearly indicating that employment contracts are not being used effectively by all employers so as to avoid litigation in this area.

Claims under the Wages Act 1986 have re-reiterated that:

- employees cannot force or 'persuade' employee to sign away their rights to their full pay.

- even if employers consider they are 'justified' in withholding cash, e.g. because the employee has broken company rules, damaged equipment etc. this will not exonerate an unauthorised deduction from pay. If the employer has a complaint it has to be dealt with via due legal process, i.e. a county court claim. The Wages Act is no short-cut! [12]

To avoid problems with the Wages Act, likely problem areas such as stock shortages, abuse of company property, unauthorised phone calls, damage to cars, leaving without giving notice, and leaving before completing a course should have been identified. An appropriate response can then be devised and inserted into the contract. If the contract documentation is merely a statement of terms, a separate signed document will need to be used to authorise deductions. The clause will not need to specify that a financial deduction will be commensurate with the harm caused but it is suggested that a grossly excessive sum may be challengeable under the Unfair Contracts Act 1974.

If the contract documentation cannot anticipate all likely problem areas, a simple form can be devised to apply to a given situation. It need only state:

- the reason for the deduction

- the amount owing

- the method and timing of deductions

Statutues dealing with tax and other matters

Payments and deductions must be made in accordance with relevant and current statutory provisions. A failure to make proper deductions may raise the possibility of illegality, in which case the whole contract may be void and unenforceable (see Chapter 3). Describing payments as 'gifts', 'auxiliary pay', 'expenses', or 'professional fees' when this is not the legal reality will not be contractually effective and may lead to criminal charges.

THE ITEMISED PAY STATEMENT

Virtually all employees are entitled to a written statement setting out basic pay, statutory and other reductions and net pay (Employment Protection (Consolidation) Act 1978 s8 and TURERA). This statement should be consistent with contract terms, otherwise it can help as evidence in claims that contracts are inaccurate or broken. Information should be provided on basic pay, statutory deductions, other deductions and net pay.

CONTRACTUAL PROBLEM AREAS: EXPECTATIONS OF PAY RISES/BONUSES ETC

Case law shows that frequent confusions and disputes arise over pay, largely because of ambiguities and the differing expectations of the parties. A contract may state that 'there are opportunities for bonus payments'. The employee might conclude, not least after talking to other employees, that bonuses are regularly or even invariably paid. Indeed, there may be a custom in the occupation for bonus payments, perhaps because basic pay is low. The employer may feel confident that the legal right is not there to pay any bonus and should the financial situation deteriorate he/she need not do so. Similarly, a term stating, 'pay is reviewed annually' may lead to the expectation of an annual pay rise especially where that has been the practical outcome for a number of years. Recession or re-organisation may affect these expectations.

HOW ARE UNCERTAINTIES RESOLVED?

Courts do not have a clear line on situations such as set out above. They may well side with the employee if a regular pattern of bonus payments has arisen. The best response is to be unequivocal in the contract, although if the word 'review' or 'assessment' or similar is used in documents the law generally sees payment as discretionary and not necessarily leading to a rise. It may be preferable to state the situation clearly and to use a clause such as:

'Your pay is £165.50 per week. Bonus payments may be made at the absolute discretion of the X Department Manager, based on your performance and commitment. There is no automatic entitlement to a bonus payment in any circumstances. Only employees who have been employed continuously for one year are qualified for the discretionary bonus scheme'.

A clause referring to 'reviews' of pay ideally needs to be explicit about the review process itself (if any). Most importantly, it must stress that the annual review does not necessarily imply a pay increase.

'Your pay will be reviewed annually by your Departmental Manager/the company's Pay Panel/the Board of Directors etc. This does not imply an entitlement to an annual pay increase'.

Similar approaches must be taken to enhanced payment through commission, overtime, performance pay etc. To avoid uncertainty the contract must define:

• Which payments are fixed, which discretionary.

• How payments are calculated; what deduction can be made.

• Who exercises discretions and according to what formula(e).

PERFORMANCE RELATED PAY

Although the trend towards linking pay with performance is most marked in senior and executive posts it is clearly being applied to an increasing number of employees. Typically, senior staff qualify for discretionary payments which are either linked to the performance/profitability of the employing organisation or to individual employee performance (around 50% of executives qualify for bonuses of typically 10% - 20% of annual salary). Mostly, this has led to pay rises, especially in the 1980s; the 1990s have seen rises generally limited or in many cases, not given at all.

In terms of employment contracts linking pay to organisational performance is relatively uncomplicated, providing there is agreement on the criteria. These can be profits, turnover, dividend to shareholders, market share, or, in the case of the public sector, the ability to attract funding, students or increased productivity. There needs also to be clarity on who qualifies - a relatively straightforward matter where there are personal contracts, but less so where collective bargaining prevails.

The key issues here are to identify:

• What is the reference point/indicator for a pay rise?

• Who qualifies?

• Is the award mandatory once, for example, the percentage profitability has been achieved, or is it still discretionary?

- If it is discretionary, who decides and according to what criteria?

- How is payment to be made? Is it a lump sum, an increased monthly salary for a specified time or paid in shares or other non cash terms?

- Is it clearly understood that if, for example, a loss is made or turnover reduces that pay will be maintained and not be cut? If the latter is envisaged this must be agreed to in order to conform with the Wages Act 1986.

These matters can be illustrated by the following clause:

'Staff at Grade x and above qualify for membership of the Incentive Pay Scheme. Percentage increases in net (gross) profits shall (may) entitle staff to equivalent percentage pay rises. Decisions on pay rises shall be made by the Chief Executive and shall be final'. or......'

Most policies linking pay to performance base it on individual employee performance. Experience of this practice is long standing, as commission payments form all or part or part of the total pay package in some sectors. It is typically linked to financial targets - sales, completed tasks, etc. - and is measurable. Bonuses or PRP are often linked to performance in a less easily measured way.

When pay contains an enhanced element such as commission it is vital to express the intention unambiguously and to anticipate possible problem areas. A clause such as the one below is not effective.

'Your pay is £ per month, payable on the last day of the month directly into your bank account. You are entitled to 10% on all your sales'.

It should have been made clear that salary is in arrears, but more importantly to clarify what the 10% relates to. Is it gross or net sales? What if an order falls through or a customer complains about the qualify of a product? Price to the customer is easier to quantify in many cases, but much will depend on organisational practices.

The clause might better read as follows:

'..You are entitled to 5% commission your total monthly sales, at the gross value of sales to customers. Should sales be disputed or revoked the company reserves the right to deduct the appropriate sum representing commission paid from a subsequent salary payment'.

The debate in many organisations, especially public sector ones, has been whether pay should be formally linked to appraisal or staff development initiatives or should stand alone. It is vital that organisations should be unambiguous about the extent to which pay is linked to personal development plans, appraisal, quality measures etc. These intentions must be clearly transmitted through the employment contract documents. It is always important to remember the requirement in TURERA, 1993 that all employees must receive precise information about pay and/or the 'means of calculating it'.

It is adequate to state that:

> 'Your basic salary is £24,700 per annum. You are covered by our performance appraisal scheme and you may qualify for additional annual payments based on the results of the appraisal scheme. Details of the scheme are attached'.

There are almost as many PRP schemes as there are organisations using them and they vary considerably regarding the extent to which they rely on quantitative analysis. Some are very formal:

> 'Our appraisal scheme requires that you are subject to an annual performance review by your Departmental Manager. This will review efficiency, attendance, productivity, attitude and personal development. An employee effectively discharging their professional tasks qualifies for 100 marks. An above average performance 110 marks and an exceptional performance 120. Failing to achieve an acceptable performance level will be awarded 90 marks, a poor performance 80. A mark of lower than 80 may lead to disciplinary action. Those achieving 100 or more marks qualify for an annual performance payment of up to 5% of annual salary as determined by the Departmental Manager in consultation with the Personnel Director'.

Other schemes are more broadly based and contract documents simply refer to overall performance:

> 'Departmental Managers review performance annually. They may recommend enhanced pay for individuals in the light of their review outcome.'

As PRP can cause pay levels to rise beyond what organisations can pay, there are growing reasons for drafting contract terms as flexibly as possible, and even to anticipate the withdrawal of a scheme. It is increasingly important to add the following clause to any merit/performance pay system where deflation is a real possibility.

> 'The company/authority etc reserves the right to withdraw the scheme at any point or to substitute terms'.

This approach is preferable to either making a management announcement 'out of the blue' distributing a press release or protracted negotiation with unions or employee representatives.

PAYMENT THROUGH ILLNESS OR INJURY

One of the central problems of the law relating to employment contracts has been defining what obligation is placed on the employee in order to earn the contractually agreed wages. Is it to work or simply to be ready to work? If it is the latter then the obligation to pay wages continues unabated through illness. Some case law (*Orman v Saville Sportswear*)[13] had indicated that unless the employer specified that pay was not to be paid through illness it remained due. Alternatively, some cases have indicated that if a custom has evolved whereby wages have not been paid through illness this is strongly indicative that to earn wages the employee should have attended the workplace at the very least (*Mears v Safecar Securities* 1982))[14]

Other cases have tended to the view that in most workplaces there will be generally implied that some pay will be due during illness, probably referred to as sick pay, to supplement statutory sick pay (SSP) (*Howman v Blythe* (1983)).[15] It is clear that the employment contract continues to operate through absence due to illness. In these unsatisfactory circumstances it is wise to specify the contractual situation when an employee is ill, and under TURERA Schedule 4 details should be provided in the written information for employees.

The question of entitlement to pay during illness, the length of its provision and mechanisms to deal with potential abuse have become urgent in the light of the Social Security Act 1994. This transfers virtually all the costs of statutory sick pay (SSP) to the employer, and as the UK has one of the highest sickness absence rates on Europe, the financial implications are considerable. However, it is extremely unwise to exclude part-timers and other groups of atypical staff because anti-discrimination legislation could be brought into play.

Contract terms ought to reflect both SSP and 'topping up' with occupational benefits. There are a number of preliminary issues to address:

• Whether, and at what rate, to provide pay during illness and injury? Should this be full wages or a lesser sum? Are there any types of illness or accidents excluded?

• Who qualifies for payment? Is it open to all employees, regardless of weekly hours or type of employment contract? Does it depend on the length of continuous service? (In this context the impact of anti-discrimination legislation must be kept in mind, especially regarding part-timers).

• How long is it to last for? Is it to decline gradually after certain trigger points or to continue at a steady level? When does it end?

• How does the right arise? Are there requirements regarding evidence of illness, will in-house occupational health practitioners play a role, are there medical examinations or other monitoring procedures?

• Is there a right to withdraw payment in specified circumstances? Are there provisions relating to failure to co-operate with occupational health practitioners or the scheme more generally? What of fraud or abuse?

- How does the contract reflect any relevant terms from a health insurance policy, (if taken out). How to ensure that any clauses limiting the obligation of the insurer to pay out, eg not covering accidents outside the usual scope of duties, work outside the UK, nor for employees above or perhaps below certain ages are reflected in employment terms. If this is not done and an employee, say, suffers an accident abroad while on company business the employer may have to provide compensation itself.

The following suggested clauses illustrate various approaches to the situation when an employee is ill or injured:

'In the event of incapacity for work due to sickness, accident or incapacity you are required to notify or arrange for notification to your manager immediately, explaining the reason for the absence and date of likely return, if that is possible'.

'If your absence exceeds a continuous period of more than 7 days (excluding Sundays or days you are not scheduled to work) a National Health Medical Certificate, signed by a doctor must be sent to the company's Personnel Department. Should the absence continue, medical certificates should also be forwarded in accordance with Personnel Department instructions'.

'You qualify immediately for the company's sick pay scheme' or 'You qualify for the company's sick pay scheme after six months continuous employment. Until such time during any period of absence due to illness, injury or incapacity you do not qualify for any payment/you may qualify for some payment at the complete discretion of the Personnel Department'.

'The company is entitled to require that you attend for a medical examination at any time after the commencement of your absence period. This examination will be carried out by a medical practitioner nominated by the Personnel Department'.

'You are entitled to payment of your normal basic salary for a period of up to three months in any continuous twelve month period. Employees who have completed six years continuous service qualify for up to six months salary during periods of absence due to illness, injury or incapacity'.

'At its complete discretion the company may extend the period of entitlement to basic salary beyond the prescribed period'.

'Where injury or incapacity has been caused in circumstances which may give rise to an entitlement to compensation from the third party(ies) responsible for causing the injury or incapacity the company requires you to pursue such claims'.

'Failure of any employee to fully comply with any requests or instructions related to sickness, injury or incapacity, howsoever caused, entitles it to withhold all or part of sick pay'.

'Abuse of any aspect of the scheme is treated as a breach of the organisation's Disciplinary Code. It may lead to dismissal'.

The regulations covering the payment of statutory sick pay need to be kept constantly under review in order to determine the current provisions for payment and rebates for employers. This is subject to frequent change, usually in April of each year.

THE HEALTH AND SAFETY AGENDA

The increasing impact of European health and safety law requires effective health surveillance of all employees, with consequent costs for employers. It is therefore important to set contract provisions relating to pay during absence in a wider context, including 'Well-Being at Work' and similar policies. Contracts must also reflect specific initiatives and policies for with groups such as pregnant women, those suffering stress related disorders, and older/ younger staff. The health of staff will inevitably come under closer monitoring and organisations have obligations respond to health concerns (RSI, stress, smoking, violence etc. (*see The Work Environment: The Law of Health, Safety and Welfare*, Patricia Leighton, Nicholas Brealey Publishing, 1991).

There must be provisions to deal with employee health concerns. The more they have 'star billing' in contracts, the readier courts become to recognise when an organisation has a firm commitment to health and safety. Sick pay schemes are an integral part of these developments, and it is important that schemes are rigorously drafted, applied and monitored - not just to prevent uncertainties or abuse, but also to ensure health problems at the workplace are detected and responded to.

MATERNITY AND PAY

Legal requirements arising out of the 1992 European Directive on Pregnant Women and Nursing Mothers require careful attention and planning by employers. The Directive was implemented in the UK by TURERA 1993. The key provisions are as follows:

- Employees are entitled to a 14-week period of maternity leave regardless of length of service or weekly hours, the employment contract continuing during this period.

- During the maternity leave period the employer must maintain all contractual rights and benefits, other than 'remuneration'. Remuneration includes salary/wages, but may perhaps exclude the company car, health care, insurance premiums and 'fringe' benefits. Employer pension contributions are probably included in 'remuneration' and technically may not need to be maintained through the leave period, but good practice suggests they should be.

- Those who qualify for statutory maternity pay at lower and higher level as provided by the 1994 Social Security Act are paid this sum by the employer.

The statutory framework for maternity leave and pay sets a minimum requirement. Many employers offer benefits beyond this and have wide discretions as to what and how they offer them.

Maternity leave and maternity pay provisions should be incorporated in the contract. In particular, the following issues need to be addressed:

- Confirmation that the employment contract subsists during the 14 week period and throughout the leave period (up to 40 weeks). Most opinions are to the effect that it does.

- Clarification of the provision for occupational maternity pay topping up the statutory minima (as appropriate). What will continue to be provided or paid during the leave. Will it cover, for example:
    travel expenses?
    company car?
    pension contributions? Will they continue as before or be suspended? What will be the employee's obligations?
    health care insurance contributions?

- Arrangements regarding enhanced pay, holiday entitlement etc.

DEFERRED PAY: OCCUPATIONAL PENSIONS

There can be few employment contract topics so complex and subject to such recent publicity as pensions. Specialist books and advice is available (and necessary) though there are a few basic legal rules and issues of management practice which underpin the topic. (See *Managing the Pensions Revolution*, Sue Ward, Nicholas Brealey Publishing, 1995).

There is no obligation to provide a pension, but employers do have to inform employees in the written information contract terms whether there is an occupational pension available to them (they cannot be forced to join), and an indication of where the detail is to be found. Clearly, pension provisions must not be discriminatory.

PAYMENT DURING PERIODS WHEN WORK IS UNAVAILABLE

The previous section dealt with the situation when the employee is unable to work, though work is there to be done. It is important to consider the reverse - the employee wants to work but there is none or only a limited amount aviailable. Unless the contract states to the contrary, pay remains due when work is not provided. The only exception is where the failure to provide work was for circumstances well beyond the employer's control, such as dramatic weather conditions or sudden and drastic power cuts. As the borderline between whether a situation was within or beyond an employer's control can be a fine one, the simplest remedy is to provide for the more obvious eventualities through the contract itself.

In many, typically manual, occupations there has been a strong tradition of not providing pay during a lay-off, leaving employees with their contracts still subsisting but with insurmountable barriers to state income support (e.g. no unemployment benefit as they are not technically available for work). This interruption to payment can also have significant knock-on effects on qualification for holiday pay, sick pay and even pension entitlement. Increased harmonisation of employment conditions, along with the decline in industries subject to much day to day interruption to work has led to an increasing number of employees being viewed by law as entitled to pay during a lay-off period.

The contract should clarify the position. For example, if there is adverse weather or a health and safety notice requiring all or part of the premises to be closed or a power failures or no work available due to lack of orders, it is important to have dealt with specific points in the contract:

- Is pay to be maintained?

- If yes, is it at full pay or a lesser sum, for example, 50% of full pay?

- What is the effect of providing less pay than usual or no pay or accrued rights, e.g. holiday pay, pensions and merit/performance pay or bonuses and commission?

- If pay is maintained is there an obligation on the employee to undertake alternative work or attend another workplace under the employer's control?

- How long will pay last - the length of the disruption or lay-off or shorter?

- Can the right to pay be withdrawn?

Suggested clauses include:

'When the employer is unable to provide work for employees, for whatever reason, there is no entitlement to payment of wages during that period'. ('The employment contract with all its other obligations and entitlements continues').

or

'When the employer is unable to provide work for whatever reason the employer will continue to pay wages at full/50% normal rate for a period of up to 14 working days'.

or

'If any staff member is unable to attend their normal workplace due to adverse weather or similar conditions they should report to the nearest office operated by this authority and make themselves available generally for work. The office manager will determine the nature of the work and if none is appropriate or available instruct the staff member to return home with no loss of pay'.

or

'If the usual workplace is partially or totally closed due to circumstances beyond the control of the employer, providing the closure does not extend beyond 48 hours there is no entitlement to pay by employees. If the closure continues the employee can be required to undertake suitable alternative work at another of .... Ltd's premises or work at home. Refusal to work disqualifies the employee from normal pay; should there be no work available the entitlement to normal pay arises'.

If the employer differentiates between full-timers and part-timers or temporary/casual staff there are clearly risks from anti-discrimination laws if the atypical groups are predominantly female.

STATUTORY GUARANTEED PAY

Section 12 of the EP(C)C Act 1978 includes provisions for statutory guaranteed pay in some circumstances where nothing is provided by the employment contract. This provides up to five days pay (with a maximum limit) in any rolling three month period. Payment is due by the employer regardless of the reason for the lay-off. Only those who have worked for four weeks qualify, but it does apply to part-timers.

There is no statutory entitlement if the lay-off was caused by industrial action at the premises of the employer or an associated employer, or the employee refuses either suitable alternative work or a reasonable condition imposed by the employer. Any payment made under the legislation can be offset against any contractual payment due. The sums provided by the statutory scheme are relatively small so that generally contractual arrangements will dominate.

TERMS RELATING TO WORKING TIME

Topics covered here are:

- **basic hours**

- **overtime**

- **shift working**

- **annualised hours**

- **night working**

- **unsocial hours**

- holidays

- **Sunday working**

The last few years have seen growing pressure to provide flexibility in working hours so as to meet demands for variable and increased work load etc. Virtually all recent surveys of labour use and employment contracts have emphasised the move away from the dominance of the standard 37 - 40 hour week, with or without overtime, towards more variable and flexible working. The move towards longer hours makes the UK unique in Europe. Ascertaining precise trends in working time is notoriously difficult; it has also to be borne in mind that many employees do not formally record their working hours at all. The tradition in the UK has been that employers are broadly free to determine weekly working hours, and few occupations have hours limited by law. Indeed, for management and senior professional staff it is becoming less common for contracts to prescribe working hours at all.

However, as considered in Chapter 2, European law-makers have aimed to establish a broad legal framework for daily, weekly, and annual breaks from work so as to ensure health and welfare at work and to avoid the associated stress-related problems. Employers will need to reflect the lessons of stress research and case law in their employment contracts. The contract should establish a framework for working hours and their effective management to establish good practice at the workplace and comply with emerging legal norms, especially from Europe. Even without statutory intervention the common law contract rules have laid down some basic rules to ensure that employees are not exploited through the device of the implied terms relating to both a safe workplace and mutual trust and confidence (see page 59).

The implications of recent case law are that contracts must not be enforced unreasonably or in circumstances where an employee's physical or mental health would be put at risk *(Walker v Northumberland CC* (1995))[17]. This is an important legal intervention, because it had been thought that if an employee freely entered into a contract with flexible (and extendible!) hours they could later complain if they disliked it, or suffered harm as a consequence of the long hours.[18] The central legal message is that managers have to indentify more precisely their business/organisational needs for staff to work at particular times. They must also be increasingly aware of legal constraints on lengthy or open-ended contract hours. The European Directive (operative November

1996) on Working Time (1993) requires the following breaks in all employment contracts:

- a consecutive break from work of 11 in every 24 hours averaged over 14 days;

- where shifts last 6 hours or more there should be a break (probably of at least 30) minutes;

- a usual weekly maximum of 48 hours, although there will be opportunities for averaging hours over a 4 month period and for employees in the UK to agree by contract to work longer, providing there are safeguards by law to prevent abuse;

- a usual weekly break of 35 consecutive hours in a 7 day period averaged over 14 days;

- at least 4 weeks paid leave for all employees in any completed 12 month period.

WHAT IS 'WORKING TIME'?

This is a vital issue for many managers. The European definition is any time that you are at the 'disposal' of your employer, i.e. time when you are not free to pursue your own interests or activities. Hence, aside from travelling to and from your usual workplace it is likely that all time will be 'working time' for legal purposes. This will have particular relevance for managers, sales staff, inspectors etc where travel to meetings and for other purposes is an important aspect of work. Contracts must be phased so as to regulate such time and ensure adequate breaks.

There are some 'derogations' for those working in residential facilities and emergency services etc. Nonetheless, the basic strategy of the European Directive must be accommodated within employment contracts.

Particular attention must be paid to the contracts of:

- senior staff

- staff on-call' 'standby' and the like

- staff working weekends

- those with highly variable hours

- homebased staff

The contract may need to require employees to record their working hours and to take breaks. 'Overworking' may need to become a disciplinary matter!

BASIC WORKING HOURS

It is not usually difficult to express basic weekly hours of work for employees.

'Your weekly hours are 35. You will work 9am to 5pm Monday to Friday with one hour break for lunch'
or
'..your normal working day will be 9am to 5pm; management reserves the right to vary these hours in accordance with company needs'
or
'Your normal working week is 40 hours. You will work an average 8 hour day between the hours of 7am and 7pm with 1 hour for lunch. Your precise working hours should be agreed with your supervisor'
or perhaps
'Your working hours are not prescribed but should be sufficient to enable you to effectively discharge your professional duties'.

The last type of clause is becoming common. It could be thought too vague to meet legal requirements for sufficient certainty and present health risks. It may though be possible to construe such a clause in the light of custom and practice.

'Your hours of work are as are necessary to carry out your professional tasks. You should record and monitor your working time. Your should not normally exceed 48 hours in any week and should ensure that you have adequate daily and weekly breaks. Guidance notes are available and should be complied with'.
'You should also ensure that other employees for which you act in a supervisory or managerial capacity are not regularly asked to exceed their normal working hours, whether paid for or not'.

OVERTIME

The key issues here concern the requirement or otherwise to undertake overtime and the basis of payment for it. For those with unspecified working hours, in principle the idea of 'overtime' in cannot arise. The major question for the employment contract is whether overtime is mandatory, i.e. if it is required, even at very short notice should the employee be required to do it? If the employer offers overtime can the employee legitimately refuse?

Typical clauses might appear as follows:

'Your normal weekly hours are 38. On occasions you will be required to undertake overtime'

'..any overtime requirements will be limited by up to 2 hours per day'
or
'Your normal weekly hours are 30. Should there be overtime opportunities the
company will offer such work to you'. 'You are not obliged to carry it out'.
or
'Your normal weekly hours are 38, 9-6 on Monday, Tuesday and Wednesday
and 9-5 on Thursday and Friday with one hour for lunch. On occasions the
employer will require you to work on either a Saturday or Sunday rather than
on one weekday. Should this occur you will receive one and half times your
equivalent hourly rate'.
or
'Overtime will be required from time to time. You should not normally refuse
a request'.

If hours have been expressed in annual terms, it is implicit that there is
normally no access to overtime (see page 121). The requirement for a contractual clause providing for time off in lieu (rather than overtime payment) must
be considered and, if appropriate, specifically stated in the contract, which
would ensure that working hours are not excessive.

Shift working

The UK is reportedly the highest user of shift work, including night work, in
Europe. Traditionally, shift working has been rewarded with enhanced pay
('premium rates', and the like) with night shifts having the highest premiums
due to the social impact of night working. In some employing organisations
shift patterns have rotated, often allowing for concentrated break periods
when shifts are being changed. However, employers have more recently
aimed to achieve a higher level of flexibility without increased wage costs.
Any changes to current practices will need to be made lawfully (see Chapter
8).
The key practical issues to determine are as follows:

*   Where shift work and night work are concerned to decide the length and
    timing of the shifts, e.g. 6-2, 2-10, 10-6, or 6-6 or perhaps 8-8 where 12
    hour shifts are used. It is essential that the timing and length of shifts
    conform with any legal rules (especially the Working Time Directive,
    from 1996 onwards).

*   How flexible/rotating the shift patterns are. How will variations be
    made and notified?

*   What the pay rates are?

*   How these hours affect part-times, and part-time pay etc?

    It is also important to reflect carefully the contract hours of employees outside traditional manufacturing where the service or function extends well beyond 9-5 (e.g. libraries, the leisure industry, teaching in further and higher education where the working day potentially lasts say from 8am to 10pm).

Here the key contractual issues concern:

- expression of the basic hours and how parts of the day are expressed, e.g. 8-12, 12-4, 4-8. Saturday and Sunday hours

- the formulae to determine when hours are worked by individual employees.

- who decides the rota.

- are there any possibilities for negotiation on an ad hoc basis?

- how formal is negotiation - can 'private' deals be struck?

- if extra hours are worked how is the employee compensated?

For example:

'Your weekly hours are 40. Our premises are open from Monday to Saturday 8am to 8pm, divided into three shifts 8-12, 12-4, 4-8. You will normally work two consecutive shifts on five days a week. You are entitled to alternate Saturdays off and one other day during the week'.

'Your work rota will be posted on the 21st day of each month to cover the next calendar month.'

'If you experience or anticipate problems with the rota, please immediately discuss the matter with your departmental manager'.

NIGHT WORK

UK employers are the most intensive users of night work in Europe. Research in occupational health is indicating there can be significant health problems with night work, a factor which prompted the European Commission to include specific provisions for night work in the Working Time directive 1993. The directive requires regular health checks for night workers, adequate welfare and medical facilities at night and a usual shift length of no more than eight hours. Any attempt to provide for 'back-to-back' shifts (double shifts) by contract or otherwise will be unlawful when the directive is fully implemented.

Although the directive provides for derogations for certain types of work, e.g. prisons, hospitals and transport, where the eight hour rule may not be easy to apply rigidly it is important to note that this does not imply the rules can be ignored. The employment contract and workplace practices should ensure time-off 'in lieu' where longer shifts are worked and ensure that this is carried out.

Overall, the planning and operation of night work will require increased attention and careful articulation in the contract. It will be inadequate to use phrases such as 'night workers qualify for premium rates at ... and are required to work such hours as our service requires'. Overtime (i.e. more than 8 hours per shift) is possible but only where carefully monitored and with compensating breaks.

A sample clause may look as follows:

> 'Your weekly hours are 40. You are required to work five eight hour shifts rotating on a fortnightly basis. The hours of shifts are 7am to 3pm, 3pm to 11pm and 11pm to 7am. In no circumstances will you be required to work two consecutive shifts'.

> 'If you are required to work overtime it will be limited to two hours per shift. Management will compensate you with an equivalent reduction in hours within 4 weeks of the overtime being undertaken'.

> 'You are reminded that all employees who regularly work at night must co-operate with appropriate medical examinations. If you are experiencing health problems which may be due to working at night you should immediately inform your section supervisor'.

> 'You are reminded that if, in the judgement of the employer you are unfit to continue night work you should co-operate with appropriate medical surveillance and may, as consequence be required to cease night work'.

It is important always to define 'night', whether extra pay is provided for night work and at what rate, and whether night work can be refused. Ensure that the operation of these contractual provisions do not infringe anti-discrimination legislation or the implied term of trust, support and confidence. This may occur, for example, when there are sudden changes to rotas, sudden demands for overtime, and peremptory rejection of explanations by employees - perhaps to do with child care - for why they can't work at night.

'UNSOCIAL' HOURS

Where working time takes place outside the 'normal' work parameters of, say, 8am to 7pm a tradition has developed in some organisations of an unsocial hours premium to compensate for the detrimental effects on home life of some working patterns. With increasing flexibility in contracts generally such payments are becoming less common, though time off in lieu for weekend or late evening working is available to some employees. If such payments are made the contract should:

*   define precisely the circumstances when it is payable;

- identify whether and by whom payment is authorised

- prescribe the amount payable

- provide for variation or withdrawal of the facility

This became a contentious issue from the late 1980s, largely through the relaxation of shop opening hours. Sunday working has become more wide-spread but often by part-time or casual employees. The EU directive on Working Time states that 'in principle' Sunday should be a part of the consecutive 35 hour weekly break. This does not ban Sunday working, and leaves the situation of employees who object to Sunday working unclear.

The Sunday Trading Act 1994 (STA) addresses the issue of the statutory and contractual rights of those who work on Sundays. It applies only to 'shop workers' who work on '...any premises usually wholly or mainly for the purposes of retail trade or business'. This covers both service facilities (hairdressers, opticians etc) as well as shops, bars, restaurants etc.

Shop workers cannot be obliged to work on a Sunday if they have 'opted out' by giving a written notice to the employer. After three months the notice comes into effect. Reasons for opting out do not have to be given. Alternatively, an employee can 'opt-in', i.e. agree in writing to Sunday working. The legislation does not apply to those who only work Sundays.

Forcing an 'opted-out' shop worker to work on Sundays or be dismissed, selecting such workers for redundancy, or otherwise causing them a detriment entitles claims to be made to an industrial tribunal. The implications for employment contracts are as follows:

- contracts for new staff which may or do require Sunday working should clearly state that specific written agreement to working on Sunday should be obtained for the avoidance of doubt.

- when existing employees who did not not previously work on Sundays are asked to do so this will amount to a contract variation. Signing an 'opting-in' notice will indicate agreement to change, and there is no legal reason why incentives cannot be offered.

- employees who refuse the change are able to claim for unfair dismissal it dismissed though they have to establish that refusing to work on Sundays was the cause.

- existing Sunday working employees can opt-out by serving the form set out below on their employer. This will operate separately from the contract but clearly establishes a contract term that Sunday working cannot be insisted on.

- the 'opted-out' shop worker is not entitled by the STA to have work provided in lieu of Sundays and pay can be proportionately reduced. This should be done carefully and fairly so as to avoid an inference of a 'detriment' or vindictive attitude more generally.

- the 'opt-outs' remain in-force during maternity leave and other periods of statutory suspensions from work.

- other measures relating to working time

STATUTORY RIGHTS IN RELATION TO SUNDAY SHOP WORK

You have become employed as a shop worker and are required - or can be under your contract of employment - to do the Sunday work your contract provides for.

However, if you wish, you can give a notice, as described in the next paragraph, to your employer which gives you the right not to work in or about a shop on any Sunday on which the shop is open once three months have passed from the date on which you gave the notice.

Your notice must:

- be in writing;
- be signed and dated by you;
- say that you object to Sunday working.

For three months after you give the notice your employer can still require you to do all the Sunday work your contract provides for. After the three month period has ended, you have the right to complain to an industrial tribunal if, because of your refusal to work on Sundays on which the shop is open, your employer:

dismisses you,
or
does something else detrimental , e.g. failing to promote you.

Once you have the rights described, you can surrender them only by giving your employers a further notice, signed and dated by you, saying that you wish to work on Sunday or that you do not object to Sunday working, and then agreeing with your employer to work on Sundays or on a particular Sunday.

STA, 1994

HOLIDAYS

With a few exceptions there is no statutory entitlement to public or annual holidays in the UK. Most other European states do have legislation providing for paid public holidays (typically around 12 per annum) and formulae for defining minimum paid annual leave (e.g. 2.5 days per month, 25 days per year).

TURERA 1993 requires that the contract documentation informs employees of their holidays entitlement and whether it is paid. It will also be important to address the following matters,

- Decide how entitlement to holidays arises, e.g. are more days given for longer periods of continuous employment?

- Decide how the terms apply to part-timers and other atypical groups; this can be especially complicated for those working Mondays but on a part-time basis.

- Whether there are mandatory periods when at least a proportion of annual holidays are taken - e.g. at least five days between Christmas and the New Year Public Holiday.

- Establish the procedures for determining the timing of holidays and for 'occasional' days: how much notice has to be given, to whom and whether a proposal can be objected to.

- Establish the parameters of the 'holiday year'. Can holiday entitlement be carried over? If so, who will authorise it and according to what criteria?

- Establish the situation when an employee is ill on holiday - do they then qualify for paid sick leave and then more paid holidays? Or is it hard luck?

The EU Directive on Working Time requires all employees have at least four weeks paid leave over each year of employment. If an employer has a reference year of, e.g., 1 April - 31 March and an employee commences work on 1 July, they will have a pro-rata entitlement as long as they receive four weeks over their actual year's employment.

An important provision is that the entitlement cannot be 'bought - out', implying that four weeks is an absolute requirement on both sides of the contract. It is also implicit from the directive that breaks from work need to be recorded and monitored (it probably needs to be a contractual requirement that holidays are formally notified, especially, perhaps by senior and professional staff) and that a culture develop within the organisation that employees do actually take breaks.

An example of how these issues can be reflected in the contract is as follows:

'You are entitled to 35 days paid annual leave, excluding public holidays. The holiday runs from 1 May to 30 April and all leave must be taken within this year. Exceptionally, your manager may authorise carrying over into the next holidays year no more than 5 days leave'.

'In order to ensure your health and safety all staff are required to take their leave'.

'You are required to take at least 5 days leave during the period 25th December to 3rd January inclusive'.

'You should agree your leave dates with your manager at least 3 months in advance if the intended leave exceeds four consecutive days. Leave of up to four days should be authorised at least one week in advance of the first day of intended leave'.

'Any variation or postponement of previously authorised leave must be agreed to by your manager'.

FLEXI HOURS

In many parts of the service sectors, especially banking and finance and parts of the public sector, flexi hours have become quite common, although there is little research indicating how popular and efficient such contractual arrangements are. In all flexi-hours contracts the following should be defined:

- are there core hours which must be performed each day? If so, what are they?

- are there outer parameters for working, e.g. 7am to 8pm?

- are there maxima or minima hours per week/per month etc?

- what is the key reference period for the scheme - three months, six weeks etc?

- are there limitations and, if so what, on 'banking' extra hours and/or carrying them over to the next reference period, alternatively, for making up shortfalls on hours.

- what are the provisions to prevent abuse of the system, e.g. claiming to start work earlier than in reality?

- what are the provisions for varying the scheme both generally or for specific groups of staff or even individuals?

TIME OFF FOR SPECIFIC DUTIES OR ACTIVITIES

Employment legislation provides an entitlement to reasonable time-off for specified duties. In the case of public duties, e.g. local government, school governor duties or as a JP, no entitlement to paid leave exists. There is such such an entitlement in the case of trade union duties. In most other European states leave is always paid, typical situations being for bereavement, child-birth, house removal, training and major domestic events, such as weddings. In the UK, the pattern is more mixed.

It is vital that employers specify in the contract:

- What events, situations qualify for leave;

- Whether that leave is an entitlement or discretionary;

- If discretionary, how and why is the discretion ever used;

- Whether the leave is paid or unpaid;

- Where the statutory leave period is to be for 'a reasonable' time off ,how reasonable is to be defined. Examples can be given.

TERMS RELATING TO JOB LOCATION

The topics covered here are:

- **job location**

- **mobility clauses**

- **secondments**

- **travel and working abroad**

JOB LOCATION

There is growing pressure to ensure flexibility over location. The popularity of re-locating away from expensive inner city locations, often re-inforced by development grants and by government policy in the public sector has sometimes caused problems because contracts were either silent on job location or too specific.

For example, a contract might describe the workplace as '28, Bridge Street, Bigtown, Westshire'. Virtually all moves would be variations of a contract term and would, if not agreed to, be a breach of contract.

If contract documentation did not include information on job location the courts or tribunals had to construct an appropriate clause if a dispute arose. This led to some odd decisions where in some cases a move two streets away would be held to be a change of job location, while other cases concluded a term could be implied that an employee could be moved within daily travelling distance.

The unpredictability of case law means that it is vital to plan for future organisational change and express contract terms appropriately. Furthermore, TURERA now requires information on job location.

Clauses which can deal with the most common situation are as follows:

'Your place of employment is at the ..... campus, Midshire University. You may be required to work on a temporary or permanent basis at any premises or facility operated by this university within the UK'
or
'You can be required to work anywhere in the UK or overseas at the direction of this university on a temporary or permanent basis. Appropriate financial support will be provided (see Handbook, Section V)'.
or
'You are employed by Bisco Ltd at its Southlodge plant. You may be required to work at any of its other South East Region Plants'.
or
'Your normal place of work is your own home. Currently this is 27 Baker Street, Bunville, Doughshire. If you move house you must notify your employer at least one month before you move'.
or
'You will be required from time to time to attend Bisco Ltd's headquarters at Garribaldi Close, Eccles, Lancs. Bisco Ltd will reimburse travel expenses at their prescribed rate'.

It is important to note that if there is a mobility clause in a contract or one that requires attendance on a limited basis at other premises the clause will be 'activated' sensitively. For example:

'You may be required to work anywhere in the UK where SPK Ltd has an operational function. If change of workplace will require re-location SPK Ltd will endeavour to provide at least one years notice of the move and will assist with re-location costs (see SPK Employee booklet, section 7)'.

SPLIT SITES

Many organisations require employees to move between different work locations. This might include manufacturing premises/local authority headquarters/distribution depots/neighbourhood offices etc and perhaps some time spent at or working from home.

The simplest way to respond to this is to draft a clause which expresses the contractual duty in terms of working at or from any employer premises and the employees' home. This is an important issue not just because the contract needs to be as accurate as possible but because some statutory duties apply to the workplace wherever it is (e.g. Health and Safety at Work Act 1974).

'Your work will be based at our........premises. You may be required to work at any of the health authority's premises or to attend elsewhere, if so directed'.

'You are permitted to work at or from home if you and your.....manager agree such an arrangement'.

TRAVEL AND SHORT VISITS

Secondments and assignments cover situations when the employee is working under the direction of another employer for a significant period, and were considered in Chapter 6. However, short assignments or arrangements involving extensive travel inside or outside the UK require different attention. Short assignments require the employer to:

- define clearly the organisation or place to which the employee is going.

- define the length and purpose of the visit.

- clarify the position regarding pay, expenses sickness and sick pay, disciplinary rules etc.

- establish any discretions or choice the employee may have.

OCCUPATIONAL BENEFITS

This is a highly complex and detailed topic. What is provided by the employer over and above basic pay depends on a variety of factors ranging from the traditions and culture of an occupation, where the organisation is based, and on organisational policy, (e.g. to recruit and retain key staff). Employees may have access to subsidised or free canteen/restaurant facilities, preferential shopping, subsidised or free travel, free access to education or training opportunities, or a company car. Once the decision has been made to provide benefits and facilities many of the basic questions are those relating to employment contracts more generally.

It is vital to decide if the benefit is prescriptive (i.e. will definitely be provided) or discretionary; who it is provided for and on what terms, and in what circumstances the benefit can be withdrawn. Many of the problems arise when the employer wants to vary or substitute a benefit, such as reduce the size of the company car or provide one of a different make or close down the canteen or sports complex.

When the contract is not explicit on the legal status of the benefit, the courts have often see the provision of benefits (especially to do with transport) as legally binding and thus more difficult to vary or terminate (*Keir and Williams v Hereford & Worcestershire* (1985))[19] on the removal of concessionary transport). There is, therefore, every reason to direct careful attention to occupational benefits even though there is no technical necessity from TURERA, 1993 to provide written information.

Some of the most widely offered benefits are:

> Subsistence and travel expenses
> Car
> Private health care plan
> Personal accident insurance
> Life assurance scheme
> Share option scheme
> School fees, child care vouchers etc
> Workplace social facilities
> Workplace medical and similar facilities such as hairdressing
> Workplace nursery
> Sporting and leisure club membership
> Free or subsidised travel
> Free or subsidised accommodation
> Removal, re-location assistance
> Subsidised mortgage etc
> Preferential shopping arrangements
> Part or full payment of tuition/examination fees, and expenses.

The detail of each of these schemes will vary from employer to employer, and the information can be consigned to a handbook. However, if it is intended to be contractually binding (and most will be) the language and style of the material must be consistent with that objective; the main contract document must cross-reference the relevant policy, handbook etc., which must be make clear:

• The precise nature of the benefit itself - is it any school fees, fees for a UK school or a named school; in a life insurance scheme is it clear what is covered and who is protected and, most importantly which organisation the policy is with;

• Who qualifies? Are all employees, regardless of length of service eligible? If not, what are the requirements? Do part-timers and casuals qualify, for example, for a preferential shopping scheme or Christmas hamper? (It would be wise to include them). Is it all staff or only those above a certain grade, such as managers, who have access to a lease car?

• Whether there are any restrictions on the benefit. For example, what, if any, is the cash limit on preferential purchases, what is the maximum number of times, if any, that the in-house dentist or hairdresser can be visited, is there a limit on the size of a mortgage where preferential repayment rates apply, how many children and of what age can use the workplace nursery. If nursery places are provided free or below cost who comes free and who has to pay;

* Whether benefits are an entitlement or discretionary. If they are discretionary the handbook must identify who exercises the discretion and it has to be decided whether the discretion is untrammelled (i.e., is absolute) or will be operated according to specified criteria. These might include length of service or employee performance and may, therefore, be directly linked to the appraisal or other performance indicators. For example, work capable of being measured either quantitatively or qualitatively may be linked with a specific occupational benefit such as a free holiday;

* Whether benefits can be taken away if the employee leaves, for example, company shares, a car or an insurance policy. This matter has given rise to some complex case law and is best resolved through the contract itself. It will also be very important to determine whether the manner of the contract's ending is relevant. For example, does dismissal for misconduct imply forfeiture of accrued rights to benefits; can any payments or opportunities be reclaimed?

* Whether benefits can be suspended. What is the position where an employee is on secondment, or maternity leave, a sabbatical or perhaps on a training programme. In view of the specific provisions relating to the 14-week period of maternity leave introduced by TURERA 1993 and the continuation of employment contract rights apart from 'remuneration' this matter is best dealt with in the contract itself;

* Whether a benefit can be ended or varied;

* Whether the range of benefits and their management is consistent with HRM policies at the workplace. Are they consistent with equal opportunities, are they reinforcing or consistent with quality initiatives, do they give appropriate emphases or priority to matters presented in mission statements or organisational culture?

Just as with HRM issues generally it is vital to review the benefits package regularly, to ensure that it is consistent, has an overall coherence, is up to date and has been working effectively. It will be particularly important to check whether changes in the workforce and its deployment have not distorted the availability and application of benefits.

Travel and Subsistence Expenses

Employment contract law implies a term that if the employee sustains a loss in executing the employer's business or service they should be fully compensated (*Coslett v Quinn* (1990)).[20] Technically, therefore, travel and accommodation expenses 'reasonably incurred' are the contractual responsibility of the employer. It will normally be necessary to prescribe a clear framework for expense claims so as to introduce the concept of the 'authorised' expense, thus implying that the employer has negated the requirement to pay 'unauthorised' expenses.

One of the major sources of employee complaints is the failure to pay expenses quickly enough. Typically, there are fewer complaints about the amount due. However, it will be vital for any scheme to have an in-built mechanism to ensure inflation, VAT, other tax increases are catered for - a petrol allowance of 5p a mile is not convincing for a 'state of the art' information technology employer in the mid 1990s!

The following are some of the important questions which should be addressed through the contract documentation:

- Are there restrictions on the type of travel for which expenses can be claimed - air, first class/standard class rail, taxis, (or not)?

- Are there restrictions on who qualifies for certain types of expenses?

- Are there financial limits on subsistence and other matters? How are they varied?

- What evidence is required of actual expenditure?

- What are the procedures for claiming expenses; how are they paid and within which time scale?

Typical clauses might read as follows:

'You are entitled to claim for travel, subsistence and other specified expenses reasonably incurred. Full details of current rates are available in Section 5 Employee Handbook'.

'The employer reserves the right to vary the level and availability of expenses and the mechanisms by which expenses are authorised and claimed. Employees are reminded that dishonest claims may be viewed as a serious breach of discipline leading to dismissal'.

Cars and Other Vehicles

Recent years have seen many changes to the practice of employers providing or subsidising cars for employees. The practice of providing cars is probably still most highly developed in the UK, despite budgetary changes diminishing its attraction. Environmental and economic concerns have forced review of the type of vehicle and its availability.

Many employers prefer to subsidise the use of the employee's own car for work purposes, to lease cars for employees or provide cars in a 'pool', i.e. lent out to individual employees as and when required. Similarly, the move to night work, longer working hours generally and relocation to rural areas has led some employers to provide transport to take employees home at night. Here the driving force has often been health and safety concerns. All these different ways of providing transport raise different contractual issues, but one feature is that employees attach great importance to their provision. Their removal or variation, unless specifically authorised by contract will probably cause disputes.

If a car is provided, the contract must address the following:

- Who qualifies for a car, of what type and whether new or no?;

- Whether there is a guarantee of replacement, over what time scale and at what level (i.e. can there be trading down or up and who decides on this; the employer or employee?);

- Who insures, services and maintains the car?

- Whether there are any restrictions on the use of the car such as who can drive it, how much can it be used for leisure, foreign travel etc;

- Whether it can be withdrawn, for example, during leave, secondment or for bad driving, a poor accident rate etc;

- Whether the employee can substitute a cash payment for a car or some other benefit on a 'cafeteria model'.

Provision of accommodation

The 'tied' house or cottage has often presented problems for employment law, particularly when the employee leaves the job or is dismissed. It is important that the employment contract fully reflects the accommodation issue, and deals with maintenance, access, sub-letting and payment. The employment contract will also set down requirements for cover and emergency call-out - often a corollary of 'tied' accommodation, though this must be consistent with the regulation of working time (see page 173).

The contract and lease must provide for vacation of accommodation in the event of the job ending, marital breakdown, redundancy, transfers etc.

CLAW BACK CLAUSES

Employers often provide financial support to help employee training and development, e.g. by paying fees for an MBA, keeping a job open during a sabbatical or supporting an employee to obtain a vocational qualification through day release or otherwise. A perennial worry is that after completing the course or qualification the employee will promptly leave. Attempts to force the employee to stay are doomed to failure as the courts will not require that people stay in employment relationships against their will. However, it is legally possible to recover all or part of monies spent on the employee if they leave, say, within two years providing the contract has made provision or a separate, legally binding collateral contract was entered into.

A clause could state:

'The company will pay any course fees and other reasonable expenses of an employee undertaking a course or programme of study approved of by the company's training manager. The amount paid shall in no circumstances exceed £10,000'.

'Should an employee leave the company's employment within three years of completing the course or programme of study they will be required to reimburse the company for all or a part of the sums expended.'

'The company reserves the right to monitor and review employee performance on the course of programme of study. If it is considered unsatisfactory the company may discontinue payment or seek reimbursement from the employee'.

EMPLOYEE PERFORMANCE

The last decade has seen a rapidly growing emphasis on quality, employee performance and performance measures. Although the broad thrust of initiatives is to stress improved efficiency the means adopted have differed widely. The traditional mechanisms for ensuring efficient performance of employees have been either through incentives (commission, bonuses, performance related pay; see page 155) or through a rigorous application of disciplinary rules including dismissal of employees who perform badly.

Although most organisations see a continuing and important role for disciplinary procedures the connection is not always made between the introduction of recent HRM initiatives and total quality management, for example, and the need to re-inforce those organisational objectives through the contractual disciplinary procedures. Indeed, there is sometimes a real reluctance to integrate disciplinary procedures within organisational human resource policy making and this in turn can relegate the employment contract to a minor role in quality/efficiency business policy re-engineering initiatives, etc.

The employment contract has a central role to play in translating organisational policies to the 'sharp end' by expressing those policies in the structure, wording and management of the contract itself. An organisation which, for example, places considerable emphasis on customer care needs to reflect that priority in the express terms of contract, especially its disciplinary procedures. In adopting a strategic approach to employment contracts it is important to bear in mind that although the 1990s have provided a climate within which 'right sizing' 'restructuring' and 're-engineering' etc have taken place with relatively little legal challenge or employee resistance, this is not always the case.

Setting different performance indicators may, without employee agreement, lead to claims for breach of contract. Employees are now less reluctant to take claims, so care must be taken with the contract.

The contract itself, through its implied terms of co-operation and mutual trust and support has mechanisms which can link the conduct, attitudes and performance of the individual employee with organisational aspirations. Case law has constantly supported employers in unfair dismissal cases who seek to establish standards of dress, courtesy and performance. For example, employers attaching importance to customer care have successfully defended unfair dismissal claims where employees have been dismissed for rudeness, bad language, inappropriate dress and personal appearance, or suspicions of dishonesty.

However, the common law rules and their application by judges is prone to variability and uncertainty in any given situation. It is preferable to deal with substantive issues through the contract, rather than leave it to the preferences of an individual judge or tribunal and the effectiveness, or otherwise, of legal representation.

What of the typical performance issues which need to be addressed through contracts? It is not easy to categorise them but, nonetheless, the main performance issues can be grouped as follows:

- *Performance issues related to employee competence and the ability to meet established performance indicators.* This is clearly closely related to appraisal in most organisations and will have a significant 'skills' underpinning. It might also be linked to quality management and other policies such as a need for flexibility or employee empowerment where increased responsibility and decision making has to be taken on board by individuals. The identification and the articulation of both the policy and appropriate express terms in employment contracts is vital.

- *Employee performance in terms of complying with requirements for attendance and commitment.* One of the most important issues for many employers is high levels of employee absence for either illness or otherwise, i.e, unauthorised absence (absenteeism). The UK is thought to have the highest absence rates in Europe and this must be a priority for managers. Absence control is clearly a core issue the contract needs to deal with.

- *Employee conduct and behaviour* relating to obeying orders, punctuality, behaviour towards colleagues and others, hygiene standards, drunkenness and drug abuse etc. Attitudes and behaviour which might have been tolerated even a decade ago are now unacceptable. Typical here is the response to harassment in sexual, racial or other grounds. The European Recommendation on Dignity at Work 1991[22] requires that employers put in place structures and procedures to deal with what would perhaps previously be considered 'horseplay' or 'high spirits', jokes, or personal idiosyncrasies. Soft porn posters as well as demands or offers of sexual favours, for example, indicate a lack of dignity for others. Employers have to deal with these issues and although workplace policy documents are developed this is another issue which, to be effective, must be recognised by the contract .

Hence, performance issues can be generated by the organisation itself and its culture but also by extraneous demands, especially those relating to fair treatment at work and health and safety in its widest source.

LEGAL ISSUES

Legal demands relating to performance are few. It is necessary to provide written information about the employee's job (TURERA, 1995 Sched 4). This can be short and to the point, or more expansive and set down in more detail the key professional tasks to be performed. There are growing arguments for more precision in terms of job content and for providing information about the context and the constraints within which work must be done. In courts and tribunals employers' decisions will inevitably be set in an economic and organisational framework. Policy documents (e.g. the TQM or 'Customer Care' or 'Customer/Patient First' etc.) will have an important part to play, even though they are not perhaps intended to be contractually binding on employees.

If the contract is to contain clauses relating to any aspect of performance such as punctuality, absence, flexibility regarding work and working time, dress and attitude, such clauses must conform to basic contractual rules. Their language must be clear and unambiguous and, most importantly, if it is intended that breaking a clause might lead to the imposition of a penalty, such a clause must comply with the contractual rules relating to effective incorporation of sources materials into the contract (see Chapter 3). An example here would be a violence, smoking or harassment policy.

It must also, if appropriate, comply with the Wages Act 1986 if sums of money or benefits might be withheld. In this case the contract must establish through the agreement of the employee the right to make deductions. It is also important to ensure that in the contract package as a whole there is an overall consistency in approach and detail towards specific issues. For example, an employer might have developed a Well-being at work policy. This might stress the importance attached to a smoke free working environment, the availability of health care facilities, the need to co-operate with health surveillance procedures, and hygiene practices. If this document is totally detached from the individual employee contract and its disciplinary rules the policy may not be taken seriously or become established in organisational culture.

It may be helpful to consider:

- Which policies, if any, need to be underpinned by contract?

- What performance issues are important enough and appropriate to be a part of the contract?

- What is the role of disciplinary procedures if any?

- How should policy documents and organisational initiatives be referenced? Should they be incorporated into the contract?

Beyond these more technical matters it is vital that contracts should reflect any organisational commitment to policies such as the following:

> 'quality'
> 'loyalty'
> 'flexibility'
> 'appropriate behaviour and standards'
> 'involvement'
> 'team work and team building'

Policies should all be carefully analysed, defined in practical terms and, if appropriate, key issues incorporated in the employment contract.

It is generally helpful when writing contract documents to include an explanation of why a term is being inserted at all. For example, many employers are putting a higher premium on health and safety policies and practices. In order to ensure adequate employee protection they have sometimes to be re-deployed or have their work varied in some way. This is especially so when they are pregnant or perhaps suffering a stress-related disorder.

An employer might consider the following type of clause:

'This company is fully committed to carrying out its health and safety obligations to staff. In order that this be done effectively employees are reminded of their own legal responsibilities regarding health and safety at work and specifically the need to co-operate with manager's instructions, including that of changes to terms of work if change are considered appropriate in health and safety terms'.

It is also important when assessing employees in the context of disciplinary rules to have a clear idea of the seriousness of specific performance shortfalls (is lateness more serious than being rude to a customer, or the same; is refusal to swap shifts or provide cover for an absent colleague in the content of a 'flexibility policy' more serious than dishonesty or violence?). If one matter is more serious than the other, why is this so.

The overall culture and priorities of the organisation must be in the forefront so that a responses to performance shortfalls are consistent with the nature and image of the employer. Clearly, it would be appropriate for a pre-school nursery employer to view as very serious any sexual improprieties but be more relaxed about a dress code. Similarly, lateness, personal hygiene and wearing uniform correctly will be serious matters for some employers whereas maintaining high and accurate professional standards, for example in the airline industry or medicine, will be priorities for others. There, even one lapse can have catastrophic consequences. Similarly, for misconduct more generally there is an overriding need to be precise. For example, is it well understood by employees what is meant by:

> 'Unsatisfactory time keeping'
> 'Absenteeism'
> 'Unsatisfactory Performance'
> 'Unsuitable Dress/Appearance'
> 'Abuse/use of alcohol and drugs'
> 'Discriminatory conduct toward fellow employees'

The three major performance categories - employee skills, attendance and conduct, have been traditionally a part of disciplinary procedures, especially employee conduct. As a preparation for developing effective contract procedures to deal with performance it is important to define organisational expectations and standards, create rules and procedures for dealing with issues and establish procedures for enforcement.

THE NEED FOR DISCIPLINARY PROCEDURES

The need for disciplinary procedures will be evident to all but the most idealistic and utopian-minded employer. As in any other relationship, things will go wrong, people will not do as they are supposed to, and there must be a structure for dealing with such situations. There is an ACAS Code of Practice (No 1) on Disciplinary Practices and Procedures in Employment, and while this code lacks the force of law, failure to follow the code will be taken into consideration when judging whether or not an employer has acted reasonably (see Chapter 9). There is a booklet, *Discipline at Work*, also published by ACAS, whose provisions are both influential and widely used.

There is no statutory provision for disciplinary procedures. However, as previously discussed employees must be given details of both disciplinary and grievance procedures in their statement of written terms of employment.

It is not enough that the employee draws up disciplinary rules and procedures. That is the easy part. It is in the interests of both employer and employee that the rules are seen as fair, procedures are enforced equitably and there is a proper system of enforcing rules. Rules that are not enforced or are seen as not being applied consistently to all employees will result in a system that is ineffective and may have a negative impact on the organisation.

As always there are advantages to be gained from co-operation of employees and/or trade unions. This will lessen the likelihood of later objections that rules and procedures are unreasonable or lacking in clarity or fairness. Even if such objections are made the employer will be able to counter them by pointing to the contribution/co-operation of employees or trade unions. In *East Hertfordshire District Council v Boyten* (1977)[21] the council's internal disciplinary procedure had been drawn up with union approval. Following Boyten's dismissal for fighting in the street with another employee it was argued that the disciplinary procedure was flawed, because witnesses had not been called by either employer or employee, although procedure allowed them to do so.

It was said by the industrial tribunal that the internal disciplinary appeal should have remedied this by calling witnesses, although there was no provision for this in the disciplinary procedure. The Employment Appeal Tribunal did not accept this. The procedure had been drawn up with the co-operation of all those involved and it was not for third parties (albeit industrial tribunals) to re-write the procedure. The advantages of enlisting the co-operation of all those involved is obvious.

THE ADVANTAGES OF FAIR AND EFFECTIVE PROCEDURES

Effective and fair disciplinary procedures will:

- Protect both employer and employee interests.

- Clarify what type of conduct is unacceptable and where and when such conduct will be unacceptable.

- Enable employees who are the subject of discipline to prepare adequate and appropriate responses.

- Reassure all employees that disciplinary procedures have been the subject of management time.

- Avoid disciplinary issues widening into wider industrial action.

- Avoid legal action by employees who feel the procedures are unfairly weighted against them.

    Disciplinary rules and procedures are not devised to:

- intimidate the employees.

- show management dominance.

Disciplinary rules must be consistent with organisation culture; they are also a product of co-operation for allowing the employer (or his representative) time to prepare a considered response to allegations.

Rules need to be effective, and are likely to be so where they are seen as reducing arbitrary, unfair and hasty decisions. Formal procedures do not favour employee over employer or vice-versa, although it is clear that there are advantages for employees where there are formal procedures and clearly laid down rules.

Given the usefulness to all parties of disciplinary rules and procedures it is important to get it right.

DRAFTING DISCIPLINARY RULES AND PROCEDURES

It is difficult to envisage a situation where any one set of disciplinary rules could be drafted that would cover all potential disciplinary situations. When rules are being drawn up two main objectives should be kept in mind:

- The efficient and safe performance of the work, and

- The maintenance of a satisfactory working relationship between

> the workforce themselves; and
> the workforce and the employer or management.
> the workforce and third parties (if appropriate).

However, particular circumstances might be required to be taken into account include:

- The type of work carried out.

- The size of the establishment, e.g. whether rules are to apply to more than one site.

- The nature of the workforce (professional, craft, skilled, unskilled).

- Specific legal or environmental restraints that apply, e.g. Regulations governing fly-tipping of chemicals etc.

Consistent with the considerations on page 195, it is useful to draw up a 'league table' of how serious certain offences are to be regarded. If alcohol abuse or drunkenness is seen as gross misconduct (e.g. where a bus driver is involved) then this should be made clear. Offences meeting summary dismissal should be indicated.

Procedures

These should identify who is entitled to enforce the rules, and are particularly important where new employees are concerned. They should explain how the disciplinary procedures operate, and that there are some vital rights open to employees.

- Right to a hearing

- Right to representation

- Right for time to prepare a response

- Right to appeal and to whom.

The procedure should provide for a fair and efficient record of disciplinary hearings/warnings and ensure that the proceedings are adequately supervised. A review or appraisal of procedures should be allowed for at regular intervals and the procedures themselves should be readily available.

Every effort should be made to ensure that employees know and understand the rules and how they relate to other policies, such as performance related pay, appraisal and, perhaps, equal opportunities. These are the 'basics' of disciplinary rules and procedure, although much of their content varies from organisation to organisation. They should be coherent, consistent up-to-date and effectively managed.

SOME TYPICAL PERFORMANCE ISSUES: APPLYING THE RULES

Some important issues to address concern employee competence, absenteeism and performance in terms of reflecting the human resource objectives of the employer more generally.

Regarding competence, the contract needs to make plain the consequences of errors, slowness etc but also the failure to obtain qualifications or participate effectively in training and development. In some organisations the performance element of the employment contract has become so pivotal that separate/collateral contracts are devised referred to variously as 'performance agreements' or 'performance warranties' and the like.

Standards must be defined and failures to meet them given prescribed consequences. The set standard may simply be expressed in terms of a number of pieces of work, or take the form of more complex marketing or selling targets. Targets may be the same or distinct from those established by a formal appraisal scheme. Staff development interviews may also be separate, or play a role. With the move to personal contracts the possibilities of bias, favour or even corruption in managing these contract procedures cannot be overlooked, and some form of review and monitoring procedure should be applied.

The quality/performance issue must be considered, not just in the contract but in other documents, and the language and presentation checked for consistency and comprehension. Another major performance issue is that of absence. This has to be addressed and requires a move away from 'old' sickness procedures. With legislation placing growing burdens on employers for social security payments, the need to keep absence levels under constant review and to have effective rules and procedures to monitor and respond to absences is self evident.

At the very least employers must establish a climate whereby sickness absence is not seen as an entitlement or a 'perk' but employees are only absent for legitimate reasons which, ought to be evidenced. Unauthorised absences have to be regarded as disciplinary matters but the 'ground rules' need to be clearly established. The provision for self-certification for social security purposes does not preclude such ground rules, examples of which are:

> 'Employees are reminded that this health authority/company etc attaches importance to attendance. If you are unable to get to work due to illness or injury you are required to contact your departmental manager immediately by telephone or arrange for a member of your family or a friend to do so, to enable your employer to provide cover or make alternative arrangements. You may be required to produce evidence of your ill-health or incapacity if requested by your departmental manager'.

> 'If your illness absence is lengthy or you are frequently away from work through intermittent illness you will be required to attend our occupational health specialist. You are reminded that the (authority/company etc) requires employees to co-operate with health surveillance procedures and in all enquiries into absences from work'.

> 'Absenteeism, i.e. unauthorised/absence from work is a disciplinary offence and the normal disciplinary procedure will be used. If, however, misleading or false statements are provided so as to explain the absence the (authority/company etc) reserves the right to view it as gross misconduct'.

LOYALTY AND COMMITMENT

The role of the contract in specifying certain activities as having legal consequences because they have the ability to damage the employer's legitimate business/organisational interests has always been an important one. Included in the topic are:

* fidelity clauses

* employee intenvions

- confidentiality

- restraint of trade

- exclusivity clauses

- 'garden leave;' clauses

- 'whistle blowers'

Because of the economic implications of divulging a new marketing or product development plan to a rival the law has had a long history of intervention. The law has sought to provide a balance between the legitimate interests of the employer without unduly restricting employees from applying their professional skills or exercising initiative. Finding the right balance has been especially problematic when dealing with employer attempts to restrict ex-employees from competing or trading after the contract has ended.

Many legal issues, such as definitions of 'confidentiality' or 'restraint' have produced complex and difficult case law. The law has not been static and cases reflect changing priorities and concerns. Most recently, 'head hunting' and the poaching of staff and teams of staff have featured in case law as well as the news.

Much of the case law has traditionally emerged from the private sector where trade secrets and competitiveness pressures have been the driving force. However, public sector employers in in education, health care and many governmental agencies employers are increasingly addressing the issues.

In higher education for example, senior employees' contracts highlight the position of royalties from publications or patents, and require employees to be more open about consultancy and related work. Sometimes such activities performed without consent are major breaches of contract. There has generally been a 'tightening' up due to the recognition that with internal markets in the public sector employers have pressing needs to protect their business interests. Most of the legal rules have equal application to contract of self-employment, although the interpretation by law of how far the employer of a consultant can restrain competition will be much more limited.

The other general point by way of introduction is that the implied term of faithful and honest service, present in all employment contracts, has been a very effective device to deal with many workplace issues. An example here would be an early case, (*Hivac v Park Royal Scientific Instruments* (1946))[22] where employees moonlighting for a rival could be stopped from doing so because there was a risk that confidential information might be disclosed. It was sufficient in law for there simply to be the risk of disclosure for the implied term of faithful and honest service to have been broken.

Similarly, the implied term has been enforced so as to prevent other potential conflicts of interests. Illustrative here is the case of *Bell v Lever Brothers* (1932)[23] where an employees shareholding in a rival company was held to have broken the term. Even such an interest by a spouse or child may be adequate grounds where the employee has a senior post or has access to confidential or sensitive material *(D.C. Foot v Eastern Counties Timber* (1972))[24].

It is generally clearer and safer to insert express terms to deal with likely problem areas than leave them to common law rules. The usual rules of certainty, illegality etc apply. Additionally, a few topics are covered by statute law, particularly intellectual property rights. The Copyright Act 1988 establishes that production of material (designs, books, advertising copy, music etc) related to the employment of the copyright belongs to the employer. This rule applies whether or not the employer requested the material, whether or not it was paid for separately.

However, problems can arise where the copyright material is drawn from the employee's own skills or experience. In this case the copyright belongs to the employees. If someone is employed as a medical researcher but composes a song or advertising jingle outside working hours, the copyright is theirs. If the demarcation between work skills and those used to develop copyright material is clear there are no difficulties. If, however, work skills are related to 'home skills' the line is harder to draw. When an employee is, for example, a textile designer, commercial artist, photographer or researcher/lecturer and material is developed of the same general type, controversy can rage. The legal approach is to see a distinction between individual 'know-how' and the legitimate business interests of the employer.

Clauses in contracts can address these issues. Insofar as they confirm the legal situation they are valid but they cannot be used to override legal rights. In other words a clause which states the following may not be effective:

> 'Any work, materials, design, or similar which is produced by you at any time or at any place during your employment with this organisation is the property of the organisation'.

It will only be adequate so far as copyright material relating to the employees' job description is concerned. It is important to draft terms which realistically address the practical issues at the workplace. This is an area where personal contracts and 'bespoke terms' do have a clear role to play.

It is legitimate to insert contract terms which clarify the legal position. It is also appropriate to reinforce them through organisational policies stressing improvement and development such as through quality circles, suggestion schemes and the like so as to remind employees that they should co-operate with organisational improvements.

EXCLUSIVITY AND CONFLICTS OF INTEREST

Clauses in contracts which purport to restrict an employee from working part-time or otherwise for someone else (or for themselves on a self-employed basis) are only enforceable so long as the clause is needed to protect legitimate business interests. Where there is doubt as to whether the proposed work of the employee will conflict the contract clause could read as follows:

'Employees are reminded that they should not undertake other work on a paid or unpaid basis unless they have received authorisation from their departmental manager. Such authorisation will not be unreasonably withheld but working without authorisation will be reviewed as a disciplinary matter'.

Similarly:

'Employees should not join any employing or other organisation where there is a possibility of a conflict of interest between their employer's organisation and the other. If employees are unsure on this matter they must seek advice from the Director of Human Resources'.

WHISTLE BLOWERS!

An increasingly important area concerns the role of contract and its management when employees divulge information about an organisation to outsiders, including the press and the police. The normal legal rule is that contracts can restrain confidential information. However, if the matter is of public concern no contract clause can be enforced. If there is concern about health and safety, TURERA Schedule 5 specifically provides protection from victimisation. Case law (*Initial Service v Putterill* (1968))[25] indicates that the confidentiality rule cannot apply where laws are being broken, in that case to do with an unlawful cartel being operated.

Attempts to 'gag' employees where information concerns criminal or other unlawful acts or policies will not be effective. A better approach might be to draft a clause which stresses the harm to legitimate and lawful organisational interests rather than 'a blanket' one.

RESTRAINT OF TRADE

This has been one of the most contentious areas of employment contracts because it restricts employees, even long after their employment has ended. The law's position is that clauses which prohibit or limit the ability of ex-employees to work for a competitor or set up in business themselves in similar work are unenforceable unless they are reasonable from the perspective of the parties and of the public. The public interest in having proper access to products and services is vital and no less so with the advent of the European Union and its emphasis on free competition.

Indeed, clauses which unduly restrict competition are contrary to Articles 85 and 86 of the Treaty of Rome 1956. Business generally has given increasing prominence to free competition, including in the public sector, a matter which law courts have rejected.

The type of issues which clauses might address include:

- prevention of competing over a defined time scale and/or within a defined radius or within a particular industry;

- prevention of solicitation of clients during or after termination of contract;

- prevention of ex-employees poaching remaining employees; restriction on publication of material about the ex-employee's employer.

When deciding whether a clause is enforceable law courts will focus on the precise need for a clause - (if there is one at all), and whether the language in the contract adequately expressed a necessary restriction or went too far or was therefore oppressive. Clauses can be drafted so that there are sections dealing with time ('*You will not set up in business as a hairdresser for two years*'), dealing with geographical area ('*Within the counties of Essex and Suffolk and Norfolk*') or by exercising certain skills ('*You will not set up in business as a designer, architect or housebuilder*').

EXAMPLE: THE PROMOTIONS MANAGER

An employee, in return for a cash payment of £5,000 entered into a restrictive covenant limited her business activities, 'Within Scotland and the North of England for a period of six months after the termination of employment, (however that comes about and whether lawful or not)'. The document also contained a clause which purported to enable the covenant to remain effective even if challenged as being unreasonable to the extent that any reasonable remaining parts could continue. The employment contract ended after 15 months and the employee alleged wrongful or unfair dismissal. The employer sought an interdict (injunction) to enforce the contract.

The interdict was refused; the Court of Session in Scotland held that the argument that the manner of the ending of the employee's contract would not affect its enforceability was lost. To allow enforcement where the employee had, say, been unfairly dismissed or perhaps subject to unlawful discrimination was unreasonable.

The court was not prepared to help re-draft contract terms where they were vaguely or too broadly drafted. Here it was clear that much of the covenant was too wide, for example, a prohibition on 'offering commercial advice to interested persons'. In addition, she only ever worked in Scotland.

Overall, the court decided that while it was reasonable to restrict the ex-employee from soliciting other staff or canvassing its customers, for a prescribed time the other attempts of the employer to 'gag' the promotions manger's business manager were unreasonable and unenforceable. (*Living Design v Davidson* (1994))[26]

If courts take the view that one part is too wide it can be struck out, leaving the valid parts intact. This is a risky and unsatisfactory approach; it is far better to define precisely what are the business needs which require protection and why, and how much the employee has really gained from the employment over and above their own professional skills (know-how versus, say, market intelligence) and what type of restraint and how wide should it be.

It is impossible to provide appropriate examples of drafting, not least because every workplace situation is different and because drafting them is a highly specialised task. However, one related area is that of restraint during notice periods where, until recently courts had been generally supportive of employers who sought to stop employees from working for others having given in their notice. The law prescribes minimum notice periods - up to three months for long serving employees. Many employers require longer periods of notice, with 12 months often being usual for senior or technical posts.

'GARDEN LEAVE' CLAUSES

The technique of 'garden-leave', i.e. paying the employee during the notice period but requiring them not to work (leaving them to tend their garden instead) was seen as legally valid in 1987 with the case of a newspaper production manager who was successfully prevented from working for a proposed rival evening newspaper (*Henderson v Evening Standard* (1987)).[27] However, support from courts will only come if the restriction is reasonable: it may also contravene European Law and the European Convention on Human Rights (freedom to work). Hence a contract may state:

'You are required to provide six months notice of termination. The company reserves the right to require the employee to serve the notice period and during such period they will be fully bound by the terms of the contract, in particular dealing with matters which the company considers prejudicial to its interests'.

Nonetheless, a court may still consider the clause too wide. A court will carefully examine and balance the interests of the parties, as well as the wording of the notice clause itself. An employee entitled to full pay during a 'leave' period can generally be restrained from working for a rival if there is sensitivity surrounding business dealings and the 'leave' period is not too long.

REFERENCES

1   See Chapter 5 and the requirements of TURERA, Sched 4
2   [1993] IRLR 591
3   Annual Reports, Central Office of Industrial Tribunals
4   1993/C/248; 1993 Com. 1993 388
5   [1982] IRLR 333
6   [1980] IRLR 210
7   [1984] IRLR 227
8   [1976] IRLR 366
9   [1978] IRLR 263
10 See 2 above
11 [1987] IRLR 26
12 See *Delaney v Staples* [1992] IRLR 191
13 [1960] 3 All ER 105

[14] [1982] IRLR 183
[15] [1983] ICR 416
[16] 85/92/EEC (Working Time Directive)
[17] [1995] IRLR 35
[18] *Johnstone v Bloomsbury Health Authority* [1991] IRLR 118
[19] [1985] IRLR 505
[20] [1990] IRLIB 413
[21] [1977] IRLR 347
[22] [1946] 1 Ch 169
[23] [1932] AC 161
[24] [1972] IRLR 83
[25] [1959] 1 QB 396
[26] [1994] IRLR 69
[27] [1987] IRLR 64

8
Changing and Managing Contracts Effectively

Employing organisations in both the public and private sector operate in a dynamic, fast changing environment. Many of the pressures on an organisation are external e.g. financial markets, government policy, technological change and changing consumer markets. Leading management writers all stress the need for businesses to adapt to the ever changing demands of the market place. Companies must for example learn to 'thrive on chaos' and 're-engineer the corporation' Those who do not will not survive.

Adapting will often involve expensive on-going investment in plant, machinery etc. Financial costs apart this is relatively straightforward. Sometimes given less consideration at the policy stage are the effects on the human resources of the organisation. Although it is often stated that people are the most important resource, they are sometimes the most easily forgotten. If staff are not fully involved in the process of change, problems are likely to arise, because organisations need to retain their employees' support. Managers who are aware of this are more likely to use the employment contract as a bond rather than a binding mechanism, or a weapon to ensure that employees are always 'flexible' and unable to resist change.

Managing this change is a creative process, with numerous pitfalls, but many of these can be foreseen and hopefully avoided. Managerial decisions almost invariably have legal implications, particularly where employees' contracts are concerned. Sometimes this is forgotten - employers will invest much time and energy in setting up the employer/employee relationship, making provisions on pay, bonuses, benefits, holidays, grievance procedures etc. but will forget other aspects of the employment contract. As the needs of the business change, the relationship between employer and employee must also adapt and change. This will involve a continual process of contract management and variation, though a well crafted and presented employment contract should have anticipated many likely changes and have made appropriate provision.

DEALING WITH CHANGE

Organisations should have in mind at least some of the following:

.   Changes in government policy, e.g. market testing, contracting out etc.

.   Changes in consumer tastes or demands, e.g. for longer shop opening hours.

.   Changes in organisational priorities, e.g. emphasis on training, language skills, flexibility.

.   Changes in technology; different skill needs.

.   Changes in markets.

.   Changes in workplace location; or the need to increase worker mobility.

.   Changes in competitive or economic pressures.

.   Changes in wider society, e.g. desire of employees to spend more time with children, work at home, move to freelance work etc.

For the organisation to adapt it clearly requires adaptation by those who work in the organisation. This may not always be easy. As Justice Walton said in *Cresswell v Board of Inland Revenue* (1984)[1] (dealing with employee resistance to the introduction of computerisation in tax offices): '... all of us... by nature desire nothing better than to be left to deepen our accustomed ruts, and hate change...'

However, most employees today will be aware of the need to change and adapt. The great pitched battles over who does what and other demarcation disputes have generally been consigned to the annals of British labour history. There will always be those who refuse to change and a smaller number who are unable to. An example of this latter was the highly skilled boatbuilder who had worked with wooden craft. When the company moved to production of fibreglass boats, despite his best efforts he was unable to adapt to the new technology (*Hindle v Percival Boats Ltd* (1968))[2]. His contract was lawfully terminated because at a time when law provided no remedies for unfair dismissal he was considered by the court to be inflexible and unable to perform his job properly. He was not, therefore, redundant. There still was a job to do building boats, and employees were still needed, it was just that boat building techniques had changed.

If the business organisation has to change along with its employees this raises a number of issues:

- What are the typical reasons for business change which have implications for employment contracts?

- What are the legal rules of effective contract change?

- How are employees covered by law when there is organisational change?

- What is the situation if employees do not want/are unable to change? Where does this leave the employer?

MAJOR REASONS FOR CHANGE

It is impossible to catalogue all the different and varied reasons which may lead to the employer seeking to vary his employees' contracts. Some changes may be welcomed by the employees, e.g. increases in pay, or shorter working hours. Changes such as these are unlikely to cause problems and need little attention. Others will often require variation of current contracts and be less popular with staff. It is helpful to categorise change affecting individuals or groups under two major categories:

CHANGES TO LOCATION, WORKING HOURS, JOB CONTENT AND PERFORMANCE STANDARDS

Location
The employer may wish to move the place of work to a new site, or concentrate the workforce on one site instead of several. This is unlikely to present a problem if the new workplace is close to the old. If not, changing the place of work may involve a breach of the express or implied terms of the contract of employment and give rise to a redundancy situation. An employee may also be required to be mobile or work abroad; drivers/delivery staff could have their base shifted and their 'area' or routes altered or extended.

Moving a workplace may involve unlawful sex discrimination (*Mende-Hill v British Council* (1995)).[2a]

Hours

There are several possibilities here. The employer may wish to increase the hours worked, or reduce them and/or change to part-time contracts. Several retail organisations in the early 1990s - e.g Burtons and Sock Shop - moved almost all their full time staff onto three day contracts. The legal validity of what almost certainly amounts to a 'de facto' unilateral variation in terms may be doubtful.

Another possibility is that the employer may wish to keep the same total hours but spread over more days (e.g. move to Sunday working). Lawful Sunday opening of supermarkets in England and Wales has already demonstrated some of the problems that can arise in this area affecting pay rates and those with firm religious beliefs. Another possibility is that the employer may wish to move to a split shift system to cover peak business periods more efficiently. Payment of a 'retainer' over holiday periods rather than requiring full attendance and full wages would be another example of the implications of a change in hours, and might occur with school domestic staff for example. Many employers have sought to reduce or eliminate overtime, sometimes as part of an annualised hours or similar policy.

Other major areas of change may involve flexible hours or abandoning defined hours altogether, placing emphasis instead on the effective performance of job tasks, regardless of the time taken (see Chapters 6 and 7).

Job content

The employer may wish to take advantage of new technology in order to operate more efficiently, e.g. by using a computer for design work.

Multi-skilling is probably now the norm, allowing employees to perform a variety of tasks and to switch from one to the other as circumstances dictate. An employer may, for example, wish electricians to carry out some plumbing or joinery work. It is still unusual to ask one skilled tradesman to carry out all the work of another type of tradesman. Where semi-skilled workers are involved, there are fewer objections. This whole area of task flexibility or multi-skilling is becoming increasingly popular with employers. Similarly, employees who are members of professions such as doctors, teachers, social workers and librarians are increasingly performing managerial as well as budgetary, marketing and personnel tasks. Nonetheless, there may be strong resistance to these types of changes.

The potential list is endless, but expanding or changing what an individual employee is expected to do to earn their wage/salary is one of the most difficult and often controversial areas of contract change.

CHANGES TO THE EMPLOYING ORGANISATION

Included here are:

- mergers and acquisitions;

. change of legal status, for example, from District Health Authority or Ambulance Service to National Health Service trust, LEA to grant-maintained schools, or privatisation of state monopolies, company re-structuring and hiving off.

. 'market-testing' and contracting out of parts or services provided to an organisation. Typical here are contracting out cleaning, catering, security and maintenance, but increasingly management services, personnel, and legal and financial services are affected.

This is an important topic. There have been many recent legal developments which require the employer to handle these substantial re-organisations, mergers/take-overs and contracting-out etc. far more carefully. The law increasingly recognises the employment rights of the employees affected: the Transfer of Undertakings (Protection of Employment) Regulations 1981 (TUPE), along with legislation dealing with changes (including job losses) often associated with transfers have considerable and practical implications, re-inforced by other EU legislation and ECJ case law.

THE BASIC LEGAL RULES OF CONTRACT CHANGE

There are different views on varying or changing the terms of a contract. Legal academics will tell you that it is a straightforward issue, and strictly speaking they are right, but for those who operate in the business world the issue is far from straightforward. Additionally, it is one of the less regularly considered employment law topics, despite being such a vital one.

When carrying out a lawful change, it is important to note whether or not the contract provides for such an action.

WHERE THE CONTRACT AUTHORISES CHANGE

If the contract itself makes provision for change, the signature of the employee is present to indicate agreement, and the contract clearly specifies how change will be made and communicated, the change will not, in principle, break the contract. In effect, the employer will have reserved the right to make changes and in altering hours, pay, job location etc. will be merely 'activating' the contract. This is typically the situation where the contracts are 'personal contracts' (see Chapter 3), and is the more usual situation in the private sector and for senior (though not the highest) posts. Having such a clause in a contract ensures that the first hurdle of effective change is overcome.

A typical clause might state:

'Clause 27'
'Management reserves the right to make changes to contract terms from time
to time. Employees will be informed of change by individual notice provided
by the Personnel Department, at the latest within 4 weeks of the change taking
effect'.
or
'Clause 27'
'X Ltd recognises the General Administrative Union for bargaining purposes
regarding the terms and conditions of all manual grades (staff grades D-F).
Any agreement with the Union automatically changes the terms and conditions of the relevant staff'..

Alternatively, the contract will authorise more limited change, e.g. to hours
of work or job location ,or key aspects will be expressed in generally flexible
terms.
For example:

'Your place of work is currently the company's premises in Bridge Street,
Cardiff. However, the company reserves the right to require you to work at
any of its UK premises'.

It is vital that the employee has agreed to this method of contract change.
Issuing a mere 'statement of terms' under Schedule 4 TURERA will probably
not suffice. Relying on such clauses constitutes the first stage of lawful change.
However, simply having a clause in the contract may not be enough for
effective legal change.

The second stage of a contract change is that the 'activation' of the contract
clause (to re-locate, change payment system, change job content etc) should
not be done in an unreasonable manner. Employees need time to adjust,
training and/or other support. To change, for example, the date when salary
is paid may affect mortgage re-payments; other changes, say to hours, may
be disruptive to family life or affect schooling, partners work etc.

Law reports provide some clear guidance on how not to introduce change
hastily and insensitively. It follows naturally that unlawful change not only
breaks the employee's contract but may lead to claims of constructive
dismissal. It must be borne in mind that peremptory or highly insensitive
conduct by the employer is also grounds for arguing that there has been a
breach of the implied obligation of trust and confidence. This may be the case
even where the employee is prepared in principle, to go along with the change
- what matters in law is the manner of change.

SOME ILLUSTRATIVE CASE EXAMPLES

A bank employee based in Leeds was told at the end of the one week to report
for work in Birmingham the following Monday. His contract contained a

mobility clause apparently covering the situation. However, it was decided that in view of the employee needing to sell his house, move his family and arrange for accommodation near to his new workplace the employer's order was grossly unreasonable. (*United Bank v Aktar* (1989))[3]

A sales representative whose job it was to raise advertising revenue was subject to a re-organisation in the operating areas of 'reps'. She was given a smaller area and this had a very bad effect on her commission earnings, which made up a large part of her overall earnings. Changes were authorised by contract but nonetheless making such a change which would have a direct and inevitable impact on earnings without giving consideration to the wider impact was grossly unreasonable. (*Star Newspapers v Jordan* (1993))[4]

An employer had reserved the right in the contract to vary contract terms, including those affecting working hours. However, the contract also provided for employee consultation before changes were made. Hours were raised from 37 to 40, without extra pay. The failure to comply with the consultation requirement, plus the general unreasonableness of the package meant that the employer had broken the contract and no change had occurred. (*Humphreys and Glasgow v Broom and Holt* (1989))[5]

Most of these problems could have avoided by thinking through the full impact of change on employees - often a 'knock on' rather than direct one, and/ or giving time for employees to reflect and adjust.

If a contract clause is relied on in the change process it is important to take care not to go beyond the scope of the clause itself. A mobility clause applying to the UK will not authorise change to Europe; a clause providing for hours of work including abolition of overtime will not of itself remove entitlement to all premium rates etc. What appears obvious or a natural consequence of one change will not necessarily be seen as such by a court or tribunal.

WHERE THE CHANGE IS NOT AUTHORISED BY CONTRACT

In most situations change is more clear-cut. Many 'variation' cases reach a tribunal or court because the employer argues that the alleged variations (e.g. to hours or working practices) were clearly covered by the existing contract terms. The employee argues, not surprisingly, that employers had not provided for change through the contract. Where this is so, a proposed change for example to hours of work, Sunday working (but see Chapter 7), introduction of a smoking policy, an alcohol policy, or a new dress code etc is seen in law merely as an offer to change. This is a process similar to the original offer of employment at the recruitment stage. The employee can then accept the offer or reject it. Acceptance can be made formally - signing a slip of paper or an amended contract.

Alternatively, an offer can be made and if an employee remains at work, receives the new benefits of the contract and does not protest after the passage of time, they will be deemed to have been accepted by conduct. The law does not specify any particular period - this depends on individual circumstances.

For example, an employee on sick-leave or maternity leave might need longer than someone working to the new terms for effective change to be deemed to have occurred. The law expects that any employees affected are individually provided with full information and have an opportunity to consider it. The fact that other employees, even an overwhelming majority, have gone along with it does not technically alter the situation.

Particular care has to be taken to provide the information to those on secondment, based at home, even suspended for disciplinary reasons. The fact that the employer has gone through a full consultation process and used a questionnaire before introducing or expanding a smoking policy, for example, will not validate a faulty procedure as between them and the individual employee.

CASE LAW EXAMPLE

Local government officers responsible for coding applications to determine entitlement to housing benefit and the like were faced with a change, from manual coding to computerised coding. This, the officers alleged, amounted to changing skill needs and a material change to their job content which they did not accept. It was decided that using computers was merely a different and improved way of coding and that the introduction of computers though not mentioned in contracts did not vary existing contract terms. (*McPherson v Lambeth LBC* (1988))[6]

In reality, perhaps in a recession or in areas or sectors with high unemployment, employees often go along with changes they strongly object to. Managers have been able to impose new contracts or have offered inducements, such as a one-off cash payment to those who agreed to change, albeit reluctantly.

However, what is the position of employees who object but continue to work? Legally, they are asserting their right to refuse the employer's offer and can continue on the 'old' contract. Indeed, in many sectors such as further and higher education, this has been the situation. The employer can decide to go along with this, especially if the employee in question is valued.

CASE LAW EXAMPLE

Robertson and Jackson were employed by British Gas as meter emptiers. They were paid according to the number of meters they emptied, and achieved high average earnings. The employer, with the agreement of the trade union, decided to change their pay policy to produce higher basic earnings but lower commission. The meter emptiers objected and after the change was introduced claimed the back pay of what they should have earned under their original contract terms. They won. (*Robertson & Jackson v British Gas* (1983)[7]

However, an employer can treat the two employee groups differently and, for example, not give any pay rises or bonuses to those on the 'old' contract unless it can be argued this breaks the implied term of trust and confidence.

To test this the employee has to give notice and claim constructive dismissal (see Chapter 9).

IMPOSING NEW CONTRACTS?

Are the problems just referred to overcome by simply dismissing and offering to re-employ staff on 'new' contracts? The answer is 'yes', and 'no'. It is possible to give notice to terminate the contracts and to make a new offer, especially if the new offer provides for continuity of employment and other accrued rights. But this of course constitutes a dismissal, and unless a reason is present to provide grounds for a fair dismissal it will potentially open up successful unfair dismissal claims. Traditionally, tribunals have been fairly sympathetic to employers using this device in the context of re-organisation to improve efficiency, productivity etc. However, if used simply as a means of cutting wages, removing occupational benefits etc the dismissal is likely to be seen as unfair.

For the recent judicial view of these tactics, see the following:

CASE LAW EXAMPLES

Mrs Wiles was employed as a telephonist - her working hours alternately each week were 8-4pm or 10-6pm. The employer sought to change the hours to 8-4 and 12-8pm the later shift having a negative effect on family commitments. Mrs Wiles objected. The employer argued that all that had happened was that they had tried to negotiate a new contract and had given due notice to terminate the original one. However, this amounted to an 'anticipatory breach of contract' and Mrs Wiles had been constructively dismissed by the employer trying to force through the unilateral change. The mere fact that the employer could give notice to end the contract (despite possible unfair dismissal claims) could not provide a 'short-cut' to proper negotiation and employee agreement. (*Wiles v Greenaway Harrison* (1994))[8]

Two employees in a confectionery manufacturing organisation were dismissed and offered new contracts. The objective of change was to increase productivity. The effect of the new contract was to remove the opportunity to earn overtime. There was no cut in basic wages. Nonetheless, this was held to be an unfair dismissal. There should have been consultation with the employees in view of the impact on their earnings. Consultation was preferred to the 'sack and re-employ' strategy. (*Trebor Bassett v Saxby and Borrman* (1994))[9]

This last case is fully in line with the emerging legal trend - to put increased emphasis on consultation and negotiation, whatever the business policy objectives in mind. It is quite clear that the EU legislative and case law priority of requiring consultation before decision making is having a general effect.

The practical points which strongly emerge are:

• to check all contracts before change is planned to be sure whether or not the precise proposed change is authorised by the contract.

• don't assume that agreement with unions will necessarily bring lawful change in individual employee contracts.

• don't assume because employees still come to work they have agreed to change; they can still protest and exercise legal rights (see below).

• don't assume that because there are business reasons for change that change can be driven through; don't over rely on the implied obligation to co-operate (see Chapter 3).

• always aim to explain, consult and negotiate change.

IMPLICATIONS OF UNLAWFUL 'CHANGE'

Any change in terms of work affecting an individual or group's contracts that is not lawfully carried out (i.e. done by one side only) amounts to a unilateral variation of the contract, usually amounting to repudiation. This can have the following potential consequences:

• The employee may terminate the contract without notice and claim that they have been constructively dismissed. However to be effective this must be done soon after the complained of act by the employer.
   or
• The employee may carry on working, note his objection to the variation and sue for damages for breach of contract in the County/Sheriff Court or the High Court (depending on how much compensation is sought).
   or
• The employee may seek an injunction (or interdict in Scotland) to prevent the employer implementing the change. It should be noted that this will only rarely be granted. It will only apply where the essential working relationship has broken down and there is practical value in a 'breathing space'.
   or
• The employee may, if appropriate, seek a public law remedy. Here, courts examine the legality of the decision-making process itself. If invalid, a decision will be quashed.

Where the change is in the status or nature of the employing organisation itself (e.g.contracting out or take-overs) the legal implications of getting it wrong can lead to:

• Redundancy claims from the employees affected.

- Claims for compensation if the correct procedures regarding changes were not followed under TURERA.

- Public law remedies.

All of the above can be costly, time-consuming and disruptive. When things go wrong it is so often not for business or organisational reasons but because the process of change, especially employee consultation, was badly handled

Very often major organisational changes are accompanied by media interest and public debate which can bring much bad publicity to the organisation.

CHANGES TO THE EMPLOYING ORGANISATION

Recent years have seen considerable changes to employing organisations. Mergers, acquisitions and the contracting out of some service needs have become commonplace. There has been considerable legislative and case law intervention on the effect of these changes on the rights of employees.

The basic legal position is that if an employer ceases to exist (e.g. through compulsory winding up or dissolution of a partnership) this operates in law as a dismissal of employees, entitling them to a redundancy payment and/or unfair dismissal claims. This is clearly an inconvenient legal approach if, after a merger or acquisition for example, for all intents and purposes other than the legal name of the employer, things go on as before. Hence, since 1965 and the then Redundancy Payments Act the law has considered such changes to be a 'transfer'. If the business or part of it was bought as a going concern and operated in the same way after the 'transfer' as before, the law will provide for continuous employment between 'old' and 'new' employer and the business change itself cannot provide grounds for a redundancy claim. Transfers have recently become increasingly important because the contractual and statutory rights of employees affected also take a very particular form.

Following the legislation and the case law arising from EPC(C) A 1978, the Transfer of Undertaking (Protection of Employment) Regulations 1981 (TUPE) (to implement the European Acquired Rights Directive (1977) and recent changes in TURERA 1993, the practical implications are as follows:

- If there is a 'business transfer' (see below) through merger, acquisition, or perhaps contracting out, the effect is to transfer employees to the new employer, along with all their contractual rights, except pension rights but probably including collective rights. Pension rights are excluded and the new owner/operator does not have to offer equivalent pension arrangements to the affected staff. (*Walden Engineering Ltd v Warrener* (1993))[11]

- If any employee is dismissed 'in connection with the transfer', i.e. got laid off before the transfer or by the new owner it will be automatically unfair, unless there are 'economic, technical or organisational grounds' for changes in the workforce, in which case the dismissal will be for 'some other substantial reason' (see Chapter 9).

- An employee refusing to be transferred loses their rights.

The practical implications of this are that if an employer cuts the workforce in anticipation of selling a business or contracting out to make it attractive to a buyer or contractor, these dismissals will be automatically unfair. If the new owner/contractor dismisses employees directly or constructively (e.g breaking their contract terms by reducing pay) unless there are objectively justifiable organisational reasons they will also similarly automatically unfair.

The key issue is the position of employees who are not dismissed and the effects on their employment contracts. In principle, their contracts are carried over. If any employee refuses to be transferred they loose any statutory right to unfair dismissal and redundancy (TURERA s53)

The contract terms are all transferred. For example, changing the date on which payment is made or pay made up will break the transferred employees' contract (*Rask v Kantineservice* (1993)).[11] In any negotiations for mergers, acquisitions or contracting out it has to be recognised that whatever contractual rights the employees have, including continuity rights, will go with them. There is some scope for subsequent change but the onus is on the new owner to establish the 'economic, technical or organisational' reason.

CASE LAW EXAMPLE

The establishment of an NHS Trust operated as a business transfer and the staff and their contractual rights moved to the new Trust. Two consultants were therefore transferred but when they were dismissed by the Trust this was held to be justified as their medical specialisms were not required by the new employer. (*Porter and Nanyakkara v Nottingham Health Care Trust* (1994))[12]

DETAILED ISSUES

What is a transfer?
TURERA 1993 applied the concept of business transfer to all parts of the public sector and private sector regardless of whether property (cash as well as premises, equipment etc.) has changed hands. It is also clear that even the transfer of a cleaning contract where there was only one employee performing the work can be a 'transfer'. Facilities management contracts, franchises, and licenses to operate, as well as the more obvious business acquisitions, can be 'transfers'. The law's emphasis is on the task to be performed (to cater, provide

security, manufacture clothes, manage a leisure centre) not the precise financial arrangements or ownership of real property. Precisely what the transferee takes on will depend on how the transfer was devised and communicated regarding employee contract terms. Negotiations will be far simpler if both the transferor and transferee have a clear understanding of the contractual rights and duties of relevant staff. The advice offered in Chapters 3, 6 & 7 will be helpful to this process.

However, the key question remains over what a transfer is, as opposed to a change which is not a transfer. Clearly, a business or part of it has to look much the same after the business change as before for a transfer. Contract caterers need to be using kitchen equipment and operating to the same or very similar demands as previous in-house staff, or those of another private contractor. This has always been a difficult legal topic but courts and tribunals have become increasingly flexible in that minor changes introduced by the new owner/operator have been disregarded and emphasis placed on whether, from a customer/consumer/patient viewpoint the business looks much the same as before.

CASE EXAMPLE

An owner in the leisure industry in Denmark offered a lease of a dance hall to a new operator on the expiry of a previous lease. The new lessee operated the facilities in a similar way as the previous lessee and employed the same staff. There was no interruption to the facility. It was held to be a 'transfer'. (*Foreningen of Arbejdsledere i Danmark v Daddy's Dance Hall A/S* (1988))[13]

Organisational, technical or economic reasons
Clearly, if the new operator/owner has significantly different skill needs the contracts of staff affected can be terminated. But if the reasons are not genuinely business driven the employees affected will be unfairly dismissed.

CASE EXAMPLE

This is probably the most important recent UK case on the topic: Forth Dry Dock and Engineering Co Ltd went into receivership. Forth Estuary Engineering Ltd was set up to acquire Forth Dry Dock. At 3.30pm on one day the entire workforce of Forth Dry Dock was dismissed, effective as at 4.30pm. Within 48 hours it was learnt that Forth Estuary Engineering was recruiting staff, but at lower wages than offered by Forth Dry dock.
The House of Lords accepted that there were no genuine organisational needs other than wage cost savings and that the main purpose of the 'transfer' had been to avoid the impact of TUPE and to drive down wages generally. (*Litster v Forth Dry Dock and Engineering Co Ltd* (1989))[14]

Therefore, the important legal tests remain:

- whether a business change is a 'transfer'. If not the employees are redundant.

- what, precisely, are 'economic, technical, organisational reasons'?

Case law increasingly emphasises the rights of employees to be 'protected' by law and that mergers, contracting out etc. are not to be used as a 'ploy' to off-load staff or an opportunity for whole sale contract change.

This section on contract change must be read in conjunction with Chapter 9, which deals with the substantive legal and practical issues presented by job security law. If employees and their contractual rights have been taken over by a new employing organisation but the new owner changes the contract without agreement or dismisses the 'new' employees, the usual legal rules will apply.

The following practical points emerge:

- Potential new owners will want to know the terms and conditions of existing staff at the negotiation or tender stage. Any vagueness or weak contract procedures will not aid this process.

- As well as obvious contractual issues such as wages, working hours and occupational benefits (excluding pension rights) a transfer will involve wider contractual matters such as negotiating rights and some workplace policies. The law is somewhat imprecise on this but it would be wise to anticipate that a significant contract package will transfer and become the responsibility of the new owner or operator.

- Any attempts to change existing contract terms to 'slim' down potential labour costs for a 'new' owner will open up possibilities of unfair dismissal claims under TUPE.

- The law is giving increasing weight to employee interests, including part-timers and a higher proportion of workforces generally.

- Should a further transfer take place, again whether or not property changes hands, the contractual rights will move again. If services revert to an in-house basis the employees and their contracts will need to be taken on again.

- ECJ case law is stressing the need for effective consultation with the workforce as a whole should contract change or redundancy be anticipated. In the area of transfers as well as contract variation more generally, the need to involve employees is paramount, even when there are no recognised unions. In effect, the legal approach requires that when individual changes are made in the context of a business transfer there is a need to keep all employees fully involved.

All this emphasises the need for effective management of employment contracts at a time of organisational and business change. Although it is tempting to focus on the TUPE regulations and the case law which has regulated change in detail, it must not be forgotten that the 'basics' of contract law and contract change need to be complied with.

R<small>EFERENCES</small>

1	[1984] ICR 508
2	[1969] 1 WLR 174
2a	Unreported
3	[1989] IRLR 507
4	Unreported
5	[1989] IRLIB 369
6	[1988] IRLR 470
7	[1983] IRLR 302
8	[1994] IRLR 380
9	Unreported
10	[1993] ICR 967
11	[1993] IRLR 133
12	[1993] IRLR 486
13	[1988] IRLR 315
14	[1989] IRLR 161

9
Ending It All

Recent years have seen British employers of all sizes shedding ever-increasing numbers of employees. The public sector, which many saw as immune from job loss, has also shed workers with the introduction of market testing, compulsory competitive tendering and other initiatives. Shedding labour has acquired a euphemistic language of its own. Employers do not talk of dismissals and redundancies, rather it is 'letting people go', 'downsizing', 'rightsizing' or presenting them with 'alternative career opportunities'.

Although such 'economically driven' dismissals are the most numerous, they are not the only type of dismissal. The other and more frequently litigated reason would be what might be called the 'behaviour driven' or 'just cause' dismissal. The law relating to the termination of contracts is obviously of major concern to employer and employee alike. The employer must be aware of legal rights and duties, many derived from contracts, when considering 'letting people go'. Although a well drafted and managed contract should have anticipated change or problems and therefore minimised the risk of disputes, it is important to recognise that even with the best crafted contract the decision to end it has to be handled carefully and lawfully.

The potential costs of ignoring the advice that follows may be high, both in economic and human terms. The former may be easier to calculate but the latter may be more significant (and ultimately financially more expensive). The potential impact of badly-ended contracts will affect not only the individuals immediately involved, but colleagues and the employing organisation as a whole - including the outside world of competitors, customers, patients, and potential job applicants.

THE COSTS OF LEGAL ACTION

This was touched on in Chapter 1, but an estimate of the costs of dealing with a claim for unfair dismissal or any of the other legal actions connected with ending contracts will depend on a number of variables. Included here will be the resources open to a claimant which will enable them to pursue a claim with rigour, using professional legal advice. Similarly, the support of a trade union or professional association increases the likelihood of a case being hard fought but might also facilitate a negotiated settlement.

Costs will also depend on the complexity of a claim, as well as the numbers of employees involved. The costs of lawyers vary considerably, especially if a barrister/advocate is used. A 'local' solicitor will often be cheaper but may not have the up-to-date and comprehensive understanding of employment law which is increasingly required. Hourly fees for city centre specialist firms start at £200 per hour, and legal bills now itemise and charge for every letter, FAX, photocopy, phone call and meeting. The more poorly prepared an employer's case is (e.g through slack procedures, lack of documents and other evidence) the more costs will rise. For most cases the employment contract and supporting documents are fundamental. Properly prepared documents, as considered in Chapter 3, will considerably aid the process. If an employee/claimant is well aware (or ought to have been) of contractual obligations, a stronger case can be made against them.

It is important to remember that the judicial process is also imprecise. Hearings are often delayed, or deferred: people often spend hours simply waiting around. All this costs money, too. A top QC can cost £1,000 a day or much more, even if they are not 'on their feet'.

A sample bill for a straightforward industrial tribunal case which involved a day's proceedings might look as shown on the next page.

However, the major costs associated with litigation will not be confined to legal advice. The involvement of senior managers, line managers, other staff as witnesses and the resources of the personnel department will be expensive. Many cases require the senior manager of an organisation to attend a tribunal personally. Where the basis of the claim is an alleged breach of discipline, it is likely that at least four or five staff will be required at the tribunal on the day.

Prior to this there will have been many internal meetings and much correspondence, as well as external meetings with lawyers and others. In an organisation with senior staff salaries averaging £50,000, a day in a tribunal will cost £250 for each manager involved, though the real cost in terms of disruption to business will be far far higher. There will also be travel and subsistence costs associated with meetings and hearings.

The total 'bill' for a relatively simple dismissal case is likely to be at least £5,000, with the possibility of appeals to higher courts or even to the European Court of Justice in Luxembourg. The process itself is always prone to delay, uncertainty and unpredictability. Pending or actual litigation will have an unsettling effect generally and will probably increase emotional and stress levels.

Disputes and litigation can never be eliminated or even avoided. However, if employment contract processes are robust and their management well informed and professional the potential damage on an organisation will be minimised.

It should be noted that even where the contract is ended 'properly' there will be a cost, but that cost will usually be foreseeable and therefore can be

De Witt & Rapier
Solicitors
Bank Chambers
High Street
Casterbridge

Ms Gladys Trench
Director of Personnel
AJ Tools Ltd
Rock Industrial Estate
Stoke Treadmill
Wessex

Dear Mrs Trench,

Re: Johnson v AJ tools Ltd

Further to a decision in the above claims in Casterbridge Industrial Tribunal on May 10th 199( ), I have pleasure in setting out our fees for professional advice and support. We have applied our usual schedule of charges as agreed.

1. Professional advice 12 x £100 per hour	1,200
2. Attendance at tribunal	800
3. Secretarial expenses, disbursements, telephone, FAXES and other overheads (see attached)	1,630
4. Counsel's fees: one conference; one day in tribunal, preparatory work	3,400
	£7,030 + VAT

budgeted for. Overall, It is always important to consider:

•   Why you may wish to end contracts and the role of the employment contract.

•   The legal requirements of lawfully ending it.

THE MECHANICS OF TERMINATION

NOTICE

Contracts of indefinite length can normally be terminated by either party indicating that they wish to bring the relationship to an end by 'giving notice' The period of notice required to end the contract is usually an express term of the contract. If there is no express provision then a reasonable period of notice will be implied by the courts. What is reasonable will depend on a variety of factors. Some factors which have been considered relevant have been the employee's age, position in the organisation, length of service etc.

It has been held that for a senior manager a year was a reasonable period of notice. Leaving notice to the uncertainty and the arbitrary nature of the courts is obviously inadvisable on economic grounds. Notice is something which should be dealt with at the contract formation stage.

Statute law (EP(C)A) makes provision for minimum periods. The employer must give one week's notice to an employee who has been employed between one month and two years. Thereafter he must give one week's notice for each year of employment up to a maximum of 12 weeks for 12 years. The statutory notice requirements for the employee are less rigorous. Employees must give at least one week's notice if employed for more than a month; the contract may have extended this.

Experience shows that employees under notice will perform poorly, and may actively work against their employer's interests. It is often advisable, once the decision to dismiss is made, to terminate the relationship immediately and offer a payment in lieu of notice. This has the advantage of getting the employee off the premises. The acceptance of pay in lieu of notice terminates the contract at the date of acceptance. It may need to go beyond the contractual minimum and include a 'disruption' element if the grounds to end the contract are not likely to be fully convincing.

Employees may be contractually bound to give a longer period of notice than that provided by statute. Attempting to hold an unwilling employee to his contractual notice is unlikely to be productive, unless the employer wishes to send a message on the nature of contractual obligations to the rest of the workforce. Where the employee resigns and gives notice there may well be no obligation on the employer to allow him to work that notice. Payment of wages or salary may be all that is required, even if there is a loss to the employee (e.g. in lost commission).

However, contracts are sometimes terminated as a result of 'head-hunting' or even poaching (which may entitle the employer to sue the 'poacher' for inducing a breach of contract) and the employer has to protect business interests.

'GARDEN LEAVE'

Problems may arise in the above situation where an employee accepts a payment in lieu of notice. As we have seen above the contract terminates once the payment has been accepted. What if the employee wishes to go off and work for the rival company, during what would have been his notice period? The law is faced with a dilemma - does it protect freedom to work by the employee or the trading position of the employer?

ILLUSTRATIVE CASE EXAMPLE

Eaglestone worked for GFI as a foreign exchange options broker. His contract of employment stipulated 'that he must not during the continuance of this agreement be engaged or interested, either directly or indirectly, in any capacity in any trade, business or occupation whatsoever, other than the business of the company', unless he had GFI's consent. The contract could be terminated by either side on 20 weeks notice. It also contained a restrictive covenant on Eaglestone's activities in the 20 weeks following the termination of his employment.

In the summer of 1993 Eaglestone decided to join a new company that had set up in competition with GFI. He sent in notice of his resignation. GFI applied to the High Court claiming that Eaglestone was in breach of contract and sought an injunction that he could not work for the rival company during his notice period. The injunction was granted. Eaglestone applied to either have it lifted in its entirety or failing that to cover less than the 20 weeks. The court said that 20 weeks was longer than was necessary to protect the employer. Twelve weeks would be appropriate. (*GFI v Eaglestone* (1994))[1]

The court tried to deal with the above dilemma in a fair way. However, the law is a bit of a lottery in this area. It would be rash to assume that employees can always be restrained from working for a rival (in the absence of a restraint of trade clause (see Chapter 7) during the notice period. The genuineness of likely damage to the employer will need to be established before 'garden leave' will be supported.

There will of course be circumstances where the employer need not concern himself with giving notice - he may be justified in dismissing summarily (without notice). This is discussed at page 226 below.

WHAT IS 'DISMISSAL'?

Dismissal (for the purposes of the legislation) is defined in EPCA sections 55(2), 56. It can take various forms, and it is vital to ensure that the procedure adopted has actually ended the contract. In addition to the forms of dismissal discussed below, a failure to permit women to return to work after confinement is treated as a dismissal.

TERMINATION BY THE EMPLOYER

'Where the contract is terminated by the employer with or without notice'
There will usually be no difficulty in recognising this situation provided that the dismissal is set forth in unambiguous language and it is clear when it is to take effect. Difficulties have arisen when it is not immediately clear whether the words spoken constitute a dismissal.

Phrases like 'You're finished with me' (*Tanner v Kean* (1978))[2] uttered in the heat of the moment by an employer as part of a vitriolic attack on an employee who had taken a van without permission, do not form an effective dismissal. In many cases the words spoken in the heat of the moment have been almost immediately withdrawn as in *Martin v Yeoman Aggregates Ltd* (1983)[3] where an employee refused to get a spare part for a director's car. In that case the judge held that it was a matter of plain common sense vital to industrial relations that both employer and employee should have the right to withdraw words spoken in the heat of the moment.

Problems may arise where it would seem on the face of it that the employee has resigned. Investigation may however show that the reality was that the resignation was forced on the employee (i.e. 'resign or be sacked'). This has been held to be a dismissal as in *Robertson v Securicor Transport Ltd*[4] where the employee who had breached a company rule was given the alternative of resigning or being dismissed. The employee must however establish that there is a certain and immediate threat of his being dismissed.

It should be noted that any attempt to get an employee to 'sign away' unfair dismissal rights will normally be ineffective. A contract cannot be used to take away statutory protections. The conclusion to be drawn from these cases is that the ending of the contract should be unambiguous and confirmed immediately in writing.

It must be borne in mind that suspending an employee does not end the contract; it simply relieves the employee of the duty to work. It is imperative if the suspension is caused by an arguable breach of contract that an investigation by a line manager or consultant is launched immediately and that contract documents are used during this process. The contract should provide the 'base-point' for the investigation.

NON RENEWAL OF FIXED TERM CONTRACTS

'Where there is a fixed term contract which is not renewed under the same terms upon its expiry'
Non renewal of a fixed term contract amounts to a dismissal. The fact that a contract provides for a period of notice will not of itself preclude it from being a fixed term contract (see Chapter 6).

CONSTRUCTIVE DISMISSAL

'Where the employee terminates the contract, with or without notice in circumstances such that he is entitled to terminate it without notice by reason of the employer's conduct'
Some employers may occasionally use a variety of means to force the employee to 'resign' when the real reason is the conduct of the employer. Typical grounds for employees alleging constructive dismissal are:

- Where the employer is in breach of the agreed contract express terms and the breach is a serious one. The failure to pay agreed wages, provide holiday pay, maternity pay, overtime rates or overseas allowance are examples. This will clearly hinge on how the terms of the contract have been set down (see Chapters 3 and 7).

- Where there is a breach of the implied obligations in the contract, for example, to provide a safe workplace, or support and confidence (see Chapter 3).

It would seem from the cases where constructive dismissal has been an issue that the employer's conduct must amount to a fundamentally material breach of contract before the employee can start to persuade a tribunal that there has been constructive dismissal. The onus is on the employee to satisfy the tribunal that the behaviour complained of, justified the employee leaving. This may not be easy.

ILLUSTRATIVE CASE EXAMPLE

A Glasgow hospital had decided to introduce a smoking policy. At first smoking was allowed in special areas but it was decided to introduce a total ban. There was widespread consultation with the trade unions and staff interest groups. What response there was, was of a positive nature. Dryden, a heavy smoker, said she could not get through the day without smoking. She resigned, claiming that she had been constructively dismissed, because she, personally, disagreed with the ban and saw it as unreasonable. She lost.

The situation would have been different had there been a contractual right to smoke (this is unlikely) but it might unusually be the case that the introduction of a no-smoking policy would be a breach of the implied term of (mutual trust and confidence) although this was held not to be the case here. (*Dryden v Greater Glasgow Health Board* (1992))[5]

SUMMARY DISMISSAL

Dismissal frequently involves 'summary dismissal', i.e. the employee's contract ended suddenly without period of notice or money in lieu. While the action may be justified the employer must be aware that such summary justice could rebound, and at a cost. Some advice may be useful here to prevent this happening. There is no simple checklist of what will or will not permit summary dismissal. A variety of circumstances will need to be taken into account, especially the express terms of the contract.

Summary dismissal will be justified where the employee's breach is 'incompatible with the contract of employment so as to preclude further satisfactory continuance of the relationship' (*Sinclair v Neighbour* (1967))[6]. A breach of the implied term of trust can undermine the essential nature of the employment relationship. Here it was taking cash from a till, though replacing it next day (see Chapter 3).

Managers must always be careful because even where the employee appears to be breaking a major express contract term, e.g. regarding working hours or job content, there may be circumstances justifying it, such as psychiatric illness or serious domestic pressures.

In the case of serious misconduct (as opposed to breach of express contract terms) the test would seem to be whether the employee's conduct is detrimental to the reputation of the business (or suggests that there is some problem that makes the employee unfit for that particular work). It has been argued that to dismiss an employee who has been convicted of some (often) minor criminal offence means that they are being punished twice. The employer though will probably feel that he has different interests to protect than those of the state.

Note should however be taken of paragraph 15(c) of the ACAS Code of Practice (No 1) which recommends that the conviction of a criminal offence away from the workplace should not automatically be treated as a reason for dismissal. The test would seem to be either unsuitability for the type of work or unacceptability to fellow employees or customers.

ILLUSTRATIVE CASE EXAMPLES

A school grounds man was convicted of incest with his daughter. He was immediately dismissed after attempts to find an alternative job were unsuccessful. The Court of Appeal agreed that the employer was correct in believing that the employee could not continue in work where he might come into even casual contact with young girls. (*P v Nottinghamshire CC* (1992))[7]

A quarryman was dismissed following a similar conviction of incest with his daughter. His subsequent dismissal was held to be unfair as it was an isolated incident that had nothing to do with his job, (which did not bring him into contact with female staff), and his fellow employees were happy to work with him. (*Bradshaw v Rugby Portland Cement Ltd* (1972))[8]

JUSTIFYING DISMISSAL

The Employment Protection (Consolidation) Act 1978 provides that an employee who has not less than two years continuous service entitled to be provided by the employer on request with a written statement of the reasons upon dismissal for the dismissal. This statement, if requested, must be provided whether or not notice is given, or whether the contract concerned was for a fixed term and is not being renewed. The statement must be provided within 14 days of the dismissal. Women who are dismissed at any stage of pregnancy or after childbirth in circumstances in which their maternity leave period ends by reason of the dismissal must be given a written statement, whether requested or not. Managers and employers should consider issuing statements even when not required to do so in the interests of clarity for all concerned.

THE CONCEPT OF UNFAIR DISMISSAL

For the majority of employees the protection afforded by the common law was weak. Now most employees have a general legal right not to be unfairly dismissed, and those who feel they have been may complain to an industrial tribunal. The legislation has 'come of age'.

WHERE DO WE FIND THE LAW?

The right to claim for unfair dismissal is now contained in the Employment Protection (Consolidation) Act 1978 (EPCA) as amended. Section 54 of EPCA provides: 'in every employment to which this section applies every employee shall have the right not to be unfairly dismissed by his employer'.

WHO DOES THE LEGISLATION APPLY TO?

It applies only to employees, not to the self employed (see Chapter 4). Not all employees, however, are covered. To bring a complaint of unfair dismissal the employee must have two years continuous service (see below), and:

• Must not be over the normal retiring age providing it is a unisex retiring age or if there is no such normal retiring age be over the statutory retiral age of 65. It will be necessary to keep in mind proposals to harmonise retirement ages though employment contracts.

• Must not be members of the police force (including prison officers).

• Must not be ordinarily be working outside Great Britain (which means England, Wales, Scotland but excludes N. Ireland, Channel Islands and the Isle of Man).

• Must not be employed on a fixed term contract where they have agreed in writing to waive their rights to claim unfair dismissal (see Chapter 6 on the effect of renewal or extension of fixed term contracts).

Employees who have been dismissed for trade union related reasons may claim even if they fail to meet the age or service criteria. Employees who claim their dismissal involved either sex or race discrimination need not meet the two-year service qualification, (nor, since TURERA 1993, need those claiming their dismissal was pregnancy related).

Two years continuous service

The rules relating to continuous service are complex though it is possible to give a brief overview here. It should be noted that it is possible, at time of writing that the requirement for two years continuous service will be successfully challenged as discriminatory against women. The two year period is also longer than any comparable requirements within other EU Member States.

It is especially important to note that even where the express terms of contract have been designed to prevent continuity, e.g. by building in breaks, the law may still override this by holding that the contract remains in existence during the 'gaps' (see below).

Key points

Only service with the current employer counts but there may be express contractual provision that service with a previous employer counts (or does not). This will probably be important where there are take-overs, mergers and contracting out. The Transfer of Undertakings Regulations 1981 apply to all employment sectors, and continuity rights are amongst the most important contractual rights carried over to the new employer as a transfer (see Chapter 8).

It is vital to check the current position from case law and legislation in circumstances where there has been a break from working because the law can view the 'gap' as retaining continuity.[8] Payment of a retainer or a 'standby contract' keeps the contract alive. Similarly, TURERA keeps the contract alive during the statutory maternity leave period of at least 14 weeks (and possibly longer for those women covered by broader provisions).

Some important issues have yet to be resolved by the courts, such as the status of zero hours or nil hours contracts when workers are not actually working. It is possible that there is continuity.

However, typical circumstances when continuity will be preserved are when:

- The current employer/sole trader dies and employee is re-employed by the personal representatives of the deceased.

- There is a change in the composition of an employing partnership but the partnership its continues. This has particular relevance to knowledge organisations.

- The employer is a corporate body which is replaced by another corporate body by Act of Parliament e.g. upon privatisation or by establishment of a new legal status such as an NHS Trust, a government agency or higher education corporation.

- There is a transfer of a business from one person to another (see earlier in Chapter 8, page 208).

- The employee is taken into the employment of an 'associated' employer (see below).

- There is a 'temporary cessation of work (see below).

WHAT IS AN ASSOCIATED EMPLOYER?

'Associated' is defined in section 153(4) EPCA 1974 as: 'any two employees are to be treated as being associated if one is a company of which the other (directly or indirectly) has control, or if both companies are controlled by a third person'. Control involves the theoretical ability to dictate events rather than actual day to day control, and is therefore determined by the number of shares held by an individual - not who, in reality, controls the company. For example, a company may be controlled in the day to day sense by someone who does not have a majority of shares. This strict legalistic interpretation of control may well work to the advantage of the purported associated employer who may be able to claim breach of continuity and thereby avoid his liabilities. This is an area where particular care and advice should be taken before dismissing.

'TEMPORARY CESSATIONS' OF WORK

One of the most contentious aspects of employment law is continuity of employment where, the employee is not actually working under an employment contract for a period of time but the law considers employment to be continuous. Illness is the commonest situation where continuity is preserved. Most problems have arisen over casual, seasonal and similar work. The legal question is whether continuity exists when a casual building, catering or agricultural worker who works on an intermittent basis is 'temporarily' away from work when not physically working continuity exists.

The law is relatively clear on how it approaches a given factual situation. It examines whether, looking at the employment relationships over a period of time a pattern of behaviour has developed whereby when work is available it is offered to and accepted by the employee in question. If the answer to that is 'yes', the next question is whether working periods are longer than those spent off work. If 'yes' again, the likelihood is that continuity will exist and, if appropriate claims for unfair dismissal or redundancy made. (*Ford v Warwickshire CC* (1983))[9]

DEFENDING CLAIMS

Once the employee has established that there has been a dismissal in the legal sense the employer must show that the reason for dismissal fell into one of five potentially fair reasons. This section focuses on dismissal relating to contractual terms, but also provides an overview of 'fair' dismissals.

POTENTIALLY FAIR REASONS FOR DISMISSAL

Managers must be aware of the circumstances which will permit them to dismiss employees and the need to bear in mind the role of the contract. They must also consider as discussed earlier the risk of the employee raising an action against the employer.

The unfair dismissal legislation gives five potentially fair reasons which may justify the dismissal of an employee. Equally important is the significance attached by courts and tribunals to the way in which the dismissal has been handled.

The potentially fair reasons for dismissal can be divided into two broad groups. The dismissal may have been:

• Behaviour driven (dismissal for cause) or

• Economically driven

The tribunal considers the reasonableness of the employer's conduct, not simply whether the dismissal could be considered unfair. This will put contractual, disciplinary and other procedures under the spotlight, but the tribunal must not substitute its view for the employer's view of what is reasonable.

The tribunal must take into account that there will often be a band of reasonable responses to the employee's conduct. The function of the tribunal is to decide if the decision to dismiss fell within this band. If it did not, the decision is unfair.

Whatever the reason for dismissal and however justified by the express and implied contract, employers must still act reasonably or the dismissal may be found to be unfair. Whether or not an industrial tribunal finds that an employer has acted reasonably will depend on a variety of factors, including the size and administrative resources of the organisation. This 'reasonableness' test is an objective one. The EAT has given guidelines for its use (*Iceland Frozen Foods Ltd v Jones* (1982)).[10]

Even where the employer has mostly acted reasonably, the tribunal may decide that he has acted unreasonably overall. Failure to follow the requirements of a contractually agreed disciplinary code would be an example. (See *Stoker v LCC* (1992)).[11] In *United Bank v Akhtar* (1989))[12] the EAT said that an employer must exercise his contractual rights in such a way that the employee could carry out his contractual obligations.

BEHAVIOUR DRIVEN AND JUST CAUSE DISMISSAL

There are several categories that may justify dismissal.

CAPABILITY OR QUALIFICATIONS

These are really two separate reasons. Capability is defined in the legislation as including 'skills, aptitude, health or any other physical or mental quality' (EPCA s57(4)(a)). Qualifications mean any degree diploma or other technical or professional qualification relevant to the position which the employee held (EPCA s57(4)(b)). 'Any other physical or mental quality' would potentially cover a very wide range of employee attributes.

However, the employer need not demonstrate that the dismissed employee actually was incapable or incompetent. It is enough that he honestly believes so on reasonable grounds (*Alidair v Taylor* (1978))[13] per Lord Denning). Except in the most serious cases of incapability, (as in Alidair where a pilot landed the plane so badly that it was damaged and the passengers and other crew frightened), the employer will normally have to show some pattern of incapability to warrant dismissal. Warnings should be given and the employee warned about the consequences of his actions (see Chapter 7), particularly in the case of probationary employees.

Increasingly important in capability dismissals are job descriptions, job evaluation, appraisal and other performance management procedures. Sometimes these procedures have been expressly incorporated in the contract. This is not vital, because tribunals are looking for yardsticks against which to judge the employer's response. Material should clearly define the skill needs required of a post and establish expectations in terms of productivity. Failure to achieve this is evidence of lack of capability, especially if re-inforced by poor appraisal scores. However, appraisals may suggest training, development and support is needed, so that despite an employee's poor performance it would be unreasonable to dismiss in the circumstances.

Policy documents relating to dignity, equal opportunities, flexibility, health and safety and re-deployment will often have a role to play. Even if they have not been directly incorporated into the employment contract, they will establish the culture and expectations of the employing organisation. These will be relevant to the decision to dismiss.

GUIDELINES FOR 'CAPABILITY' DISMISSALS

If there are indications of poor performance before dismissing the following should be done.

- obtain clear data from the contract, supporting documents and surrounding material about the job demands.

- satisfy yourself in what way and over what period employee performance has fallen below required standard: obtain and check performance monitoring documents; interview relevant manager(s).

- determine whether there are any reasons for declining performance; if so will the reasons likely continue or ease.

- assess whether with support, training etc. the employee's standards will improve; is re-deployment possible?

- follow fully the contractual procedures where they apply to performance management.

GUIDELINES FOR 'QUALIFICATION' DISMISSALS

The contract should clearly specify the need to have or obtain particular qualifications and also any time scale involved.

- Employees who have lied about their qualifications at interview/application may be summarily dismissed. They should be warned of this.

- Some qualifications (e.g. a driving licence) need not be expressly required if it is an obvious requirements, e.g. employing a motor mechanic. If lost, then dismissal will usually be fair.

ILL HEALTH

Ill health will often constitute grounds for dismissal for lack of capability. The employer must be allowed to consider his own needs as well as the employee's. Both long term illness and persistent short term illnesses may be involved. It may well be the case that a long term illness 'frustrates' the contract. Frustration in the legal sense covers a situation where either party to a contract is unable to carry out their part of the contract due to circumstances beyond their control (e.g. illness.) The courts have not been keen to find frustration except in a few cases because it denies the employee the possibility of claiming unfair dismissal, as there would in law have been no dismissal

A well-prepared contract and/or sickness absence policy will have clarified the following;

- procedures for notifying illness;

- procedures for providing medical information and for medical examinations;

- provision for payment during absence, including rate and length of occupational sick pay;

- implications of failing to comply with procedures.

Dismissal where the employee is considered incapable of continuing to work must follow these procedures.

Assuming the medical prognosis is bad and it is unlikely that the employee will be able to fully comply with the demands of their job, the following provide guidance on whether a decision to end the contract was fair.

Needs of business
Different workplaces will suggest different responses. For example, small firms, organisations with very specific skill needs, and those dependent on fitness/mobility, will be able to tolerate illness less easily than larger organisations where an employee could be re-deployed.

Nature of the illness
This will be tied in with the likely absence but there may be difficulty with illnesses such as AIDS, particularly from the other employees. Regard should be had to the possibility of alternative work for all employees, but as was stated in *Taylorplan Catering (Scotland) Ltd v McInally* (1980)[14] an employer is under no obligation to create a new job or offer alternative employment more suited to the employee's health.

Likely period of absence
It is advisable that the employer attempts to establish from the employee when he is likely to be able to return to work. The need to co-operate with health procedures should have been established in the contract.

Medical reports
The employer should base any decision on valid medical information. This should be obtained from the employee, his/her doctor, and the employer's medical advisor. Employers should be aware of the provisions of the Access to Medical Reports Act 1988, which requires the employee to be informed that a report is being sought and his/her consent obtained.

A well drafted contract will have emphasised the employee's obligation to co-operate with health monitoring procedures.

Should disciplinary procedures be used for medically unsupported short term illnesses?
The general answer is 'no', because an employer's approach should be based on sympathy and understanding. However, some factors that the employer should consider include:

- Nature of the illness and the likelihood of it recurring or of another illness arising.

- Lengths of absences and spaces of good health between them.

- The contractual provisions.

- The need to have the work done by the particular employee and the impact of the absence on fellow employees.

- The extent to which the difficulty of the situation and the employer's position has been made clear to the employee.

  - Warnings on possibility of dismissal.

Where an employee has been lying or has been misleading the employer about health matters, the absence is 'absenteeism' (i.e. unauthorised absence) and can be dealt with as a disciplinary matter.

Alcohol or other substance abuse is now usually seen as a medical problem rather than a disciplinary one. Continued abuse will entitle the employer to dismiss fairly, particularly where safety of the public or fellow employers is an issue. It is advisable that detailed guidance and procedures are drawn up with regard to attendance for treatment.

Changes in the Social Security Act 1994 making employers substantially liable for statutory sick pay provision (as well as occupational 'top-ups') mean this is an important issue. From April 1994 the Government withdrew the previous 80% reimbursement to large employers (those paying annual National Insurance contributions of more than £200,000) of their statutory sick pay costs, though there is some flexibility. It should be noted that the dismissal of an employee who is within his contractual 'sick pay' period will not necessarily be unfair. Ultimately dismissal is a personnel rather than a medical function and in the event of a conflict of opinion the views of the former should prevail.

Not all matters relating to the employee's capability can be covered at the formation stage of the contract, but as much provision as possible should be made, particularly if the job entails an element of flexibility and multi-skilling. There will always be some employees who are unable to adapt to changes in technology, with a consequent impact on their workplace performance. It will be much easier to fairly dismiss such employees if there is an express term in the contract relating to adaptability and versatility for the needs of the organisation.

It will not be possible to cover all possibilities in the contract. In any case it should not be forgotten that any demands made of the employee will be subject to a reasonableness test even if not specifically mentioned in the contract.

Conduct

'Misconduct' is not defined in the legislation, probably because it covers such a wide range of behaviour. It should be noted that it is not only serious acts of misconduct (what might be called gross misconduct) that may amount to a potentially fair reason for dismissal, but also a series of less serious acts of misconduct which would not ordinarily justify dismissal if taken separately. This is something which should be dealt with as far as possible at the contract formation stage. Not all examples of misconduct can be covered, but matters such as dress, substance abuse etc. can be specified, thus avoiding problems later. 'Misconduct' can involve a breach of either an implied or an express term of the contract (see Chapter 3). As stressed there, it is important to express in the disciplinary rules which 'offences' are grave and those less so.

Some examples of misconduct have included:

Dishonesty
This should not only cover cash but also deceitful or misleading behaviour.

Gross acts of disobedience
Refusals to carry out duties are prima-facie grounds for dismissal. Special care should be taken now in regard to orders where the workplace may not be safe or equipment safe (Sched 5 TURERA). Care should also be taken to issue orders which are challengable on racial or sexual grounds. Other acts include:

* Sexual offences, including harassment;

* Dress and appearance generally;

* Disloyalty or disclosing confidential matters especially if expressly defined by the contract;

* Unauthorised use of equipment and breaches of other express terms of contract (see Chapter 7).

Proving misconduct
Generally speaking a misconduct dismissal will only be fair if the employer has a genuine and reasonable belief in the employee's guilt. Clearly, the wording and emphasis in the employment contract can have considerable importance, especially if backed up by a clear procedure for investigation.

CASE LAW EXAMPLE

Mrs Burchell had been dismissed because it was thought she was fiddling the staff discount scheme. The case decided that such a dismissal will only be fair if:
1 The employer has a genuine belief in the employee's guilt.
2 The employer has reasonable grounds on which to sustain that belief.
3 There was as much investigation into the matter as was reasonable in all the circumstances of the case. (*BHS v Burchell* (1978))[15]

This test has been widely used in later cases, and its effect is that an employee who is subsequently found not to have committed the act complained of will, provided the employer satisfies the test, have been fairly dismissed. This is something that should be addressed in the Disciplinary Code.

It must be emphasised yet again that even where the employer has fair grounds for dismissal, a correct contractually-agreed procedure must be followed or the tribunal could find the dismissal unfair on procedural grounds. Procedure will be of lesser importance where the employee is 'caught in the act' and summary dismissal is justified.

BREACH OF STATUTORY DUTY

The employer may be able to show that the employee has been dismissed because his continued employment would be contrary to the law. The most common situation would be the driver who loses his licence. However, it will not automatically be fair to dismiss in such situations. The employer must act reasonably having regard to length of service, length of the ban, the employee's need to drive, the possibility of re-deployment etc. There have been relatively few cases under this heading. Loss of driving licences is the most common but others have included failure to pass a test for hearing aid dispensers, refusal to shave a beard when working with food, and withdrawal of a work permit. If such requirements are specified in the contract, the situation will be easier.

OTHER SUBSTANTIAL REASONS FOR DISMISSAL

There are reasons why an employer might seek to dismiss which do not slot neatly into any of the above four categories. The main one has been where organisational changes have taken place to achieve improved efficiency. In recent years this has been an effective defence. Many contracts specifically require flexibility, co-operation with change or increased productivity (see Chapter 7). Others specify the need to work well with colleagues on job sharing contracts, for example.

ECONOMICALLY DRIVEN TERMINATION

The major economic reasons for the termination of employment contracts are that the employer has gone into liquidation, shifted location, introduced labour-saving machinery, or simply recession or a failing business or service. However, it is crucial that both employer and employee are aware that the word 'redundancy' has a very precise legal definition. An employee who is redundant within the legal definition will have rights which the employee made 'redundant' in lay language may not.

It should also be noted that there is a close overlap between redundancy and unfair dismissal. Many redundancies lead to claims for unfair dismissal because proceedings were handled badly. However, remedies and levels of compensation differ significantly between redundancy and unfair dismissal, with the latter generally being higher. This often leads to a dispute between employer and employee as to whether there was a redundancy dismissal or some other kind.

The law relating to redundancy is to be found in the Employment Protection (Consolidation) Act 1978 which makes provision for redundancy payments in certain circumstances. (It is also covered in Handling Redundancies by Sue Morris). There may be additional or substitutional contractual provisions for redundancy payments in the employment conract.

WHO THE ACT COVERS

For the Act to apply, the employee must:

- have been dismissed (as opposed to voluntarily resigning).

- have been continuously employed for two years since he age of 18 (i.e. the provision doesn't cover under 20s).

- not be over the age of 65 or the company's normal retiral age if it is less than 65.

- have submitted a claim for a redundancy payment within six months of the dismissal. There is provision for this period to be extended for a further six months if the employee can demonstrate good reason for not having claimed within the original period.

Well-drafted employment contracts anticipate business change, especially the following:

- re-location

- multi-skilling

- changes in job content

- re-training

Most contracts build in flexibility to enable the employer to cope with such changes more easily. Redundancy in the legal sense is now more confined to situations where the organisation is suffering an overall decline in demand for services or product.

THE LEGAL DEFINITION OF REDUNDANCY

The definition of redundancy (as defined by EPCA s81) covers three possible situations:

- The employer has ceased business altogether and has therefore no further need for employees. This situation is easily recognised, and should pose no legal difficulty. 'Business' covers not only commercial organisations but all employers, (e.g. local authorities, charities etc).

- Where the employer's business is carried out at more than one location and the site at which the employee works will be closed. Whether the employee in this situation will be redundant will depend on whether work at a different location is offered, and if it is, on any 'mobility' clause in the contract (see Chapter 7).

- Where there is a reduction in need for employees of a particular type, for example because of increased employee productivity or new technology. The Act defines redundancy as 'a reduction or diminution in demand for employees to carry out work of a particular kind'.

If an employee is dismissed in circumstances outside the legal definition of redundancy, it it will usually be an unfair dismissal. With employment contracts spelling out requirements for flexibility, mobility etc., the question of whether work of a particular kind has declined or ceased has become both more complex and difficult.

Take the following examples:

McCrea was the manager of a company which was in financial difficulties. While he was ill his work was done by the managing director. The MD was able to combine his own and McCrea's work without difficulty and McCrea was dismissed on grounds of redundancy. McCrea argued that he had been unfairly dismissed because there was no reduction in the amount of work done. The legislation however does not talk about a 'reduction in work' but 'a reduction in demand for employees to do that work'! McCrea's work still needed to be done but it was being done by another employee (the MD), in addition to his own work. There was a need for fewer employees and therefore a redundancy situation. (*McCrea v Cullen and Davison Ltd* (1988))[16]

Rawat was one of four staff employed in a restaurant. He was employed as a kitchen assistant. The restaurant owners also owned an off licence and a shop. The shop was closed and the shop employees moved to the restaurant. Rawat was dismissed to make way for them. He claimed unfair dismissal. The employers claimed the reason for the dismissal was redundancy. The EAT said this was not so - there had been no reduction in need for employees at the restaurant. (*Babar Indian Restaurant v Rawat* (1985))[17]

Pink was employed as a making and finishing room operative. He was however usually employed as a sole layer/pre sole fitter. The workforce had to be reduced. Three employees including Pink were selected. He claimed the dismissal was unfair as there had been no reduction in the need for sole layers/ pre sole fitters. The employers argued that there had been a reduction in the need for making and finishing room operatives. Pink had been employed in his contract as a making and finishing room operative. It was immaterial that at the time in question he was employed on other work. He was redundant. *Pink v White & Co (Earls Barton) Ltd* (1985))[8]

These cases illustrate the importance of the contract in defining the work to be performed and its parameters. If the contract spells out a range of responsibilities/duties, even though if not all are not actually performed an employee will not be redundant if there is still a demand for skills which the contract indicates the employee can be required to do. Contracts which are too widely or too vaguely drafted, especially in large organisations will some-times prevent legally robust 'redundancies' and put the onus on the employer to re-deploy. Similarly, a job content defined too narrowly will make it easier for the employee to resist re-deployment or other change and to claim a redundancy payment. These issues require anticipation and response.

'BUMPING'

This is where an employee who is redundant in one job is moved to another job, thereby displacing another employee, usually one with less seniority or skill.

The displaced employee has been held entitled to a redundancy payment even although there has been no diminution in the work he did (*Gimber v Spurret* (1967)).[19] There have however been contrary decisions and the issue could best be described as confused and unsettled, which of course is of little use to either employer or employee. The lessons here are that redundancy procedures in employment contracts should anticipate 'knock-on' effects as well as immediate ones and avoid 'bumping'.

HANDLING REDUNDANCY

Chapter 8 considered some of the major implications of organisational change, both in relation to the terms of work of individuals or groups of employees and regarding the organisation itself. Change may have caused employees to be declared redundant, following appropriate consultation. After agreement to the redundancies the following procedures must then be complied with, assuming that circumstances allow.

OFFERS OF ALTERNATIVE EMPLOYMENT

If vacancies exist a redundant employee may be offered an alternative job, and a new employment contract. Before making an employee redundant the employer should establish there is no work available that the employee would be expected to perform. Reference must be made to the contract which will often specify flexibility of post and location. If this is so, the express terms can be 'activated' and the employer should look beyond the employee's current post and location.

This should always be done sensitively and reasonably, and the need for is obviously less in small single-site organisations. Even where there is no alternative post that could be offered within the parameters of the contract, it has been held that an employer who does not make a reasonable attempt to find alternative work, although not contractually bound to, may be held to have been dismissed unfairly.

The employee may be happy to accept the alternative. If, on the other hand, the employee rejects the offer of alternative employment, opting instead to take the redundancy money, the money may be withdrawn. This is because an employee who unreasonably refuses an offer of suitable alternative employment will not be entitled to a redundancy payment. Refusal to accept an alternative job may also be seen as lack of flexibility on the part of the employee.

The offer may be made by either:

• The existing employer.

• An associated employer, e.g. a subsidiary or holding company.

• A new employer to whom the business has been transferred.

Any such offer need not be in writing but must specify any differences between the new job and the old. The offer must be made before the original contract ends and the new contract must take effect no later than four weeks after the end of the original one. 'Suitability' includes not only pay benefits, status and job demands but also the likely impact of job change on family life and other aspects of lifestyle.

THE TRIAL PERIOD

In effect this puts the employer and employee into a new negotiating position, i.e. of offers and acceptances. Whether an alternative job is suitable or not is a matter for objective assessment by the tribunal. A recent decision has indicated that where the terms of an alternative offer, such as a major pay cut, could give rise to a constructive dismissal then as a matter of law the offer is incapable of being suitable. Care must therefore be taken (*Sennitt v Fysons Conveyors Ltd, EAT* (1993))[20]. Each case will be looked at on its own merits. Some of the factors that have been considered are:

Pay
If the money in the new job is substantially lower than in the old then the new job will not be a suitable alternative. Pay includes overtime, bonuses and

fringe benefits (see *Sheppard v NCB* (1966))[21] where it was held that loss of overtime in the new job was not as important as the loss of fringe benefits. Losing these made the alternative job unsuitable.

Status

Any alternative job offer which involves a loss in status will make the alternative unsuitable. Examples include the headmaster offered supply teaching (*Taylor v Kent CC* (1969))[22] It does not matter that salary, wages etc. are preserved.

Skill

It is highly unlikely that any alternative offer that involved a skilled or semi-skilled worker doing unskilled work would be regarded as suitable.

Place of work

A change in location may make the alternative unsuitable. Much may depend however on whether the employee is subject to a mobility clause, either express or implied (see Chapter 3).

Hours of work

Alternative employment which involves a significant change (e.g. from day to night shift) will usually be unsuitable, but there may be a need for the employee to demonstrate flexibility.

Nature of work

If the alternative job is completely different from the old then it will be unsuitable (e.g. a hospital hairdresser offered alternative work as a clerical officer (*Nairn v Ayrshire & Arran Health Board* (1990))[23].

If the alternative offer differs in its terms and conditions from the original contract terms, the employee may be concerned about its suitability. There is statutory provision for a four week trial period (longer by agreement). The six month period for submitting an industrial tribunal claim runs from the end of the trial period. If either the employee or the employer decides, with good reason, to terminate the contract during this trial period, the employee will be treated for redundancy purposes as having been dismissed on the date the old contract ended.

If the employee turns down the job, whether the refusal is unreasonable or not will be assessed subjectively - i.e. it is more a personal than a suitability test. It may well be that objectively the job is suitable, but the employee may still be found to be reasonable in refusing it, thus keeping his right to a redundancy payment. Some factors which have been seen as reasonable grounds for refusal have included:

- Domestic difficulties, e.g. a spouse who is unwilling or unable to move, or having to look after elderly parents.

- Poor travel facilities, e.g. if the alternative job involved a much lengthier journey to work.

- Lack of suitable educational facilities, e.g. if a child needs special schooling because of a handicap or special skill.

- The temporary nature of the alternative, e.g. if it was clear that the alternative job would definitely last only a short time. It would be considered unreasonable, however, if an employee refused an alternative job because it might not last a long time.

It should be noted that although suitability and (un)reasonable refusal are two separate issues it has often been said that 'it is confusing to draw too rigid a distinction between suitability and reasonableness because some factors may be common to both aspects of the case'. It is important however that the employer takes personal matters into consideration when offering alternative work. He will not be able to save the cost of the redundancy payment by offering any old job. When the employee accepts an alternative offer from an existing or associated employer, or a new owner of the business, there is no break in service for the purpose of determining continuous employment.

Consultation

Statutory requirements exist for formal consultation with unions, and such procedures should be incorporated into individual employee contracts. The statutory procedures apply if the employer proposes to make more than 100 employees redundant within a 90 day period, when there must be consultation at least 90 days before the first dismissal takes place. If the employer proposes to make more than 10 employees redundant at one establishment within a 30 day period, there must be consultation at least 30 days before the first dismissal takes place.

However, TURERA has tightened up the situation and even if only a few redundancies are involved, there must still be consultation as soon as possible before the first dismissal takes place. It is now important to note that employers need to consult even where they do not recognise unions. The employer may issue notices of dismissal during the consultation period provided they do not take effect until the end of the consultation.

Before moving to consult over the criteria for selecting staff, consultation must be undertaken with a view to 'reaching agreement' on the following:

- ways of avoiding redundancy

- reducing the number affected

- minimising the impact of redundancy on individuals.

The Act originally referred to consultation, not negotiation (but see below). These are very different but in redundancy situations it will be usual for the borders between consultation and negotiation to be blurred. The employer must disclose to employees and/or their representatives.

- the reasons for the proposals.

- numbers and descriptions of those to be made redundant.

- total number of employees of each discipline employed by the employer at the establishment in question.

- the proposed method of selection.

Redundancy agreements and procedures now increasingly establish selection criteria for redundancy. Typically they now include:

- job skills held/needed.

- flexibility/adaptability in the light of future business plans.

- special qualifications.

- general employment record, including absence, productivity.

- Work performance/achievement, for example, as judged by appraisal.

Such procedures can be expressly incorporated into contracts; failure to follow them will amount to a breach of contract.

OTHER ISSUES SURROUNDING THE ENDING OF EMPLOYMENT CONTRACTS

There are man circumstances surrounding the termination of contracts of employment, not all of which can be covered in this book. For example, the dismissal of a woman who is pregnant, a trade union representative, or an employee who complains about health and safety standards will generally be fraught with problems.

The number of claims is rising, as are the number of situations where it is automatically unfair to dismiss. The costs of legal action and compensation levels are also increasing. The following must always be borne in mind:

- Industrial tribunals are dealing with breach of contract issues alongside claims for unfair dismissal. Their expertise will grow and contracts will increasingly be placed under the spotlight.

- Claims in other courts can be made where damages are unlimited. The county/sheriff courts, as well as the higher courts, deal with breach of contract cases all the time.

- Ending contracts of self-employed staff is simpler (no claims for unfair dismissal/redundancy etc.) but nonetheless has to be done in accordance with the contract terms. If a notice period and procedure is specified, it should be complied with. Failure to do so will involve a breach of contract. These claims can only be made in the ordinary law courts.

GUIDELINES FOR LAWFUL TERMINATION OF CONTRACTS OF SELF-EMPLOYMENT

- Identify the precise reasons for the early termination.

- If it is alleged that the self-employed person was in breach of contract, in what way did this happen?

- Identify the contractual basis for performance standards and further evidence of the alleged breach.

- End the contract with notice, but decisively and with written reasons.

REFERENCES

1   [1994] IRLR 119
2   [1978] IRLR 110
3   [1983] IRLR 49
4   *Robertson v Securicor Transport Ltd* (unreported)
5   [1992] IRLR 469
6   [1967] 2 QB 279
7   [1992] IRLR 362
8   [1972] IRLR 46
9   [1983] IRLR 126
10   [1982] IRLR 439
11   [1992] IRLR 75
12   [1989] IRLR 507
13   [1978] ICR 445
14   [1980] IRLR 53
15   [1978] IRLR 379
16   [1988] IRLR 30
17   [1985] IRLR 57
18   [1985] IRLR 489
19   [1967] ITR 308
20   [1993] EAT 297/93
21   [1966] KIR 101
22   [1969] 2 QB 560
23   [1990] Glasgow Industrial Tribunal (unreported)

Endpiece

WHAT DOES THE FUTURE HOLD FOR EMPLOYMENT CONTRACTS?

In recent years employment relationships and the contracts which create them have responded to a variety of ideas and pressures. As considered at various points in this book, the call for flexibility has lead to a variety of ideas and pressures. It has led to a major reconsideration of the traditional full time contract of indefinite length, often regulated by collective agreements as well as law. Employment contract types which were a rarity less than 20 years ago such as fixed term, nil/zero hours and task contracts have not only become well established but are the norm in some employment sectors and organisations.

Technology has also had the effect of making more people work from home, and there has been a significant and probably irreversible decline in the numbers of semi and unskilled workers who typically were employed on the regular and relatively static employment contract.

It is tempting to see the future as continuing these changes. Indeed, some writers see the inevitability of continuing change leading to the end of employment contracts as we have known them. William Bridges in *Jobshift: How to prosper in a workplace without jobs* (1995), anticipates this future with advice on work relationships defined by contracts of self-employment rather than the traditional contract of employment. In this vision, negotiation skills as well as the ability to contract effectively becomes even more crucial. The individual is the business and the business is the individual, so the balance of contracting shifts from defining how a worker fits within organisational needs and culture to providing a contract which meets the demands of the individual.

Bridge's vision is a radical one: it may be hard to apply to nurses, librarians, teachers and administrators for example, but it can provide a clear blueprint for an increasing range of occupations and activities. Even without such a radical vision, others see change as endemic within organisations constantly searching for improvement and quality (see e.g. Hammer and Champney, *Re-engineering the Corporation* (1993)). This searching will also lead to constant review of the nature and role of employment contracts themselves.

But is this really what the future holds - will it be 'more of the same'? Some argue that the next few years will be characterised by a need to review how these constantly changing and increasingly less stable employment relationships are affecting family life and the ability to plan and invest. Charles Handy in *The Empty Raincoat* (1994) reflected on the possible implications of precarious work, as well as overwork by some and unemployment for the rest.

Most importantly, a growing number of researchers and occupational health specialists are highlighting the growing incidence of stress and other work-related disorders. Amongst the typical causes of stress are long working hours, excess work pressure, unsupportive and/or remote management on one hand, and insecurity and fear of unemployment on the other. Evidence is mounting that outsourcing for skills provided by agencies or contractors has led to a decline in wages and shorter or casual contracts. This has taken place in a context where the financial savings of outsourcing are at best negligible and the costs of the bureaucracy required to support constant negotiation, contracts and transactional management are considerable.

One senses that there are some major issues to be decided over the nature and form of employment relationships, not just in the UK but throughout the world over the next few years. It is possible that some of the early structures which shaped employment relationships, such as collective bargaining, career management and training policies will be revisited. Some will see this as putting the clock back, others as a return to sensible employment practices. In the meantime there is the likely evolution of European employment law to be considered, although there are also considerable uncertainties here.

The issue of employment contracts will remain in the spotlight and the likelihood is of increased demands for careful negotiation, definition and management. Whatever the future holds, they will remain the cornerstone of employment law and people management.

Index

Academic Tenure 147
ACAS 18
Acceptance 28,33; communicating 34; non-appearance 34; time 33
Accommodation 189
Addison & others v London Philharmonic Orchestra (1981) 81
Akhtar v United Bank (1989) 68, 211, 231
Alidair v Taylor (1978) 232
Annual hours contracts 121; contract terms 122, 123; legal issues 122
Appraisals 23, 137, 165
Atkinson v Hellyer Brothers (1994) 128

Babar Indian Restaurant v Rawat (1985) 239
Bell v Lever Brothers (1932) 200
Benefits, see: Occupational Benefits
BHS v Burchell (1978) 236
Botel (1992) 112
Bradshaw v Rugby Portland Cement Ltd (1972) 227
Business organisations; downsizing 220; insolvency 215; managing changes 9, 58, 205, 206; restructuring 58; transfer 216

Capper Pass Ltd v Lawton (1976) 159
Cars 188
Casual Workers 102, 132
Changing conditions; contract changes 209, 211; hours 208; job content 208; location 207; managing 9, 58, 205, 206; organisational 208, 215
Christmas working 63

Civil Servants 146
Claw back clauses 190
Common law 26
Company handbooks 52, 88
Conduct 235
Confidential information 57
Conflicts of interest 200
Consideration; requirement 5
Consultants 102, 103; confidentiality 104; contracts 143; payment withheld 104
Continuous service 229
Contract, see also: Employment Contract; appearance 4, 13, 17; basic elements 4, 24, 26, 93; binding 34, 92; breach 20, 34, 57; categories 107; certainty 6, 30, 40; European comparisons 17; flexibility 9, 22, 40, 44; implied terms 56, 58; purpose 4, 8, 12; renewing terms 213; self-employment 7; termination 222, 224, 237, 244; variation 209, 211, 214
Contract package 88, 89
Contract terms 43, 44, 150; clarity 151; collective agreements 48, 50, 52, 96, 98; confidentiality 199; defining 150; duration 125; exclusivity 200; express 45, 88, 226; implied 56, 58, 88, 226; incorporation 49; interpretation 47; legality 152; location 183; management issues 152; negotiated 46, 50; presentation 152;

provision for change 209;
self-employment 80; sources 52
Contract type 44; special types 105;
standard form 45
Contracting out 97
Cresswell v Board of Inland Revenue
(1984) 206

De-recognition 22, 51, 94
Disciplinary procedures 97, 137,
194, 195; drafting 196;
enforcement 197
Discrimination 14, 18, 22, 31
Dismissal 220, 224, 225;
constructive 225,
continuous service 229,
ill health 233; justified 227;
legal costs 220, 221;
legislation 228; misconduct 227;
qualifications 233; reasons 230;
statutory duty 237; summary 226;
unfair 131, 217, 228
Disputes 18, 221
Documentation; contract package 88;
coverage 88;
fixed term contracts 129;
legal rules 91, 95; legally binding
92, 93; part-timers 98, 113;
presentation 99, 153; review 94, 98;
statement of terms 92;
written contracts 88, 93, 94
Dryden v Greater Glasgow Health
Board (1992) 226
Duration

East Hertfordshire District Council v
Boyten (1977) 195
Employees; behaviour 192, 231;
competence 64, 231; conduct 235;
dignity 16; disputes 10, 11, 18, 221;
duties 62; expectation 9;
flexibility 58; honesty 64, 236;
intermittent workers 82;
loyalty 61, 198; obedience 236;
obligations 57; performance 12,
191, 232; remedies 214;

restraint 65, 199, 201;
rights 14, 16, 218; role 74;
statutory protection 16; trust 59
Employers; associated 230;
control 78; obligations 57, 65
Employment contract, see also:
Documentation, Termination;
appropriate 107; benefits 35;
binding 92; categories 74;
content 42; correct 10; disputes 18;
formation 28, 87;
future developments 246;
importance 8, 10;
legal context 14, 21; renewing 98;
role 12; self-employment 79;
special types 105;
wording 36, 42, 87; written 93
Employment relationships 73;
academics 147; appropriate
contract 107; business test 81;
employees' role 74;
intermittent workers 82;
public sector workers 145;
self-employment status 78, 84;
status 143
Enderby v Frenchay HA (1993)
156, 160
Enforcement 27
Equal pay 157; claim 160;
comparisons 160; definition 158;
legislation 158, 159
European Commission v United
Kingdom (1982) 157
European (EU) law 15, 40;
collective agreements 17;
contract terms 95; health & safety
65, 66, 169; labour codes 17;
movement 15, 17;
social dumping 15;
working hours 173, 174
Exclusivity 200
Expenses, see: Travel Expenses

Fidelity clauses 198
Fissher (1994) 112
Fixed term contracts 125;

advantages 125; contract terms
   129, 130; documentation 129;
   employment status 128;
   legal issues 127; purpose 128;
   renewal 225; waiver clauses 131
Flexi hours 182
D C Foot v Eastern Counties Timber
   (1972) 200
Ford v Warwickshire CC (1983) 230
Foreningen of Arbejdsledere
   i Danmark v Daddy's Dance Hall
   A/S (1988) 217
Formation 28
Fraud 39
Freelance contracts 7
Freelance workers 102

Garden leave 203, 223
Gardiner and Taverna v Nethermere
   Ltd (1983) 136
GFI v Eaglestone (1994) 224
Gimber v Spurret (1967) 240
Government policy 12, 109, 110
Grievance procedures 97, 137

Hall v Lorimer (1994) 82
Harris v John Menzies (1994) 82
Health & safety 15, 23;
   group application 23; policy 53;
   safe workplace 65;
   self-employed 23, 144
Health insurance 168
Hedger v Davey & Co Ltd (1974) 63
Henderson v Evening Standard
   (1987) 203
Hindle v Percival Boats Ltd
   (1968) 207
Hivac v Park Royal Scientific
   Instruments (1946) 199
Holiday entitlement 96, 180
Homeworkers 135;
   communication 136;
   contract terms 136;
   legal issues 136; training 135
Howman v Blythe (1983) 167
Human resources; policies 53

Humphreys and Glasgow v Broom
   and Holt (1989) 211

Iceland Frozen Foods Ltd v
   (1982) 231
Illegal contracts 38, 39; impact 40
Illness; dismissal, 233, 234;
   health insurance 168;
   medical reports 234;
   payment entitlement 166
Imperial Group Pension Ltd v
   Imperial Tobacco Ltd (1991) 60
Implied terms; agreed wages 67, 226;
   developments 56, 58;
   legal rules 60, 61;
   safe workplace 65
Incorporation 49
Industrial relations 110
Industrial Tribunals 18; appeals 19;
   jurisdiction 20
Information leaks 201
Initial Services v Putterill (1968) 201
Injury; payment entitlement 166;
Insurance protection 11

Jenkins v Kingsgate Clothing
   (1981) 112
Job advertisements 29
Job descriptions 36
Job offer, see Offer
Job security 15
Job sharing; alternative work 120;
   characteristics 116; contracts 118,
   119; definition 115;
   development 115; legal issues 117
Job title 96
Johnstone v Bloomsbury Health
   Authority (1991) 67

Keir and Williams v Hereford &
   Worcestershire (1985) 186
Kowalska v Hamburg (1990) 112

Labour costs 108
Labour market 109

Lassey v Salterville Nursing Home (1988) 46
Laverack v Woods of Colchester (1966) 127
Lawful orders 62
Lay off period 170
Lee v Chung (1990) 81
Legal action 11, 220
Legal aid 18
Legal relationship 34, 49
Letter of appointment 91
Litster v Forth Dry Dock and Engineering Co Ltd (1989) 217
Living Design v Davidson (1994) 202
Location 68, 69, 86, 134, 183, 207

Management policies;
    casual contracts 22;
    contract terms 152;
    external constraints 110;
    impact 8, 9, 22, 37; innovation 59;
    organisational objectives 58;
    personal contracts 22, 30
McCarthys Ltd v Smith (1980) 158
McCrea v Cullen and Davison Ltd (1988) 239
McLaren v Home Office (1990) 146
McPherson v Lambeth LBC (1988) 212
Managers; contract handling 10, 205;
    discretion 69;
    employment relationships 84;
    enforcing rights 68;
    fixed term staff 126;
    performance review 166
Market Investigators v Min of Social Security (1969) 81
Marley v Forward Trust (1986) 50
Martin v Yeoman Aggregates Ltd (1983) 225
Maternity leave 169, 170
Mears v Safecar Securities (1982) 167
Mende-Hill v British Council (1995) 207
Mergers 215, 218
Mihienstedt v Barclays Bank (1991) 60

Mobility 68, 69
Mulox IVC Ltd v Geels (1994) 143
Multi-national companies 17, 110, 139
Mulrine v University of Ulster (1993) 131

Nairn v Ayrshire & Arran Health Board (1990) 242
NCB v Galley (1958) 41
Negotiated core hours 124
Night work 177
Nil/zero hours contracts 131, 133
Notice provisions 96, 223

Occupational benefits 114, 120, 151, 185; categories 186 ending 187;
    government policy 187
Offer 28, 29; binding 31; oral 31;
    process 32; uncertainty 30
O'Kelly v Trust House Forte (1983) 83, 132
Oral contract 4
Orman v Saville Sportswear 167
Overtime 63, 172, 175

P v Nottinghamshire CC (1922) 227
Page v Hull University (1993) 147
Part time workers 98, 111;
    characteristics 111;
    contract terms 113, 114;
    job sharing 117; legal issues 112;
    occupational benefits 114, 115;
    training 114
Pay; contract terms 151, 155;
    deductions 162; deferred 170;
    equal pay 157; guaranteed 172;
    illness 166; injury 166;
    lay off period 171; legal issues 156;
    maternity 169; negotiating terms 156; performance related 164;
    reviews 164; wages agreed 57, 67;
    wages legislation 161, 192;
    withholding 20
Pension schemes 59, 96;
    occupational 170

Performance; consultants 102;
    contract terms 151, 190, 193;
    dismissal 232; efficient 190;
    legal issues 192;
    measuring 74, 191, 193; quality 198;
    related pay 164;
    secondment contracts 142;
    standards 197
Performance related pay 164
Pink v White & Co (Earls Barton) Ltd
    (1985) 240
Place of work 96, 151
Porter and Nanyakkara v
    Nottingham Health Care Trust
    (1994) 216
Prison officers 146
Production capacity 108
Public sector workers 145;
    documentation 147;

Quality management standards 23
Quinnen v Hovells (1984) 159

R v Derby CC ex parte Noble
    (1990) 146
R v Sec of State for Employment
    ex parte EOC (1994) 113
Rainey v Greater Glasgow
    Health Board (1987) 161
Rask v Kantineservice (1993) 216
Redundancy 215, 238;
    alternative employment 240, 241;
    bumping 240;
    consultation, 243, 244;
    legal definition 239
Remedies 214
Remuneration, see Pay
Repudiation 214
Restraint Clauses 7, 65, 114, 199, 201
Robertson v Securicor Transport
    Ltd 225
Robertson and Jackson v British Gas
    (1983) 50, 212
Roy v Kensington and Chelsea FPC
    (1992) 146
Rule books 52, 88

Safe workplace 65
Sagar v Ridehalgh (1863) 30
Scally v Southern Health Board
    (1991) 60
Secondment contracts 139;
    briefing 141; contract terms 141;
    injuries 141; legal issues 140;
    performance 142; travel 185
Sec of State for Employment v ASLEF
    (No2) (1972) 36, 58
Selection interviews 31
Self-employment;
    advantages 77, 78, business test 81;
    contract terms 69, 143, 144;
    documentation 98, 102;
    legal tests 83; oral contracts 143;
    status 7, 76, 77, 81, 84;
    termination 245;
    working patterns 80
Sennitt v Fysons Conveyors Ltd EAT
    (1993) 241
Sheppard v NCB (1966) 242
Shields v Coomes (Holdings) Ltd
    (1978) 160
Shift working 176
Sick pay 166
Sinclair v Neighbour (1967) 226
Smoking policy 55
Social dimension 16
Split sites 184
Star Newspapers v Jordan (1993) 211
Statement of terms 92, 95
Statutory protection 15, 16
Stoker v LCC (1992) 231
Stress 10, 23, 247
Sub-contracting 75
Sunday working 179

Tanner v Kean (1978) 225
Task contracts 134
Taylor v Kent CC (1969) 242
Temporary cessation 230
Tenure 147
Termination 222, 224, 237, 244
Thomas v University of Bradford
    (1986) 147

Time off 182
Training contracts 148
Transfer of undertakings 16, 215, 216
Travel expenses 188
Trebor Bassett v Saxby and Borrman
   (1994) 213

Unsocial hours 178

Variable hours contracts 124
Variation of contract 209, 211;
   unlawful 214

Wages, see: Pay
Walden Engineering Ltd v Warrener
   (1993) 215
Walker v Northumberland CC
   (1995) 173
White v Reflecting Roadstuds
   (1989) 69
Wiles v Greenaway Harrison (1994)
   213
Wishart v RSPCA (1990) 29
Working hours 151, 172; basic hours
   175; changes 208; defined 174;
   flexibility 173